Japanese Foreign Trade

Japanese Foreign Trade

Thomas R. Kershner
Union College

Lexington Books
D.C. Heath and Company
Lexington, Massachusetts
Toronto   London

Library of Congress Cataloging in Publication Data

Kershner, Thomas R.
   Japanese foreign trade.

   Bibliography: p.
    1. Japan—Commerce—Pacific area. 2. Pacific area—Commerce—Japan.
3. Japan—Commerce. I. Title.
HF3828.P3K47   382'.0952   73-11659
ISBN 0-669-85472-7

To my mother and father,
with love
They Showed Me the Way

Contents

List of Tables

Preface

This book is the result of a number of years' research on the role foreign trade has occupied within the Japanese economy. In the course of this work it quickly became apparent that some appreciation of Japan's essential complementarity with the generally resource-rich and increasingly developed countries of the Pacific Asian region was central both to an understanding of Japan's trade network and, less well understood if no less important, to an understanding of a principal explanatory factor behind the broad pattern of economic success most countries in the Pacific Asian region have achieved during the last decade. Because there were few analyses in English of these two-way trade flows and of the accompanying movements of capital from Japan to the region, it seemed useful to attempt to set forth the broad outlines of those economic relations as they have developed from approximately 1960 onward.

This book represents one result of that attempt. While I am responsible for the analysis and for the conclusions put forward here, a number of individuals contributed greatly to the development of this book. John Maher and Sheldon Appleton first sparked my interest in economics and East Asia while I was an undergraduate at Oakland University. At Harvard, Dwight Perkins first encouraged me to look at these questions, and he has been a source of assistance and guidance in a number of ways. I also learned much from Simon Kuznets, John Kenneth Galbraith, Ken Deitch, and Walter Falcon.

Union has provided an agreeable and stimulating environment in which to work. Throughout my years here I have benefitted from the support and encouragement of a number of colleagues. In particular, I would like to mention Martin Lichterman, Erik Hansen, and, especially, Bob Herman. I have also learned much from and been stimulated by my students over the years.

David M. McKeown, Jr., deserves special mention for his continuous involvement in this project and for his steadfast support and encouragement. Among other things, he was the source of many thoughtful suggestions as the work progressed, and he took responsibility for all the computer programming.

Virtually everyone at Schaffer Library helped on this project at one time or another, though Gertrude Antemann and Loretta Walker should be singled out for special thanks. Esther Miller cheerfully and ably handled all the key punching. Others who have assisted in the preparation of this manuscript include Barry Markman, Steve Pierce, Bill Fellows, Dave Twigg, and Andy Paul. Clara Mozgawa typed the final draft of the manuscript, and I have benefitted considerably from her able assistance in all phases of this work.

A generous and timely grant from the Department of Health, Education, and Welfare financed a trip to Japan last winter that enabled me to gather additional data and to test the principal themes of the book with a number of Japanese scholars and government officials. Among the many persons that were kind enough to spend considerable periods of time with a visiting economist from the United States, I particularly want to acknowledge Hisao Kanamori, Akien Akimoto, Yoriko Kawaguchi, and Shinsako Sogo. Union College also provided several Faculty Research grants that were helpful in allowing this book to be completed.

This book was essentially completed in the spring of 1974. All during 1974, there were unmistakeable signs that the OPEC countries were succeeding in changing international economic relations in ways that were fundamental if still unclear. My immediate instinct was to revise this book, particularly with reference to the discussion of Japan's projected future levels of trade and capital flows. The reader should know that I successfully resisted that temptation.

Finally, it is customary to thank one's wife and children for providing support and encouragement in order that the book be completed. Such cursory thanks, in this case, would be totally inadequate. Niffy and Kim helped in more ways than they will ever know. Becky participated in this project from its inception, and I owe her a special debt for the understanding and patience she showed during the time I've worked on this book. Becky willingly served as a sounding board and as a source of constructive suggestions throughout, and it is fair to say that, without her assistance at every stage, this book would not have been written.

1

Introduction

By the end of 1973, the Japanese economy was one of the largest in the world. Japan achieved this impressive economic performance despite a sharply limited domestic natural resource base. Because the country is so poorly endowed with many industrial raw materials, foreign trade has played a critical role in her economic development by providing large shares of many key industrial inputs.

Much of this trade has centered among the developing East and Southeast Asian countries. While many of these countries had traditionally enjoyed major trading relationships with the Japanese, the purpose of this study is to investigate the expansion of Japan's trade with twelve of these "Pacific Asian" countries over the last ten to fifteen years, with a view toward explaining some of the underlying factors that have shaped the magnitude and commodity composition of this trade. The countries studied along with Japan include ten developing countries in Asia—Republic of Korea, Thailand, Hong Kong, Singapore, W. Malaysia, Indonesia, the Philippines, the Republic of China (Taiwan), Burma, and Mainland China—and two relatively developed countries in the Pacific area—Australia and New Zealand.[a] A major contention of the study is that these trade patterns were almost perfectly complementary. Japan provided important foreign trade markets for the largely raw material and lightly processed, primary export products of the region. The Pacific Asian countries, by the same token, were major buyers of Japanese exports of machinery, transportation equipment, and manufactured products.

The importance of foreign trade, and of Japan, to many of these Pacific Asian economies cannot be emphasized too strongly. The 1960s were to have been the "Decade of Development." These were the years during which the Pacific Asian countries were to have achieved sustained per capita rates of economic growth of 3 to 4 percent annually. Primarily agricultural (which sometimes included mining and forestry) in structure, the Pacific Asian countries relied relatively heavily upon imported capital goods, transport equipment, and manufactures to augment their domestic economic production. Imports supplied key industrial inputs that their domestic economies were often incapable of providing in sufficient quantity. Imported manufactured products were also important to help satisfy diversified consumer needs, as the standard of living of these countries generally was rising steadily.

---

[a]The Indo-Chinese countries of North and South Vietnam, Laos, and Cambodia were excluded because internal warfare in these countries for some or all of the period under discussion radically distorted their economies and made it difficult to separate and assess the "recurring" aspects of their trade with Japan.

1

Why were Australia and New Zealand incorporated into the study? Both nations are "developed," high-income countries. As such, their inclusion in the study is initially seemingly awkward and may be open to question. Yet several common parallels to the other Pacific Asian countries can be cited to support their retention here. Both countries lie geographically within the Pacific periphery. Both are turning increasingly to Japan and the developing countries in Asia for their major commodity markets. Both also have economic structures relatively heavily weighted in favor of the agricultural and industrial raw material production that characterizes much of the rest of Pacific Asia. Furthermore, their commodity trade (export) structures closely parallel the other countries in the study. Lastly, both Australia and New Zealand are moving towards political and economic status as vital parts of the concept of Pacific Asia discussed below. Their future, even more than their past, may be inextricably bound with the Pacific Asian region.[b]

It is fundamental that imported goods must be paid for. The import capacities of the Pacific Asian countries in recent years, given that their foreign-exchange reserves were typically small and not growing rapidly, were highly dependent upon their export earnings. Yet, neither their export performance generally nor their prospects in the 1960s were regarded as bright.[1] While there were important individual exceptions, the growing substitution of synthetic materials for raw materials, changing technologies, the lower growth in foreign demand for key raw material exports, and unfavorable price trends all limited the export prospects of the majority of the Pacific Asian countries.[2] During the early 1970s, moreover, additional pressures, largely emanating from the United States and Western Europe in the form of additional trade barriers and exchange-rate instabilities, further dimmed the immediate export outlook of these countries. Failure to sell sufficient agricultural and industrial raw materials abroad, it follows, would force a reassessment of development strategy. If a major external reliance on trade had to be scrapped in favor of an attempt to rely primarily upon a domestically produced, import-substitution strategy, not only would the gains from trade be reduced but the prospects for economic growth would themselves be sharply altered downward.

In terms of foreign trade, Japan proved to be the major exception for the Pacific Asian region during the last decade. A major finding of this study, which will be repeatedly stressed, is that Japanese-Pacific Asian trade has grown at virtually unprecedented rates during the last fifteen years. Put somewhat differently, in the absence of the Japanese trade, Pacific Asian trade and development prospects would have been far more pessimistic than they were and are.

---

[b]Paul Hasluck, Minister for External Affairs in Australia, asserted that much of his country's trade was complementary with Japan. He also suggested that Australia was increasingly turning to the Pacific region for trading partners and that her economic and political interests and technical assistance would be expected to grow commensurately. Hasluck, "Australia and Asia," *Oriental Economist* 35, no. 680 (1967), pp. 373-5.

What factors account for this growth in trade? Partly, it can be explained on grounds that Japanese industrialization and development continued to require large, rapidly growing industrial raw material and agricultural imports, many of which the Pacific Asian countries could, and did, supply. In turn, the Japanese economy was in an excellent position to provide much of the machinery and manufactures that Pacific Asian development strategies required. Furthermore, there are indications that Japan's small-scale business and labor-intensive technology closely approximated Asian factor proportions, which thus makes both Japanese technology and embodied capital equipment more suitable for importation by Pacific Asia.[3]

What advantages has the Pacific Asian trade offered Japan? While the domestic Japanese economy has been less dependent upon foreign trade than most of the countries of the world,[4] the foreign sector has necessarily played a major role in Japan's own growth and development since World War II. Relatively poorly endowed with natural resources, Japan has been forced to import many of the minerals, ores, woods, petroleum, and related industrial raw materials she has required. Japanese industry has fabricated them, and then Japan has either consumed the finished products domestically or re-exported them, often with considerable value added. In addition, Japan has been required to export to earn foreign exchange so that she could pay for needed imports.

Japanese producers have also turned to export markets when domestic cyclical economic downturns made home sales more difficult and when excess domestic inventories built up.[5] During the study period, Japan did become somewhat less dependent upon foreign trade than she had been a decade earlier. Moreover, trade clearly played a smaller quantitative part in her economy than it had and still does for most Pacific Asian countries. Nonetheless, the extraordinary growth Japan maintained, taken with the commodity structure of her import needs and export expansion, emphasizes and reinforces the importance of the Pacific Asian countries to Japan.

A central theme of this study is that the economic growth and welfare of *both* Japan and Pacific Asia has been dependent upon and stimulated by international trade. The *prima facie* case for extended trade between the two can be easily made: (1) they are geographically proximate, (2) their traditional trade flows have been major and long-standing, and (3) relatively underdeveloped, resource-rich Pacific Asia is best able to export many of the very industrial raw materials and agricultural products that resource-poor Japan requires for its heavily industrialized economy.

Pacific Asian nations attempting to grow and industrialize have offered rapidly growing markets for key Japanese exports of machinery, equipment, and chemicals. Pacific Asian attempts to transform and modernize its agricultural sectors have relied upon technology, farm machinery, and fertilizers and other imports from Japan. Finally, it is also clear that the outward-looking focus that trade with Japan has conveyed to Pacific Asian countries not only provided significant opportunities to rapidly expand exports but permitted these countries to acquire the skills and transmitted technology that reinforce their economic climates. In this process, the gains from commodity trade as a lever for growth and development were doubly enhanced.[6]

The potential gains from trade have not gone unnoticed. Formal national and international groupings have been proposed to facilitate increased trade and economic contacts. A host of multinational regional agencies and proposed trade associations have been developed or been actively discussed among the Pacific rim countries.[7] All recognize the potential economic complementarities noted above. Many also strengthen the region's anti-communist tendencies through informal economic cooperation and increased trade and contacts. Most proposals, however, stop short of thorough-going attempts at economic integration. They typically contain a membership that includes both developed and developing countries. Most, furthermore, urge reciprocal or non-reciprocal tariff reductions and other trade preferences for the developing countries as the basis for future cooperation.

The study would be incomplete if, in the emphasis on economic factors, it did not also reflect several political factors that have accompanied the substantial growth in Pacific Asian-Japanese trade flows. Chief among these political influences has been the somewhat vague, though highly evocative notion of an "Asia-Pacific Zone" first articulated in 1966 by Takeo Miki.[8] While this concept exists only in outline form, two central themes seem to re-emerge continually in any discussion of these matters. First, it has been proposed that Japan create a privileged zone of economic and political activity for itself in the Pacific Asia area. Concomitantly, Japanese political efforts would be focused upon organizing and stimulating an international cooperative undertaking aimed at developing the entire region.[9] Such a concept would benefit Japan, in that she would avoid economic isolation without being forced into seeking alliances or regional groups with political or stridently ideological overtones. An "Asia-Pacific Zone" would enable Japan to preserve and strengthen economic relationships with countries that were not only geographically proximate but economically complementary.

But the benefits were not to be confined to Japan. These trade preferences would also meet the needs of countries that retained few of their earlier colonialist-inspired trading ties with Western developed countries. It would also meet the needs of a set of countries that found themselves unencumbered geopolitically in an increasingly regional, bloc-oriented world.

To spur the region's development, Miki's strategy also emphasizes Japan's *responsibility* to contribute to growing prosperity in Asia. Using a combination of non-reciprocal tariff preferences, public and private capital flows, and technical assistance, Japan would promote the mutual prosperity of the countries in the region, not simply maintain Japanese economic hegemony.[10] Pacific Asian countries would be helped materially in their efforts to grow and industrialize.[11] Over time their economies would be stronger, which would be beneficial for them—and which would also further increase their capacity to trade with Japan. The dynamic benefits may ultimately come to outweigh the static gains.

In addition to the commodity trade, a considerable amount of financial resources have flowed from Japan to many of the Pacific Asian countries. This has been especially true since Japanese overall balance-of-trade constraints were eased beginning in about 1967. During the late 1950s and early 1960s Japanese reparations, including both formal and informal financial flows,[c] constituted the greatest part of this capital inflow. In recent years, Japan's stronger international economic position and her growing trade surpluses with the Pacific Asian countries enabled her to offer direct economic assistance, extend export credits, and send technical personnel to many of the developing countries in the region. Japanese direct private foreign assistance has also grown rapidly. Moreover, there are signs of a fundamental shift in Japanese thinking that gives promise of greatly increased direct, private foreign investment during the 1970s. It will be argued that these financial flows can be explained partly by forces within Japan, partly by implementation of the "Pacific Asian" concept, and partly by a need to offset the liquidity problems many Pacific Asian countries are encountering as they attempt to finance an ever-expanding trade volume.

The advantages of these largely one-way capital flows for both Pacific Asia and Japan are obvious. Furthermore, in a political context, Japan's assistance serves as an affirmation of the enormous success she has attained in rebuilding her own economy after its wartime devastation. Realization of a gradual, peaceful Pacific Asian concept as a mutual collaboration would also enable her to realize many of the real and psychic benefits she had hoped to attain from earlier ill-fated attempts to form the Greater East Asian Co-Prosperity sphere.[12]

Organization of the Study

In view of this background, this study focuses on several key questions, which subsequent chapters explore in some detail: What has been the role of trade in the Pacific Asia countries? How important a factor has it been within their respective economic networks? What can be said about the magnitude, commodity composition, and balance of this trade? All these questions must be asked, of course, in terms of both the world and Japan. How important has Japan been to each of these countries? Since this is fundamentally a two-sided inquiry, the same questions are in turn asked about the impact of trade, and Pacific Asian trade specifically, upon the Japanese economy. Given the apparent complementary relationship between the two regions, how can the broad outlines of this trade be placed in proper focus? What does each stand to gain from the greatly enlarged economic contact?

[c]For a discussion of "informal" reparations agreements, see Chapter 7 of this volume.

To assist in answering these questions, a methodology designed to analyze the trade flows has been developed. Breaking the two-country trade flows into SITC 3-digit classification levels, this study attempts to explain changes in trade from one period to another in terms of overall demand, structural (individual commodity or commodity group) demand, and changes in a country's competitive strength. Both the theoretical background of this approach and a discussion of the strengths and weaknesses inherent in this methodology are explored in some detail. The empirical findings are then presented in a series of tables. The two-way trade flows (both imports and exports) are explained by reference to the calculated coefficients of the model. Data on the trade magnitudes, commodity structure, and commodity trade concentration for Japan vis-à-vis each (and all) of the Pacific Asian countries are presented and analyzed. The balance of trade and Japanese financial assistance is considered. Finally, the prospects for future imports and exports are qualitatively and quantitatively assessed.

Conceptually, the study can be divided into three parts. The present chapter serves as an introduction and prologue. The first part, consisting of Chapters 2 and 3, develops the role of trade, with emphasis on Japan, for the Pacific Asian countries. It then investigates the role of trade, with special emphasis upon the Pacific Asian countries, for Japan. These chapters rely heavily upon summary empirical data, although some qualitative factors are also considered.

The second part of the study, which consists of Chapter 4, develops the methodology and the reasoning behind it. The final part, including Chapters 5 through 7, presents and analyzes the findings for both the magnitudes and commodity structure of the two-way trade flows. These explanations of Pacific Asian-Japanese trade are further supported by data on commodity concentration. The prospects for future trade are assessed. Chapter 7 presents an analysis of the balance of trade and Japanese capital flows. Particular emphasis is put upon the ways Pacific Asia can minimize the constraints imposed upon it that stem from the countries' negative trade balances. Finally, Chapter 8 attempts to summarize the major points raised during the whole study.

2

Trade and the Japanese Economy: The Contribution of Pacific Asia

Japan by the start of the 1970s had become a major factor in world trade. Such status, however, was not fully anticipated. During the 1950s, when the Japanese economy was completing its postwar recovery, the extent to which the Japanese economy could rely on international trade was by no means clear. In the prewar and immediate postwar years, most of Japan's foreign trade had been narrowly directed among the countries this study has called Pacific Asia. Yet in view of the enormous social, political, and economic changes that had occurred within the region since the war, Japan's ability to resume trade at prewar levels, let alone steadily increase it, could hardly be taken for granted.

Japan continued to need growing quantities of industrial raw materials. Her ability to provide the capital goods and manufactured products required by these developing, largely non-industrial countries probably insured that some trade would take place. The key question, therefore, is to ask how much trade would occur? What factors, within the Japanese economy, served to stimulate or retard these trade flows? For that matter, what trends within Japanese trade activity influenced the direction and the composition of this trade?

The factors and data analyzed in this chapter, as well as the method of argument, are similar to those that will be used in the next chapter, where the analysis turns to the Pacific Asian countries. This is done principally to facilitate comparisons and contrasts between Japan and that region. A major focal point discussed below is the question of foreign trade's composition and impact upon the Japanese economy. Parallel to this discussion is an analysis of Pacific Asia's place within Japan's trade network. Both the quantitative magnitudes and the content of these trade flows are presented and contrasted to Japanese trade with the rest of the world.

The principal argument of this chapter is that Japan's trade with Pacific Asia grew enormously over the last decade or so but that, despite this growth, the region barely succeeded in maintaining its share of Japanese trade. Measured in terms of relative trade shares, furthermore, Japan's trade dependance upon Pacific Asia was only half as large as it had been during the prewar era. What factors were responsible for these trade patterns? It will be argued that a partial explanation is that the direction of Japanese trade has changed in favor of developed countries. Within the context of the less-developed regions alone, Pacific Asia has more than held its own. The commodity patterns of this trade, which have remained complementary to a high degree, are sharply distinct: Japan exports machinery, transportation equipment, and manufactures and imports industrial raw materials and some food products. In every case, Pacific Asia emerges as a major but hardly dominant supplier to and customer of Japan. By the end of the 1960s, earlier tendencies toward import-saving (really industrial raw material-saving) patterns of industrial growth had been halted or even reversed. As long as Japan's demands for these industrial raw materials continues to increase, further growth of this two-way trade does not appear to be threatened.

Foreign Trade and the Japanese Economy

How large an impact, quantitatively or even qualitatively, has foreign trade had upon the Japanese economy? Two different approaches can be used to demonstrate foreign trade's role within the Japanese economy. The first starts with an examination of Japanese exports and imports to the world over the last fifteen years. The basic data are presented in Tables 2-1 and 2-2. Unlike the trade data presented in Chapter 3 for some of the Pacific Asian countries, the published Japanese trade data are widely perceived as being highly accurate and internally consistent.

The most striking observation that emerges from these tables is the extremely rapid rates of growth that characterized Japanese trade flows throughout the last fifteen years. As Table 2-1 clearly reveals, Japanese exports rose nearly tenfold—from $2.9 billion in 1958 to more than $28.4 billion in 1972. The corresponding import growth, which is shown in Table 2-2 for both Japan and the world for several years from 1958 to 1972, is nearly as impressive. Japanese imports from the world were $23.4 billion in 1972, which represents an eightfold increase from the $3.0 billion level in 1958. The absolute magnitudes, especially by the end of the period, were enormous.

How has Japanese trade grown when compared to world trade levels? Tables 2-1 and 2-2 show, in line 2, estimated totals of world exports and imports for the same years.[a] Japan's share of the world's exports, which are calculated in line 3, rose from 2.6 percent in 1958 to 6.5 percent in 1972. Her percentage shares of the world's imports also more than doubled. Japanese exports increased somewhat more rapidly than imports. Yet, the rising Japanese shares of world trade point clearly to Japan's ability to expand its foreign sector far more swiftly, in proportional terms, than the rest of the world. By any aggregate measure, the rates of increase of Japanese trade are virtually unprecedented, not only in comparison with any previous Japanese era but to the rest of the world, developed and less-developed alike.

[a]The world totals, while fairly reliable with respect to trends over time, are only estimates. They may be biased downward somewhat since some communist countries' exports and imports to other communist countries are not fully reported.

Table 2-1
Japanese and World Exports, 1958-1972 (Millions of U.S. Dollars)

Exports	1958	1960	1962	1964	1966	1968	1970	1972
Japan	2,876.	4,054.	4,917.	6,678.	9,779.	12,999.	19,317.	28,419.
World	109,747.	128,200.	142,470.	172,900.	204,100.	240,100.	312,400.	415,000.[a]
Japan's Percentage Share of World Total	.026	.032	.035	.039	.048	.054	.062	.065

[a]Estimated.

Note: The world totals were revised upward to include estimated exports from communist countries in Eastern Europe, Asia, and Cuba.

Source: Data taken from International Monetary Fund, *Direction of Trade: A Supplement to International Financial Statistics* (Washington, D.C.). Several annual editions, including 1958-1962, 1964-1968, 1968-1972, were used.

Table 2-2
Japanese and World Imports, 1958-1972 (Millions of U.S. Dollars)

Imports	1958	1960	1962	1964	1966	1968	1970	1972
Japan	3,033.	4,491.	5,634.	7,947.	9,522.	12,984.	18,881.	23,395.
World	114,705.	134,500.	148,996.	181,600.	213,300.	252,000.	326,800.	430,000.[a]
Japan's Percentage Share of World Total	.026	.033	.038	.044	.045	.052	.058	.054

[a]Estimated.

Note: The world totals were revised upward to include estimated imports from communist countries in Eastern Europe, Asia, and Cuba.

Source: Data taken from International Monetary Fund, *Direction of Trade: A Supplement to International Financial Statistics*. Several annual editions, including 1958-1962, 1964-1968, 1968-1972, were used.

The weight of these findings would seem, at least ostensibly, to point to the rapid growth in Japanese trade having come in response to widespread attention to and promotion of foreign trading opportunities. The role foreign trade would play in the postwar era has been argued elsewhere in great detail, and only a brief summary will be offered here. A number of economists, of whom Nakayama was one of the first, have argued in favor of sharply outward-looking, ultra-trade conscious policies for Japan.[1] Partly this reflects the domestic needs of a resource-poor country; antarky is simply not viable for a country lacking so many key raw materials. Partly, too, it recognizes the key role trade outlets can play within a rapidly expanding domestic economy.[2]

The case against trade pivots on the uncertainties surrounding external dependance. Since some raw materials must be imported in any event, in practice these arguments must be understood as stressing the dangers associated with an excessive reliance on trade—whatever that may mean. The core arguments advanced in this context include concerns as to the reverberations of cyclical developments abroad and questions about how the terms of trade would change over time. How *certain* and how large, it is asked, are the gains from trade likely to be?[3]

From the point of view of this study, however, the key issue is to ask whether—and if so, how—trade contributed more broadly to Japan's postwar economic recovery efforts. This in turn leads directly to the question of what the magnitude and scope of Japan's postwar recovery was. How did Japan's domestic economy perform during the last fifteen years?

Japan's economic achievements have become widely known, and the basic outline of her exceptionally rapid growth during this period is clear to all who care to look.[4] In Japan, economic recovery from the dislocations caused by World War II required, because of the huge wartime destruction of Japan's physical plant, massive rebuilding efforts, and Japanese production did not really begin to reach its prewar levels until the late 1950s. By 1958 or 1960, however, the recovery phase was essentially completed, and the postwar expansion with which this study is primarily concerned began.

Few things point up the significance of Japan's economic achievements more clearly than the summary trends of some key measures of economic performance since the war. Data for 1955 to 1972 are presented in Table 2-3. Several measures are presented; each points to an extraordinarily impressive domestic economic performance. First, Table 2-3 shows that Japan's gross national product essentially doubled between 1955 and 1960; it more than doubled between 1960 and 1965; it rose one and one-third times between 1965 and 1970; and it rose sharply again in 1972. Clearly part of these increases were due to rising prices. Yet, the major portion of these gains are in real terms. While the data in Column 1 of Table 2-3 does somewhat overstate the real magnitudes involved, the broader picture of Japan's large and sustained growth in marketed goods and services emerges clearly.

Table 2-3

Basic Japanese Economic Magnitudes, 1955-1972 (Billions of Yen, Current Prices)

	Gross National Product	Gross Domestic Fixed Capital Formation	G.D.F.C.F. GNP (Percent)	Employment
1955	8,624	1,705	17.8	41,720
1960	15,499	4,682	30.2	44,630
1965	31,787	9,767	30.7	47,450
1970	70,982	24,921	35.1	52,030
1972	90,489	31,524	34.8	–

Source: Data for 1955-1970 taken from K. Ohkawa and H. Rosovsky, *Japanese Economic Growth: Trend Acceleration in the Twentieth Century* (Stanford, Calif.: Stanford University Press, 1973):

Columns 1, 2	Basic Statistical Table 5, Columns 7 and 3 (p. 287);
Column 3	Calculated by author;
Column 4	Basic Statistical Table 15, Column 7 (p. 311).

Data for 1972 taken from OECD, *Economic Surveys: Japan* (Paris, June 12, 1973) p. 77.

What accounts for these economic gains? Another key feature of Japan's overall economic performance throughout this period is the huge increases in gross domestic fixed capital formation. These magnitudes are shown in Column 2 of the table. Japan's capital stock was decimated during World War II; what this data points up is the rapid build-up that occurred throughout the study period.

By 1955, the rate of Japan's capital formation, expressed as a percentage of GNP and presented in Column 3, had reached 17.8 percent. This compared very favorably with most industrial countries. What was far more impressive, however, were the rates at which capital formation rose during the entire period examined. These data show that capital formation virtually doubled between 1955 and 1960 by rising to 30.2 percent. By 1970 and 1972, capital formation grew still further, to a point where it accounted for approximately 35 percent of Japan's GNP.

It is not the purpose of these comments to trace the precise effect of these levels of capital formation. Clearly it was necessary for Japanese wage earners to postpone some of their consumption and to save substantial amounts of their income to finance this investment. Clearly, too, coordinated efforts on the part of government officials and financial intermediaries were required in order to accommodate the huge business expansion pointed up by this data. Yet, it is difficult to imagine that Japanese postwar growth would have approached these magnitudes in the absence of the levels of capital formation discussed above.

One cannot explain all Japan's growth in terms of capital formation. Among other principal factors, changes in the size, skills, and composition of the labor force are also basic to an understanding of Japanese economic history. The comparatively slow rates of Japan's population growth have attracted wide attention, and little more than a reminder of those trends is needed here.[b] Still, the corresponding increases in Japan's labor force is not so widely known. The basic data on Japanese employment is presented in Column 4 of Table 2-3. The narrative is straightforward; Japan's labor force increased by a quarter between 1955 and 1970. Put somewhat differently, the rise of more than 10 million employed workers was nearly as large as the total rise in population. A major explanatory factor was the strong labor demand and very low unemployment rates throughout the period.

From the above discussion, it is apparent that both the labor force and the capital stock available to the Japanese economy grew sharply during these years. What happened to GNP and to GNP per capita in real terms over these years, and how does the more recent Japanese economic growth compare with her experience during earlier periods?

Whatever the precise measure used to pin down real Japanese GNP over time, it is clear that the levels of GNP growth since 1956 were very high by historical Japanese standards. The data in Table 2-4, taken from Ohkawa and Rosovsky's major study, present the summary averaged magnitudes. From this data, it is apparent that Japan's post-1956 growth was quite unlike what she had experienced in the first half of the twentieth century. No attempt is made here to explain why Japan grew so much more slowly before 1956, or, more to the point, why post-1956 growth was so rapid. But the differences, no matter which smoothed and/or averaged procedures are used and whatever periods are chosen, are striking and inescapable. Population *growth* declined by a quarter, to one percent annually, while real GNP and GNP per capita rose to more than 11 and 10 percent, respectively. At no previous time in Japan's modern history was anything even approaching those rates of growth achieved.

Table 2-4
Japan's Gross National Product, GNP Per Capita, and Population: Average Rates of Growth, 1917-1969

Period	GNP	GNP Per Capita	Total Population
1917-1931	2.75	1.42	1.33
1931-1937	5.71	4.31	1.40
1937-1956	1.83	0.53	1.30
1956-1962	10.72	9.69	1.03
1962-1969	11.91	10.90	1.01

Note: This data represents average compound growth rates between successive trough and peak years of the smoothed series of long swings of Japan's GNP in real terms.

Source: Data taken from Ohkawa and Rosovsky, *Japanese Economic Growth*, Table 2.1, p. 25. Panel A data is shown.

[b]Japan's population increased from 89 million in 1955 to 103 million by 1970.

Table 2-5
Japanese Import and Export Trade Dependence, 1958-1973 (In Percentage Terms)

| Year | Nominal | |
	Export Dependence	Import Dependence
1958	11.44	9.98
1959	11.85	10.75
1960	11.45	11.05
1961	9.72	11.50
1962	10.10	10.13
1963	9.60	10.68
1964	9.99	10.51
1965	11.15	10.00
1966	11.31	9.95
1967	10.25	10.26
1968	10.70	9.85
1969	11.31	9.93
1970	11.65	10.55
1971	12.52	9.88
1972	12.19	9.10

Source: Data from 1958-1970 taken from Ohkawa and Rosovsky, *Japanese Economic Growth*, Basic Statistical Table 5 (p. 287). Data for 1971-72 taken from OECD, *Economic Surveys: Japan.*

An excessive focus on gains in domestic output, however, obscures much that is relevant to the argument that foreign dependance rose or fell. How has Japanese trade, in terms of her domestic economy, actually grown over the past fifteen years? For example, did the high, unprecedented per capita rates of domestic output outstrip the growth rates in Japan's foreign trade? The answer to that question is no, although this answer depends somewhat upon whether nominal or real magnitudes are examined. The core data are presented in Table 2-5.

Two major points emerge immediately from the data. The first is that over the fifteen-year period shown, Japan's nominal export and import trade dependence[c] remained within a relatively narrow band. As can be seen by looking first at the proportion of exports to GNP, although the export shares peaked in 1971, the shares have hardly risen over their 1958-59 levels. Three discernible shifts in these trends can be identified. First, exports averaged about

[c]Trade dependence is estimated to be the appropriate X/GNP and M/GNP ratios. This is clearly a crude approximation, however, since it does not touch upon the essential non-substitutability of many commodities Japan imports. Petroleum is perhaps the clearest case in point.

11.5 percent of GNP for the years 1958 to 1960. In the second phase, from 1961 to 1964, the average share of exports to GNP fell by nearly two percentage points, to about 9.8 percent. By the mid-60s and early 1970s, finally, export dependency data had regained its earlier levels and moved in a range around 11 percent.

The most striking observation that emerges from the import data is that the percent shares of the nominal values of imports to GNP have been constant and, in fact, have fallen slightly since the late 1950s. As Table 2-5 clearly displays, trade dependence for imported products reached its height in 1961 when imports were 11.5 percent of GNP. Throughout the 1960s, imports averaged only about 10 percent of GNP. In no year since 1961 did import dependency again reach 11 percent. In sum, these results suggest clearly that the trend for the entire fifteen-year period has been stable or slightly downward. The lowest dependence levels of the entire period was recorded in 1972.

Second, these figures clearly show the extent to which export shares of GNP have remained virtually stable in the face of the enormous upward trends in the absolute magnitudes of both time series. In fact, given the changes in the huge absolute magnitudes of all of Japan's principal economic indicators, stability of the type displayed here is remarkable. Many have argued that foreign trade expansion lies at the core of the explanation for Japan's economic success. If this is so, how can the stable trends noted in Table 2-5 be accounted for?

This record is the more surprising in view of the many forecasts that pointed to Japanese trade dependence ratios rising throughout the 1960s. It seemed hard for many to imagine that Japan's foreign sector would not grow significantly faster than domestic goods and services.[d] It would be interesting to speculate on why this disproportionate growth did not occur.

Given that Japan's *nominal* foreign trade was roughly unchanged in proportion to domestic output over these years, the next question is to ask whether the behavior of foreign versus domestic prices helped to explain the stable trade shares in GNP? How did import and export price indices change in comparison to Japanese domestic prices? How tangible were the widely expressed fears of sharp declines in the terms of trade as, and if, the magnitudes of imports and exports grew sharply?

These questions are especially relevant because, as Chapter 5 discusses in fuller detail, for a number of key industrial commodities the role of foreign trade was very significant. For raw materials like petroleum, nickel, and coal,

---

[d] In 1961, for example, when the Japanese government announced its New Long-Range Economic Plan, covering the 1961-1970 period, the projected target growth rates for the ten years forecast average annual rates of growth of 7.8 percent for GNP, 9.3 percent for imports, and 10 percent for exports. It should be noted in addition, however, that Japan's domestic industrial production was forecast to increase at an annual rate of 11.9 percent—somewhat faster than imports. For a detailed forecast of these and other magnitudes, see Japan Economic Planning Agency, *The New Long-Range Economic Plan* (Tokyo: Office of the Prime Minister, 1961).

Japan domestically was poorly endowed. To the extent that Japanese industry steadily expanded its production of a number of major products throughout the years covered in the study, raw materials imported from abroad were required as key inputs. This was broadly true somewhat independently of price trends. One must be clear about this. What is argued here is that especially for those Japanese manufactured products whose foreign, raw material costs constituted only a small share of the product's total cost, considerable upward price pressures from abroad would be tolerated in the short run. This was because in the short run, few if any substitutes—none of which were domestic—were available to Japanese industrialists. In the intermediate term, of course, sharply rising input prices might well induce the Japanese firms to reduce or suspend production in the absence of competitively priced substitutes. Seen in this context, unfavorable import and export price trends *could* act as a deterrent against sustained and expanded trade flows. The question is, did they?

If foreign prices put pressure on the degree of external dependence Japan's economy experienced during the 1960s, the evidence is difficult to find. If anything, the trends in export and import price levels are remarkable in that they were roughly in balance with domestic Japanese price trends. From 1958 until 1969, real export dependence was virtually constant. It was not until 1970 and after—during which period successive Japanese yen revaluations took place—that any tendency toward rising real levels of dependence, with export prices increasing even slightly faster than domestic prices, began to be felt. The basic data are presented in Table 2-6.

But the key question turns not on export but on import price dependence. In Table 2-6, the results of a crude attempt to measure the terms of trade as well as import price dependence are also presented. The principal finding is that between 1959 and 1972 real import dependence was essentially unchanged. Further, by the early 1970s, the proportions of real imports as compared to real GNP was significantly below the corresponding levels of the real export proportions. The gap, in fact, reached its peak in 1971 and 1972.

To be sure, it could be argued that this was achieved in spite of relative price trends. The data on terms of trade shown in Column 3 of Table 2-6, however, do not support that hypothesis. This is because the terms of trade were stable or rose slightly during the last decade, which makes it hard to claim that price trends moved *away* from Japanese industrialists (though the rising real export ratios could be read in support of the hypothesis that the export sector was not as profitable as domestic sales. This is a theme, parenthetically, that deserves much more attention than it has so far received).

To argue that trade proportions are modest must not be read in support of the view that the trade was in any sense of declining importance to Japan. The data discussed above, for example, underplay Japan's essential need for some imported raw materials that are simply unavailable domestically. These magnitudes are abstracted from Japan's political relations with many of her principal

Table 2-6
Japan's Real Export and Import Dependence and Terms of Trade, 1958-1972
(In Percentage Terms)

	Real Dependence		Terms of Trade
	Exports	Imports	
1958	11.18	8.76	89
1959	11.43	10.0	96
1960	11.47	10.98	99
1961	10.49	11.96	96
1962	11.63	11.40	96
1963	11.39	12.29	96
1964	12.27	12.27	95
1965	11.18	10.30	96
1966	11.71	10.20	98
1967	10.97	10.99	100
1968	11.76	10.84	100
1969	12.59	11.08	100
1970	13.23	12.13	101
1971	14.69	11.80	–
1972	14.74	11.72	–

Source: Data from 1958-1970 taken from Ohkawa and Rosovsky, *Japanese Economic Growth*, Basic Statistical Table 5 (p. 287). Data for 1971-72 taken from OECD, *Economic Surveys: Japan.* (1973).

trading partners, with the result that economic trends disguise fundamental and far-reaching changes in Japan's social and political relations with her neighbors. Still, the outline sketched above does roughly portray the summary magnitudes of trade's impact upon the Japanese economy during the last fifteen years and more.

Yet one central theme of this chapter is that whatever the *prima facie* case some may put forward for large and growing trade dependency, Japan's actual experience has been quite different. Trade has grown in concert with the major, continuous gains recorded in Japan's domestic economy. While foreign trade has made significant contributions to growth since the late 1950s, its postwar quantitative impact upon the Japanese economy has been less than half the comparable prewar level.[e] Export and import gains seem to have followed, as much as led, domestic Japanese production.

Several things are clear from this analysis. The most striking is that contrary to widely held beliefs that the Japanese economy is extraordinarily attentive to and dependent upon foreign trade,[5] an examination of cross-national compara-

[e]The loss of Japanese colonies has undoubtedly contributed something to this decline. See Angus Maddison, *Economic Growth in Japan and the U.S.S.R.* (New York: W.W. Norton, 1969), especially pp. 66-69.

tive data points to the observation that Japanese trade dependence has consistently been relatively low in comparison to many "high-income" and "low-income" countries in the world.[6] In fact, the stable or falling import dependency ratios signify that the Japanese domestic economy has generally expanded at a faster rate than imports, while exports have grown roughly in proportion to the domestic economy. Although trade has been important, postwar Japanese industry has been more attentive to domestic than to foreign customers, a tendency that if anything has increased modestly during the last fifteen years.[7] (Unchanged gross dependency figures, however, may disguise a growing dependence on one or a few individual commodities within the total for which domestic substitution would be increasingly costly, of which more below.)[8]

Further support for the stable trade/domestic output shares comes from some recent work of Houthakker and Magee.[9] In their cross-national studies of the income and price elasticities of international trade for several industrial countries, including Japan, they found that Japan's import income elasticity was 1.23 (at the lower end of the countries studied), while her export income elasticity was 3.55, without question the highest. One limitation of their findings was the time span selected. Their observations covered the years 1951 to 1966, and it should be remembered that Japan was still engaged in massive postwar recovery efforts in the early years of that period. The resulting changes in their broad economic aggregates over the 1950s were enormous. Accordingly, the import income elasticities, already relatively small, would be expected to decline if the period measured was limited to the decade of the 1960s. The export income elasticity, while superficially implying ultra-trade consciousness on the part of Japan, in fact is not particularly meaningful until changes in domestic Japanese national accounts are contrasted with the other countries' income levels. Japan grew much more rapidly than the other 25 countries in the study. The high export income elasticity coefficient, consequently, is interpreted here more as a reflection of faster Japanese (vis-à-vis foreign) growth in production and economic performance than as a pronounced change in trade dependency.

A principal finding of this section has been that although the growth in Japanese trade flows has been enormous, foreign trade itself has remained proportionately closely tied to domestic output. Further, from a longer-term perspective stretching from the 1930s, it can be shown that postwar trade shares of GNP were smaller than their prewar levels. If past trends are any guide, furthermore, these findings, together with the Houthakker-Magee work, raise the possibility that export dependency may rise as, and if, the rate of Japan's domestic growth lessens significantly.

**The Role of Pacific Asia
in Japanese Trade**

If aggregate Japanese trade was growing continuously, the Pacific Asian countries continued to play a key role within Japan's world trade network. The central purpose of this portion of the chapter is to put forth the broad aggregates of Japanese imports from and exports to the twelve Pacific Asian countries. It will be argued that even though both the structure and the geographical direction of Japanese trade flows with the world had undergone fairly far-reaching changes by 1973, her trade with Pacific Asia generally was able to keep pace with each shift.

To state that Japan's Pacific Asian trade largely maintained its share in Japan's overall trade flows is, however, to reverse the traditional expectation regarding trends in the direction of a developed, high-income country's trade. It is customarily held that the direction of trade will shift over time away from less-developed countries and in favor of higher-income, developed nations.[10] Japan was thought to be no exception. The case for the anticipated trade shifts can be easily made.[11] On the export side, the reasoning is as follows: developed countries' incomes grow faster; faster growth permits more rapidly rising import capacity; and finally, export flows will be larger and grow more quickly where import capacity has expanded the most rapidly.

Many economists have thought that the import demand of countries like Japan from less-developed countries will also grow relatively slowly. The key arguments are that (1) the composition of the developing countries' exports (largely concentrated among industrial raw materials and foods) have low-income elasticities of demand, (2) synthetics are systematically being substituted for some raw materials, and (3) the structure of domestic Japanese production has changed, with services (presumably with a low raw material content) assuming relatively more importance than manufactured products (whose raw material content may often be quite high).[12] Clearly these arguments could be extended in considerably greater detail. Doing so, would not, however, materially influence the broad outlines of the reasoning nor affect the rather pessimistic implications for future trade flows.

Thus the key issue here is to ask whether Japan's Pacific Asian trade followed along the rather pessimistic lines developed above. Several different measures can be used to show that, broadly speaking, it would appear that the increases in Japanese trade flows to Pacific Asian more than matched her corresponding totals to the rest of the world.

Taking Pacific Asian totals in its entirety, however, obscures much that is relevant to an examination of the long-term flows. Did, for example, much of Japan's trade growth depend heavily upon just a few individual customers? The answer to that question is clearly no. Data in Table 2-7 suggest that if anything Japan's exports to virtually every country have increased at least fivefold over the last thirteen years. Tables 2-7 and 2-8 present comparable data on Japanese exports to and imports from the twelve Pacific Asian countries. The Japanese import pattern was somewhat more uneven, but again the data show that import gains were generally distributed among virtually all the Pacific Asian suppliers.

An examination of Japanese export flows to the twelve individual Pacific Asian countries reveals the pattern of trade among the countries over time. The most striking finding in Table 2-7 is that Japanese exports came close to

Table 2-7
Japanese Exports to Pacific Asia, 1958-1972 (Millions of U.S. Dollars)

Country	1958	1962	1966	1970	1972
Australia	61.2	138.5	298.2	589.7	728.4
Burma	46.4	53.4	46.6	38.7	44.0
China	50.5	38.5	315.2	568.9	608.9
Hong Kong	99.7	192.5	369.2	700.3	909.7
Indonesia	48.6	115.3	118.6	315.8	615.5
Korea	56.7	138.2	334.8	818.2	979.8
Malaysia	14.3	38.7	94.6	166.5	263.9
New Zealand	7.4	26.8	59.0	114.1	165.3
Philippines	87.7	120.0	278.3	453.7	457.4
Singapore	77.3	105.0	137.9	423.0	701.5
Taiwan	90.0	118.5	−	700.4	1,909.6
Thailand	83.0	148.6	300.9	449.2	522.2
Totals	722.8	1,234.0	2,353.3	5,338.5	7,087.2

Source: Data taken from International Monetary Fund, *Direction of Trade: A Supplement to International Financial Statistics.* Several annual editions, including 1958-1962, 1964-1968, and 1968-1972, were used.

doubling between 1958 and 1962; they doubled from 1962 to 1966; doubled again from 1966 to 1970; and rose substantially by 1972. Throughout the last fourteen years, the expansion of exports overall to Pacific Asia was sustained at very high levels. The largest recipients of Japanese exports in 1968 were, in order of magnitude, Hong Kong, Taiwan, the Philippines, Thailand, and Singapore, each of which purchased between $77 million and $100 million of goods. Malaysia and New Zealand, on the other hand, comprised the smallest markets.

By 1972, however, this overall pattern of growth obscured several major shifts in country shares. Taiwan, which accounted for the largest single market for Japan, purchased nearly $1.1 billion of exports in 1972. (This total, by way of contrast, easily surpassed Japan's aggregate exports to all twelve Pacific Asian countries just thirteen years earlier.) Korea, Hong Kong, Australia, and China were the other major markets for Japan. In terms of growth, exports to New Zealand (which started from a very small base) and Korea exhibited the most rapid increases.

With these export returns in mind, it is useful to turn to an examination of the sources of Japanese imports from Pacific Asia. Table 2-8 shows that the rate of growth of these imports was slower than the comparable export figures, an observation that holds for each four-year interval as well as the entire twelve-year period. Import distribution was highly concentrated in 1958, as three countries (Australia, Malaysia, and the Philippines) accounted for nearly two-thirds of Japan's total imports from the twelve countries. In 1972, however,

Table 2-8
Japanese Imports from Pacific Asia, 1958-1972 (Millions of U.S. Dollars)

Country	1958	1962	1966	1970	1972
Australia	225.5	435.6	679.7	1,507.7	2,205.2
Burma	12.3	16.3	14.8	12.6	23.8
China	54.3	46.0	306.3	253.8	491.1
Hong Kong	11.5	18.9	47.1	91.8	119.4
Indonesia	36.1	91.2	175.9	636.6	1,197.5
Korea	11.0	28.5	71.7	229.0	426.0
Malaysia	158.3	186.3	171.3	418.9	395.5
New Zealand	18.9	34.0	113.2	157.6	248.5
Philippines	99.7	184.0	325.0	533.5	470.4
Singapore	12.7	22.7	30.3	86.5	120.9
Taiwan	75.6	61.4	147.4	250.8	421.9
Thailand	21.7	71.7	153.2	189.2	252.1
Totals	737.6	1,196.6	2,235.9	4,368.4	6,372.3

Source: Data taken from International Monetary Fund, *Direction of Trade: A Supplement to International Financial Statistics*. Several annual editions, including 1958-1962, 1964-1968, and 1968-1972, were used.

import concentration declined slightly, and Australia, Indonesia, and China had become Japan's principal suppliers. Yet in 1972 Australia and Indonesia provided half of Japan's imports from the entire twelve-country region. These data are highlighted because they underscore a key difference between Japanese exports and imports; namely, while Japan exports a huge volume of a broad range of products throughout Pacific Asia, her imports remained more concentrated among a few key suppliers. The fastest rates of import growth, finally, were provided by Korea and Indonesia.

How reliable are these trade flows? Japanese data generally are highly consistent among a number of sources, and these data (particularly in comparison with other Pacific Asian countries) are often used as benchmarks against which other countries' estimates are measured. For 1958, 1962, 1966, and 1970, these aggregate country flows were taken from annual compilations of the United Nations series, *Commodity Trade Statistics, Series D*. These data have the prime virtue of being subsequently reported in extremely disaggregated form, to the SITC 4-digit classification level. The *Commodity Trade Statistics* returns for 1972 are not yet available. That year, consequently, utilizes data from the International Financial Statistics *Directions of Trade*. Comparing returns from the two sources has resulted in insignificantly small differences in trade totals. These can be easily accounted for by differences in timing and reporting procedures. The two series have, accordingly, provided essentially interchangeable sources of data, and both series are used throughout the study.

How does the growth in Japan's overall exports to and imports from Pacific Asia compare with their trends in trade with the rest of the world? Data on Japan's percentage shares of exports and imports from Pacific Asia are presented in Table 2-9, and the export data make clear that no single country in Pacific Asia constituted a prime export market for Japan. The largest trade share was Taiwan's, which in 1972 accounted for only 3.8 percent of Japan's total exports. Put another way, each country's share, in and of itself, was relatively insignificant within the context of Japan's world trade network. (This finding, of course, will stand in sharp contrast to the dominant role for which Japan's shares in the respective Pacific Asian exports and imports will account, which is discussed in Chapter 3.) Indeed, it is plausible to suggest that Japan's share of most *individual* Pacific Asian countries' trade was greater than the *total* Pacific Asian trade's share of Japanese world trade.

If export shares to the individual Pacific Asian countries were small, the aggregate shares of Japanese exports to Pacific Asia as a whole were remarkably constant over the twelve-year period. To be sure, some countries' individual totals did fluctuate, but on balance, relative gains in some countries were just about canceled by relative declines in others. Slightly more than 25 percent of Japanese exports went to Pacific Asia in 1958. Export shares then rose to 26.7

Table 2-9
Pacific Asian Shares of Japanese Exports and Imports, 1958-1972 (In Percentage Terms)

Country	Exports			Imports		
	1958	1966	1972	1958	1966	1972
Australia	2.17	3.04	2.56	7.44	7.14	9.43
Burma	1.61	.48	.15	.41	.16	.10
China	1.76	3.22	2.14	1.79	3.22	2.10
Hong Kong	3.48	3.78	3.20	.38	.49	.51
Indonesia	1.70	1.21	2.16	1.19	1.85	5.13
Korea	1.97	3.42	3.44	.36	.75	1.82
Malaysia	.50	.97	.93	4.19	1.80	1.69
New Zealand	.26	.60	.58	.62	1.19	1.06
Philippines	3.06	2.85	1.61	3.29	3.41	2.01
Singapore	2.69	1.41	2.47	.42	.32	.51
Taiwan	3.13	2.61	3.84	2.49	1.55	1.80
Thailand	2.90	3.08	1.84	.72	1.61	1.08
Totals	25.12	26.68	24.94	24.32	23.48	27.24

Source: Data taken from International Monetary Fund, *Direction of Trade: A Supplement to International Financial Statistics.* Several annual editions, including 1958-1962, 1964-1968, and 1968-1972, were used, plus computations by author.

percent in 1966 before declining slightly to 25 percent in 1972. All of this was in the face of the enormous structural and quantitative changes in Japanese trade discussed above.

This apparent recent stability should not be allowed to disguise the considerable shift in the direction of Japan's trade over the last four decades. Kanamori has argued that on average during 1934-1936 Asia and Oceania together accounted for 67 percent of Japan's exports.[f] While the Southeast Asian totals undoubtedly include countries not included in this study's concept of Pacific Asia, it is reasonable to suppose that at least 60 percent of her exports formerly went to this region.[g] Much of this decline can be explained by the loss of Japanese colonies in Korea and Formosa and by a contemporary Chinese government wholly different in character and outlook from the China of 1934-1936. Seen in a longer-term perspective, accordingly, the Japanese export shares to Pacific Asia have declined considerably from earlier decades but have maintained their shares in recent years.

What about the pattern of Japanese imports from Pacific Asia? Table 2-9 also shows Japan's import shares from each of the twelve countries for selected years. It can be seen that Australia was the major supplier of Japan's imports over this period, with its share fluctuating between 7 and 9 percent of the Japanese totals. No other country, except Indonesia in 1972, accounted for a share of more than 5 percent in any given year (and only Malaysia in 1958 was greater than 4 percent). These shares again emphasize the disproportionate weight of Australia within Japanese imports, as Australia alone accounted for a third of Japan's total imports from Pacific Asia.

Japanese imports from Pacific Asia displayed many of the same properties of constancy that the corresponding export totals had maintained. What these figures emphasize, however, is that Japanese import shares from Pacific Asia were not only maintained but grew slightly. Put somewhat differently, this means that the Pacific Asian exporters fully maintained their shares of the Japanese import markets throughout the decade.

How do the shares of Japanese imports compare with the prewar shares from Pacific Asia? Measured in terms of prewar levels, the Kanamori data, averaged for the 1934-1936 period, show that Japan had previously purchased a considerably larger share of her imports from the region.[13] It is difficult to make precise comparisons, but it seems plausible to estimate that between 50 and 60 percent of Japan's prewar imports had come from the Pacific Asian countries, with 60 percent being the upper limit if all of the Southeast Asian

---

[f]Korea and Formosa, 25 percent; China, 18 percent; Southeast Asia, 19 percent; and Oceania, 3 percent. See Hisao Kanamori, "Economic Growth and Exports," in L. Klein and K. Ohkawa, *Economics Growth: The Japanese Experience Since the Meiji Era* (Homewood, Ill.: Richard D. Irwin, 1966), p. 377.

[g]The Korean total must also be revised, since only the Republic of Korea (South Korea) has been included here. North Korean trade with Japan, it may be noted has been only 4 to 6 percent of the South Korean totals.

24

countries were included.[14] The parallels between the import flows and export trends discussed above are striking. Japanese export totals to Pacific Asia were consistently larger than imports. For both, however, these findings show that although Japanese trade shares to the region declined considerably from comparable prewar levels, both import and export shares have stabilized since the postwar Japanese economic recovery. The result is that the region accounted for about a quarter of Japan's trade with the world during the most recent decade.

Inequalities in the Distribution of Regional Trade

The existence of Pacific Asia did not result in a situation where each of the other regions of the world also held stable trade shares with Japan. Instead, among the other regions there were pronounced shifts in the patterns of Japanese trade. Earlier this chapter articulated the widely held hypothesis that predicted Japanese trade with the less-developed regions would progressively decline. The question is, did this happen?

Two questions are interesting in this context. The first is, what happened to the direction of Japanese trade between developed and underdeveloped countries? Did it shift along the lines predicted? If so, secondly, how can the stability of Pacific Asian trade shares with Japan be explained in light of these shifts?

To analyze the first question it was necessary to disaggregate Japanese trade along somewhat different lines. The country breakdowns used here are "industrial" and "non-industrial," with all countries in the world assigned to one of the two groups. All such classifications are somewhat arbitrary. The industrial classification is slightly more restrictive than "developed" countries. (In practice, the latter equals the former if Australia, New Zealand, and South Africa are excluded.) This classification was put forward here because it attempts to focus primarily upon productive structure rather than per capita income. The key point is that the non-industrial countries concentrate somewhat more heavily upon primary products or lightly processed raw materials, which are key imports for resource-poor Japan and a principal focus of this study.

Data in Tables 2-10 and 2-11 show clearly that Japan's trade has in fact undergone a fundamental shift in direction between 1958 and 1972. Further, there are few if any signs that this shift is leveling off. By dividing the world into industrial and non-industrial countries,[h] Table 2-10 reveals that Japanese exports

[h]Every such classification has its arbitrary elements. To reflect industrial structure as much as per capita income, the Eastern European communist countries were classified with the developed group, and the Asian communist countries, together with Cuba, were less developed. Communist trade has accounted for about 5 to 6 percent of Japanese trade in recent years.

Table 2-10
Japanese Trade with Industrial and Non-Industrial Countries: Exports,
1958-1972 (Millions of U.S. Dollars)

	1958	1962	1966	1968	1970	1972
Exports:						
Industrial Countries[a]	1,085.9	2,294.9	4,843.8	6,385.0	9,947.2	19,138.9
Non-Industrial Countries[b]	1,790.8	2,393.0	4,935.2	6,614.2	9,370.4	9,480.9
Total	2,876.9	4,918.5	9,779.0	12,999.2	19,317.6	28,619.8
Percentage Shares:						
Industrial Countries	37.7	46.7	49.5	49.1	51.5	66.8
Non-Industrial Countries	62.2	53.2	50.5	50.1	48.5	33.2

[a]This category comprises totals for the IMF "Industrial Countries" together with "Other Developed Areas" and the Eastern European Communist Countries.
[b]This category includes all the less-developed areas, Cuba and the Asian Communist Countries, and the resource-rich areas of Australia, New Zealand, and South Africa.
Source: International Monetary Fund, *Direction of Trade, Annual, 1958-1962, 1966-1970, and 1968-1972.*

to the industrial countries grew several times as rapidly as the totals for the non-industrial countries did. In 1958, more than 62 percent of Japan's exports were directed to less-developed countries. By 1970, however, that figure fell to one-third, thereby reflecting the disproportionately slow growth trends in exports to the less-developed, non-industrial regions. It follows that Japanese exports were increasingly being reoriented to developed countries, with their respective shares growing from 38 percent to nearly 67 percent by 1972. These trends are particularly pronounced between 1970 and 1972, when virtually all Japan's export gains came from the industrial countries. It must be emphasized that Japan's exports to the non-industrial countries did rise from $1.8 billion in 1958 to $9.5 billion in 1972. These magnitudes were very large and, by any measure, this trade was of major importance to Japan. What *did* occur here was that trade with the developed countries grew so fast that the relative importance of the less-developed countries' trade declined steadily.

The same tendency to shift the direction of trade to industrial countries cannot, however, be observed for Japanese imports. Data in Table 2-11 show that the non-industrial countries share of Japanese imports moved within a narrow range over the fourteen-year period. The shares declined from 52 percent in 1958 to only 43.5 percent for the non-industrial countries by 1972. During the same years that imports from less-developed countries rose impressively— from $1.6 billion in 1958 to nearly $3 billion in 1962 and then to more than $10.2 billion in 1972—imports from developed countries grew from $1.5 billion to more than $13.2 billion. In sum, as export trade shares shifted continuously

26

Table 2-11
Japanese Trade with Industrial and Non-Industrial Countries: Imports,
1958-1972 (Millions of U.S. Dollars)

	1958	1962	1966	1968	1970	1972
Imports:						
Industrial Countries[a]	1,451.1	2,811.9	4,348.4	6,069.0	9,147.7	13,281.0
Non-Industrial Countries[b]	1,582.3	2,819.4	5,161.4	6,195.5	9,733.4	10,212.9
Total	3,033.5	5,634.7	9,522.5	12,894.5	18,881.1	23,493.9
Percentage Shares:						
Industrial Countries	47.8	49.9	45.7	46.7	48.5	56.5
Non-Industrial Countries	52.2	50.0	54.2	53.3	51.5	43.5

[a]This category comprises totals for the IMF "Industrial Countries" together with "Other Developed Areas" and the Eastern Communist Countries.
[b]This category includes all the less-developed areas, Cuba and the Asian Communist Countries, and the resource-rich areas of Australia, New Zealand, and South Africa.
Source: International Monetary Fund, *Direction of Trade, Annual, 1958-1962, 1966-1970, and 1968-1972.*

away from the non-industrial regions during the past ten to fifteen years, import shares were stable throughout much the period.

In could be argued that other, equally plausible classification criteria could be introduced. Australia and New Zealand, for example, could be classified as "developed" rather than non-industrial countries. Switching some individual countries from one group to another would affect the precise totals. The broad trends, however, remain unmistakable.

From the calculations of stable or declining trade with the less-developed, non-industrial regions above, it would be seemingly plausible to infer that the trends in Japan's Pacific Asian trade moved in similar directions. But since it was shown above that Pacific Asia's trade shares with Japan have been virtually constant, it follows that the burden of declining less-developed trade shares has been borne by some or all of the other principal less-developed geographic regions of the world. Which other regions have been displaced, and which have increased in importance? How does Pacific Asia's aggregate trade contrast with these other regions?

A partial answer to this question is provided when the regional distribution of Japan's foreign trade is analyzed. Data in Tables 2-12, for Japanese exports, and 2-13, for Japanese imports, show that there were major disparities in the regional trade impact upon Japan. For these purposes, Pacific Asian trade is shown separately in both tables, and in addition, there is a separate category of data covering a smaller, ten-country Pacific Asian subset that excludes Australia and

Table 2-12
Japanese Exports to Less-Developed Region, 1958-1972 (Millions of U.S. Dollars)

Region	1958	1962	1966	1970	1972
Pacific Asia	722.8	1,234.1	2,608.7	5,338.5	7,087.2
Ten Less-Developed Countries–(Pacific Asia)[a]	654.2	1,068.8	2,251.5	4,634.7	6,193.5
Latin America	205.0	345.2	517.6	1,112.2	1,810.1
Africa[b]	369.6	254.9	254.0	485.1	660.3
Middle East	137.1	165.8	361.6	557.1	958.9
Other Asia	273.6	442.8	704.8	865.0	727.4
Total to Less Developed Regions[b]	1,681.7	2,393.0	4,450.4	8,337.1	10,923.4

[a]Excluding Australia and New Zealand.
[b]Excluding South Africa.
Source: International Monetary Fund, *Direction of Trade Annual, 1958-1962 and 1966-1970* (Washington, D.C.).

New Zealand. Those latter two countries, parenthetically, have significantly higher per capita incomes than the other ten countries, and it was judged that a more accurate picture of *less-developed* regional comparative trade flows would emerge by concentrating the analysis upon only the ten countries. Among the other regions, the Latin American, African, and Middle Eastern areas are straightforward and unambiguous. Other Asia, in this context, includes all the remaining East and South Asian nations that have been heretofore excluded from consideration.[i] The exceptions were minor, including unclassified trade and other countries whose totals were insignificant.

Among the less-developed regions, the evidence in Table 2-12 shows unmistakably that Japanese exports to Pacific Asia (either the ten- or twelve-country subsets) were of a much larger order of magnitude than to any other less-developed region. It is easily seen that these exports rose from $650 million and $720 million in 1958 to more than $6 billion and $7 billion, respectively, by 1972. Where in 1958 about 40 percent of Japanese exports to the less-developed regions went to Pacific Asia, in 1972 more than 60 percent of the total was directed there. For the other regions, briefly, Japanese exports to each rose sharply. Among these other regions, the absolute volume of the African trade grew at the slowest rate during the last fourteen years while Latin America and, especially in recent years, the Middle East grew the most rapidly.

The principal finding here emerges clearly. Even though Japanese exports had undergone a fairly large shift in direction in favor of more-advanced countries, Japan was able to increase her exports to the Pacific Asian region much more

[i]India and Pakistan accounted for the largest trade flows for these residual countries.

Table 2-13
Japanese Imports From Less-Developed Regions, 1958-1972 (Millions of U.S. Dollars)

Region	1958	1962	1966	1970	1972
Pacific Asia	737.6	1,196.6	2,235.9	4,368.4	6,994.2
Ten Less-Developed Countries—(Pacific Asia)[a]	493.2	727.0	1,443.0	2,703.1	4,540.5
Latin America	259.3	477.3	781.2	1,368.7	1,267.2
Africa[b]	37.9	88.0	243.8	706.0	721.4
Middle East	342.2	592.0	1,232.8	2,292.5	3,221.6
Other Asia	158.6	302.2	508.7	605.5	739.7
Total from Less Developed Regions[b]	1,321.8	2,230.9	4,211.6	7,727.4	9,523.7

[a]Excluding Australia and New Zealand.
[b]Excluding South Africa.
Source: International Monetary Fund, *Direction of Trade, Annual, 1958-1962 and 1966-1970.*

rapidly than to any other less-developed area. (That finding would hold whether or not Australia and New Zealand were included.) Put another way, if Japan had been unable to rapidly expand export sales to Pacific Asia, the shifts in the direction of Japanese trade to advanced countries would have been far more pronounced than they were.

Table 2-13 shows that the Pacific Asian region accounted for similarly large and rising shares of Japanese imports from less-developed regions from 1958 to 1972. Most of these gains were, however, concentrated in the period after 1970. Thus, even though the Pacific Asian (ten-country) group maintained its position as the largest regional source of imports for Japan, the growth rate of these imports did not quite keep pace with the overall volume of Japanese imports from the developing regions of the world in the period before 1970—that is, while imports from the revised less-developed regions rose from $1.3 billion in 1958 to $9.5 billion in 1972, Japan's imports from the ten-country Pacific Asia region increased from about $493 million to $4.5 billion. In terms of other regions, an argument is frequently made that Japan's expanding petroleum requirements forced her to import oil from the Middle East in ever-growing amounts. Whatever the precise pace of oil needs, imports from the Middle East (which consisted almost entirely of petroleum) were found to have grown only slightly more rapidly than imports from the less-developed regions as a whole.[j] The major relative *gains*, accordingly, came from African imports. The biggest relative displacement, on the other hand, was suffered by the other Asian

[j]Events in 1973 make it unlikely that, looking ahead, the modest Middle East trends will continue, however.

countries, whose share in 1972 was slightly more than half the 1962 proportion of less-developed imports.

Needless to say, if Australia and New Zealand are included in Pacific Asia, its share of Japanese imports from non-industrial sources more than holds its own. The twelve-country group, in any event, accounts for nearly half of the Japanese non-industrial import totals. Yet, either set of figures in Table 2-13 points in the same direction; namely, it is clear that Japanese imports from the less-developed Pacific Asian countries have been smaller, relatively and absolutely, than their corresponding export totals to the region. Further, import shares from Pacific Asia and developing regions generally have been stable.

Japan's Commodity Trade Patterns

Up to this point in the discussion, Japanese exports and imports have been treated on an entirely aggregated basis. No formal attention has been given to the detailed commodity content of this trade. While the two-way commodity trade flows between Japan and Pacific Asia are broken down into 3- and 4-digit levels of classification and then analyzed in subsequent chapters, the bulk of that discussion concerns particular goods in terms of particular countries. The question that concerns us here is whether the major (1-digit) commodity categories in this two-way Pacific Asian trade were comparable to Japanese commodity trade flows with the rest of the world. The answer to this question depends upon changes in the trade within the major commodity groups, upon supply and demand patterns in the Pacific Asian region, and upon the nature of the trade itself. For example, did Japan export a different pattern of goods to Pacific Asia than she did to the rest of the world? Did Japanese imports from the region consist chiefly of a narrow range of goods, or were they more widely distributed among the major commodity classifications? In the brief discussion that follows, the chief concern is to identify the principal commodity patterns in this trade over the last decade. With a knowledge of the commodity trends, it is then possible to make some general remarks about whether the Pacific Asian region's shares of particular commodity groups increased or decreased over time and what effect, if any, these changes had on the overall commodity patterns of Japanese trade.

The relevant data on Japanese trade commodity patterns, in terms of the Pacific Asian region, are contained in Tables 2-14 (for exports) and 2-15 (for imports). These data are disaggregated to the SITC 1-digit levels, for a total of ten major commodity groups and were taken from selected numbers of the United Nations' *Commodity Trade Statistics, Series D.* For Japan, the data compare very closely with the International Monetary Fund's *Direction of Trade*

Table 2-14
The Commodity Composition of Japan's Exports to Pacific Asia, 1960-1970
(Thousands of U.S. Dollars)

Commodity Category	1960		1965		1970	
Food	39,886	(15.3)	46,983	(14.1)	210,704	(33.3)
Beverage & Tob.	502	(7.6)	507	(4.5)	685	(4.4)
Crude Materials	17,427	(14.1)	69,559	(31.2)	147,983	(45.3)
Mineral Fuels	11,344	(68.1)	18,702	(62.3)	34,937	(73.4)
Oils & Fats	4,987	(16.6)	2,907	(70.2)	10,482	(40.8)
Chemicals	88,033	(51.8)	296,504	(54.2)	599,835	(48.6)
Basic Manu.	586,758	(31.9)	1,009,995	(29.5)	2,140,788	(33.1)
Mchs., Trs. Equip.	277,104	(29.6)	652,363	(24.7)	1,818,903	(23.2)
Misc. Manu.	67,916	(70.1)	129,682	(11.1)	311,165	(12.1)
Other	–	(_)	12,661	(26.3)	41,293	(26.7)
Totals	1,094,461	(27.0)	2,240,471	(26.5)	5,317,155	(27.0)

Note: Figures in parentheses are Japanese exports to the Pacific region expressed as a percentage of total Japanese exports of the commodity group.
Source: United Nations, *Commodity Trade Statistics, Series D*, Vol. X-XX (New York: Statistical office).

statistics that have been chiefly relied upon heretofore.[k] Since the *Commodity Trade Statistics* is the principal source of thoroughly disaggregated trade statistics for a large number of countries, the fact that both data sources tell largely the same story is reassuring.

In Table 2-14, data are presented on Japanese exports to the Pacific Asian region as a whole. The figures in parenthesis represent the share of Japan's total trade in a given commodity classification for which the region has accounted. The categories are self-explanatory, with the "other" classification generally so small as to be insignificant.[l] The advantage of this breakdown is that the years 1960, 1965, and 1970 would highlight any shifts in the major categories over the decade.

Two major points emerge immediately from the data. First, for all three years examined, Japanese exports were highly concentrated among two of the ten categories, Basic Manufactures and Machinery and Transportation Equipment. In 1960, approximately 80 percent of Japan's exports to the Pacific Asian region were composed of these two commodity groups, and by 1970, they still

[k]Trade returns of, for example, Japanese total trade with a given country are available from both sources and can be easily compared. Where discrepancies exist, they are typically less than .1 percent of the total. For these purposes the differences are insignificant and can be ignored.

[l]"Other" includes shipments of armaments and goods not elsewhere classified by kind. As such, it largely comprises a residual category.

Table 2-15
The Commodity Composition of Japan's Imports from Pacific Asia, 1960-1970
(Thousands of U.S. Dollars)

Commodity Category	1960		1965		1970	
Food	154,892	(29.2)	455,272	(32.1)	658,770	(26.5)
Beverages & Tob.	27	(.1)	2,071	(3.8)	4,229	(4.6)
Crude Materials	730,302	(33.7)	995,295	(31.4)	2,187,744	(33.2)
Mineral Fuels	90,876	(12.3)	211,143	(13.0)	714,611	(18.3)
Oils & Fats	5,812	(15.3)	7,945	(14.8)	20,420	(26.1)
Chemicals	6,822	(2.6)	25,516	(6.3)	80,279	(8.0)
Basic Manu.	41,916	(16.7)	112,989	(20.5)	337,823	(18.1)
Mchs., Trs. Equip.	1,259	(.3)	1,849	(.3)	36,072	(1.7)
Misc. Manu.	1,255	(2.0)	16,315	(9.9)	111,961	(26.4)
Other	–	(–)	3,494	(20.4)	24,151	(26.4)
Totals	1,033,519	(23.0)	1,832,828	(22.4)	4,176,656	(22.1)

Note: Figures in parentheses are the imports from the Pacific region expressed as a percentage of total Japanese imports of the commodity group.
Source: United Nations, *Commodity Trade Statistics, Series D.*

accounted for three-quarters of Japan's regional exports. Further, this Pacific Asian trade generally fit the patterns of Japanese trade with the rest of the world. We can confirm this by comparing the shares of exports in these commodity groups the Pacific Asian region purchased with their share of Japan's overall exports. If Japanese world export patterns were not broadly similar, the relative shares could not also be similar. Further examination shows that chemicals and miscellaneous manufactures accounted for much of the remainder of this trade.

Second, the figures in parentheses show that with a very few exceptions, Pacific Asia has not generally become a dominant customer for Japan in any major commodity group. Chemicals are the chief exception. The data reveal that about half of Japan's exports of chemical products have consistently been directed to Pacific Asia.[m] Among the two chief categories, by way of contrast, Japan's export shares to Pacific Asia held relatively steadily at between a fourth and a third of the comparable world totals. (This does not ignore the high shares in the Mineral Fuels category or, in 1965, in the Oils and Fats category. These categories were quantitatively so small, however, that their impact upon the Japanese economy was hardly significant.)

With these basic trade patterns in mind, a third point is that it is also possible to support the assertion that the export patterns Japan established with the

[m]Yet chemical exports to Pacific Asia only constituted 5 to 6 percent of Japan's total exports over the decade. The trade has clearly been sizable but hardly of crucial importance to Japan.

Pacific Asian region allowed her to become slightly more diversified. Put somewhat differently, Pacific Asia provided Japan's major market for mineral fuels and chemicals, and more recently for fats and oils and crude materials. In the absence of this trade, Japanese exports of these products would have been even more miniscule. The result would have been that Japanese export patterns would have been somewhat more highly concentrated along the basic pattern noted above.

What can be said about Japanese commodity import patterns? Data in Table 2-15 show that Japanese imports have been centered almost exclusively upon industrial raw materials and food products. A principal finding, accordingly, is that the commodity pattern of Japanese imports from Pacific Asia was highly complementary to her export patterns with the region. More than 90 percent of Japan's imports came, in order of magnitude, from the Crude Materials, Foods, and Mineral Fuels categories—all of which consist of industrial raw materials or lightly processed products. These trends, further, were maintained throughout the period. Among the other 1-digit commodity classifications, Table 2-15 shows that only basic manufactures represented a significant import volume. At its peak in 1970, however, Japanese imports of basic manufactures were only $337 million. When those imports are compared to the corresponding Japanese export volume to Pacific Asia of $2.14 billion for 1970, the resulting gap is enormous. The absolute magnitudes were widening steadily throughout the decade of the 1960s.

A second major observation that can be made from the data is that throughout the 1960 to 1970 period the Pacific Asian region as a whole never accounted for more than 34 percent of Japan's total imports within any single commodity group. While a case will be made later that one or several countries in Pacific Asia accounted for very large shares of individual commodities (at the 3-digit level), these data show that such a case cannot be sustained for the major commodity groups. The smaller stable Japanese import shares from Pacific Asia also could be said to stand in sharp contrast to the dominant supplier role Japan occupies within the region's import markets.

It is an interesting question whether Japan's imports from Pacific Asia can expand significantly into other commodity groups.[15] The trends in basic manufactures were noted above. It seems plausible to hypothesize that the Miscellaneous Manufacturing category also offers considerable potential to these countries.[n] Following the customary factor-proportions argument, labor-intensive commodities would appear to offer the greatest scope for Pacific Asia. It is also possible to imagine very sizable increases in imported foods, including rice

[n]In terms of labor-intensive production industries (weaving, electronic assembly parts, and so forth), the limited scope for future automation means that Japan is rapidly outgrowing a competitive position in these industries. ". . . Japan is likely to be in the process not only of pricing itself out of that business, but also in a literal sense outgrowing it." Joseph Reday, "Far East Business," *Oriental Economist* 39, no. 728 (June 1971), p. 19.

and vegetables. There is considerable evidence in support of the view that restrictive Japanese import policies, rather than Pacific Asian supply conditions, have been the key operative variable in limiting this trade in the past.[16] If one assumes that Japan will continue to liberalize her import restrictions, it may well be plausible to expect Japan to import a growing quantity of more diversified imports from Pacific Asia in the years to come.[17]

Industrial Raw Material-Saving
Patterns of Industrial Growth

In the sections above, this study has shown that the Pacific Asian region generally maintained its share of Japanese imports throughout the 1958 to 1972 period. Collectively, the region accounted for nearly a quarter of Japan's total imports. In some ways this stability is surprising. This is because a commodity pattern that was heavily concentrated upon industrial raw materials, and to a lesser extent, food products was common to a majority of the Pacific Asian countries. A conventional argument put forward by many economists has been that the requirements of industrial growth have tended, over time, to reduce the degree of Japanese dependency upon imported industrial raw materials.[18] Given the Pacific Asian export composition together with the expected import-using patterns of Japanese industry, it seems plausible to speculate that the results would lead to a general decline in the region's relative trade shares with Japan.[19] Such a decline cannot be found in the data for most of the 1960s, and the purpose of this section is to attempt to resolve this seeming anomaly.

The case for the region's trade with Japan to worsen, at least relatively, is easy to make. It had been widely predicted that Japanese industrial requirements would shift away from relatively heavy use of industrial raw materials during the 1960s.[20] Within the Japanese economy, industries that utilized import-saving (in practice, industrial raw material-saving) patterns were expected to grow more rapidly than industries that relied heavily upon imported industrial raw material inputs.[21] Several other factors, including the increasing substitution of synthetics and technological change with a bias toward reducing the rate of raw material consumption per unit of output, could also be cited to support the argument that trends in imported industrial raw materials were generally expected to lag corresponding trends in Japan's domestic industrial activity.

Evidence in support of these predictions can be readily assembled. During an eight-year period centering upon the 1950s further, many of these expectations were realized. Constructing a crude measure of industrial dependency upon imported raw materials helps illustrate these trends. Data in Table 2-16, taken from Kanamori, shows that when indices of Japanese industrial production were compared with consumption indices of imported industrial raw materials, there were sharply declining trends in the levels of dependency of Japan's industrial

34

Table 2-16

Japanese Industrial Production and Its Dependence upon Imported Raw Materials, 1954-1961

Fiscal Year	(1) Industrial Production Index	(2) Imported Raw Material Consumption Index	(3) Column 2/ Column 1
1954	25.7	44.7	174
1955	26.1	45.0	173
1956	37.8	57.6	152
1957	52.6	67.1	128
1958	56.5	59.1	105
1959	72.6	79.0	109
1960	100.0	100.0	100
1961	129.0	118.2	92

Source: Ministry of International Trade and Industry, Seisan Dotai Tokei, in Kanamori, "Economic Growth and the Balance of Payments," R. Komiya, ed., *Postwar Economic Growth in Japan*, trans. by R. Ozaki (Berkeley: University of California Press, 1966), p. 91.

production upon imported raw materials. Indeed, Column 3 shows that between 1954 and 1961, imported raw materials grew only half as fast as industrial production. For some individual industries (e.g., cotton textiles, leather, rubber) imported raw material dependence continued to be very high. Nonetheless the overall picture that emerges is that the Japanese demand pattern for imported industrial raw materials was steadily declining in terms of her industrial production.[o]

Against this background, how can the Pacific Asian region's relatively stable import shares be explained? It seems clear that in the absence of a more diversified commodity export structure by the Pacific Asian countries to Japan, a partial explanation is that Japan's import requirements of industrial raw materials must have shifted significantly. Data in Table 2-17 confirm this hypothesis and make the changing trends more apparent. Comparison of an index of manufacturing industrial activity with indices of both unprocessed and processed imported raw materials makes clear that at least from 1962 to 1970, the rates of growth of imported raw materials were roughly proportional to manufacturing output generally. Indeed, processed imported raw materials (which were weighted much smaller quantitatively than unprocessed materials) grew considerably faster than industrial production.

[o]As the Japanese economy shifted from a heavily industrial structure to one in which the service sector was increasingly stressed, imported raw materials as a share of GNP would be expected to decline even more sharply. See Argus Madison, *Economic Growth in Japan and the U.S.S.R.*, Chapter 5.

Table 2-17
Japanese Manufacturing Activity and Its Dependence upon Imported Raw
Materials, 1962-1970

Year	Manufacturing Industry Index	Consumption Index of Imported Unprocessed Raw Materials	Column 2/ Column 1	Consumption Index of Imported Processed Raw Materials	Column 4/ Column 1
1962	74.2	72.5	97.7	55.2	89.2
1963	82.9	79.1	95.4	81.1	97.8
1964	96.3	92.6	96.2	128.1	133.0
1965	100.0	100.0	100.0	100.0	100.0
1966	113.4	111.2	98.1	108.8	95.9
1967	136.0	134.9	99.2	151.4	111.0
1968	160.4	150.1	93.6	175.7	109.0
1969	187.8	175.0	93.2	219.5	117.0
1970	218.5	201.2	92.1	219.9	100.6

Note: Column 3 = Column 1 divided by Column 2; Column 5 = Column 1 divided by
Source: *Oriental Economist, Japan Yearbook 1971* (Tokyo, 1972), selected tables,
statistical appendices.

These trends are even more striking when a crude index of the domestic industrial sector's dependency upon processed and unprocessed raw materials is constructed. While unprocessed raw materials declined slightly, from .97 to .92 (Column 3), the dependency upon processed raw materials actually increased substantially, from .89 to 1.00 (Column 5). Dependency was higher for several intermediate years. Overall, the principal finding that emerges is that unlike the 1954-1961 findings, the degree of foreign raw material import dependency fell much more slowly between 1962 and 1970. Put another way, whatever potential tendencies for import-saving patterns of industrial growth existed during the 1960s, an examination of the actual trade returns offered little support for the hypothesis that import- (industrial raw material-) saving patterns were being realized.

Chapter 6 offers a detailed explanation of Pacific Asia's actual export trade experiences with Japan. The chief purpose of this section, however, has been to establish the plausibility of rapidly growing Japanese import requirements, centered on several key commodities used for industrial inputs. These growing requirements help to explain why imports from Pacific Asia grew largely in proportion to Japan's imports from the rest of the world over the decade of the 1960s.

The existence of Japan's rapidly growing demands for imported industrial raw materials did not occur in isolation. Instead, a key factor was the virtual stability of price trends for these imported raw materials and, for that matter, for imports generally. Data in Table 2-18 show the import price trends for composite imports and for three groups of commodities: textile raw materials, metal ores and scraps, and other raw materials. For the 1959 to 1970 period, the price trends for textile raw materials and metal ores (except for 1970) were virtually constant. The Other Raw Materials category also shows an increase of an average of .5 percent per year until the last two years. Since most of these goods consist of, at best, lightly processed raw materials, it is difficult to make definitive statements about quality. It seems plausible to assume, however, that there was either little deterioration or little improvement in the quality of many of these commodities.[p] If this was in fact the case, then the price trends in imported industrial raw materials stand in sharp contrast to Japanese consumer prices, which were rising fairly steeply throughout the decade.[q]

Import prices are not a key issue here. In the methodology developed in Chapter 4, it is not necessary to isolate and analyze commodity price trends in and of themselves. From the point of view of the study, the central question this section asks is whether Japan's needs for industrial raw materials from abroad have grown or declined. From the data discussed above, it would appear that the industrial raw material needs have grown rapidly. The flat, unchanging overall

Table 2-18
Selected Prices Indices for Japanese Imported Raw Materials, 1959-1970

Year	Composite Imports	Textile Raw Materials	Metal Ores, Scraps	Other Raw Materials
1959	95.9	92.4	97.9	97.8
1960	97.1	99.6	100.9	102.1
1961	96.2	102.2	102.6	97.4
1962	94.5	101.0	97.8	96.8
1963	95.6	103.4	89.4	95.5
1964	97.9	108.3	95.8	94.5
1965	100.0	100.0	100.0	100.0
1966	100.7	100.1	102.8	104.2
1967	100.4	95.5	98.4	103.9
1968	99.0	95.6	97.8	103.2
1969	98.8	95.0	99.0	107.3
1970	103.7	90.1	108.4	111.1

Source: *Oriental Economist, Japan Yearbook 1971* (Tokyo, 1972), selected tables, statistical appendices.

[p]Growing international competition and the high degree of substitutability between countries (and sometimes commodities) could be expected to help Japan insure that quality standards would not be eroded.

[q]The consumer price index rose from 74.0 in 1960 to 115.0 in 1968, with 1965 = 100. Japan Bureau of Statistics, *Statistical Handbook of Japan 1970* (Tokyo: Office of the Prime Minister, 1971), p. 110.

price trends in the imported raw materials categories reinforced these import-using industrial patterns. At the least, they did not constitute ever-growing pressures upon Japanese industrialists to adopt import-saving methods or to produce only goods whose import dependence was small, because rapidly growing input prices were eroding industrial profits.

Conclusion

From the discussion in this chapter, it is apparent that foreign trade generally continued to be of major importance to the Japanese economy. Japan continually extended her share of world trade from 1955 to 1972, so that by 1972 she was accounting for more than 6 percent of world trade totals. External dependence was scarcely increased, however, since Japanese national income accounts grew proportionately. It seems more plausible to argue that the strong, sustained Japanese domestic growth pulled trade along rather than to assert that foreign trade comprised a pivotal, leading sector within Japan's economy.

The overall growth in Japanese international trade should not be allowed to obscure considerable shifts in the direction and composition of that trade. Exports particularly were increasingly directed towards industrial countries. Trade with the Pacific Asian region, by way of contrast, accounted for remarkably stable shares of Japan's exports and imports to the world. Measured in terms of other less-developed regions, on the other hand, Japan had by 1972 increased her shares from the Pacific Asian countries somewhat from 1955-1958 levels. In no way, however, did the region regain its prewar importance to Japan. Examination of the commodity composition of the two-way trade flows reveals the almost perfectly complementary nature of this trade. A major finding is that Japan's earlier tendencies toward raw material-saving patterns of industrial growth had been halted or reversed. A key factor in explaining the rapidly growing Japanese imports from Pacific Asia, accordingly, is that their demand for Pacific Asia's primary exports was growing, by the start of the 1970s, roughly in proportion to their domestic industrial activity.

If the reasoning put forward in this chapter is generally correct, then Japan's "traditional" trade with Pacific Asia generally continued within accustomed channels. To be sure, the *rates* at which that trade increased were substantial, and they were clearly much larger than comparable levels from previous periods. What is probably most striking is that the opportunities to expand this trade rose so continuously.

3 Pacific Asian Trade Flows: The Influence of Japan

Between the mid-1950s and the early 1970s the Pacific Asian countries' foreign trade more than doubled. Ten of these twelve countries were and are low- or, at best, middle-income countries for whom foreign trade has provided a major stimulus to domestic employment, production, and economic growth.

A central proposition of this study is that the continual trade expansion, critical to sustaining economic growth in these Pacific Asian countries, became increasingly dependent upon Japan during the period studied. The expanded trade flows, which have been set in the context of the region's trade with the rest of the world, require relatively brief discussion beyond presenting the basic data and analyzing the key trends. It is asserted below that although Japanese trade was relatively unimportant to some of these countries at the start of the 1960s, Japan had become the dominant trading partner for virtually every country in Pacific Asia by 1970 or 1972.

A parallel theme is that on the supply side, the greatly enlarged trade flows between the region and Japan were generally limited rather narrowly to long-established trade patterns. This meant that Pacific Asia continued to export chiefly industrial raw materials and food products to Japan. The Pacific Asian region's import demands, on the other hand, consisted largely of Japanese machinery, manufactures, and chemical products. By the early 1970s, paren-thetically, Japan had become a key supplier of capital goods to most of Pacific Asia.

This chapter is divided into three parts. The first section attempts to establish the plausibility of an outward-looking, externally oriented economic strategy for Pacific Asia. Since many of these arguments have appeared elsewhere in considerable detail, only a brief summary case is presented here.

The second portion of this chapter presents the summary trade data for the Pacific Asian countries. The region's trade flows are contrasted against other developing areas in order to assess their relative growth in trade. A crude measure of trade dependency is developed, and shifts in the terms of trade are also examined.

The chapter ends with an analysis of the growing Japanese role in trade. Data concerning both absolute and relative trade flows are offered. The implications of the expanded trade with Japan are analyzed by contrasting the Pacific Asian trade flows to other developed regions.

Throughout this chapter some basic reservations about the accuracy of this data will be raised. A more detailed examination of the comparability, as well as the accuracy, of the data, however, is presented in the Appendix.

39

**The Role of Foreign Trade in the
Pacific Asian Countries**

Two sharply different arguments with respect to the possibilities for international trade for developing countries have been widely represented in the literature in recent years. The first begins with the premise that developing countries are likely to export mostly primary products and import manufactured goods and machinery. A hypothesis that the elasticities of demand facing exporters of food stuffs and lightly processed raw materials are typically apt to be low is next put forward. Extending this argument suggests that the export prospects for primary products are simply not promising. Gunnar Myrdal has made this argument with particular respect to Southeast Asia.[1] If trade is actively pursued, this reasoning continues, what also happens is that imports of machinery and manufactures rise sharply. Given the expected higher income elasticities of demand for these imports, it follows that a major reliance on trade is accompanied by steady declines in the terms of trade. This consequently requires that an ever greater volume of primary products be exported in order to pay for imports.[2]

It remains for Myrdal to state the case of trade for Pacific Asia in perhaps its most pessimistic form. He argues:

There is no longer any significant stimulus to be derived from export markets.[3] In fact, demand for most of South Asia's traditional exports is expected to rise hardly at all. . . . If development is to occur in the South Asian countries, it will not come as a response to foreign demand for the products in which the region has traditionally had a comparative advantage.[4]

Indeed the main thesis of Myrdal's discussion of foreign trade is that "the spontaneous growth-inducing stimulus of a relatively free and expanding international trade is no longer present."[5] Successful development efforts, he argues, must accordingly be internally based.

The second argument starts with an assertion that foreign trade generally can play a key role in a nation's economic growth and development. Hla Myint, more than perhaps anyone else, has been identified with this pro-trade position.[6] These claims are particularly relevant to Pacific Asia, it is contended, because most of these countries have several physical and structural characteristics that make them unusually well suited to benefiting from specialization and foreign exchange.[7]

The potential appeal of international trade to the Pacific Asian region can be readily demonstrated. First, even though levels of production and per capita income differ widely, the region as a whole can be accurately portrayed as having a relatively abundant, although considerably underexploited, natural resource endowment. Also, particularly if parts of Mainland China, Singapore, Hong Kong, and the island of Java are excluded, these countries are not overpopulated. Whatever the actual levels of economic achievement, prospects do not appear to have been sharply constrained by adverse pressures of population on a limited, inadequate land/natural resource base.[8] In this context, it is plausible to argue that a major economic problem for most Pacific Asian countries, certainly unlike other less-developed regions, has been to bring additional land and natural resources into more productive use.

Secondly, again with a few exceptions, the Pacific Asian countries' relatively small population and geographic size, together with their limited purchasing power, have resulted in modest domestic markets for most products in these countries. The resulting effective demand has typically been of insufficient size to warrant the build-up of large-scale domestic manufacturing industries or major capital goods expenditures.[9] Indeed, there is considerable evidence that the smaller the country and the lower its productive capacity, the greater the role that the foreign trade sector would occupy in its economy.[10]

The large, underexploited resource base and small internal national markets, taken together, make a strong *prima facie* case for an outward-looking development strategy that relies heavily upon international trade. A more important question, however, is to ask whether the domestic structure of these economies would lend itself to large-scale trade. Is trade a viable strategy for the Pacific Asian countries to explore?

All of this leads Myint to conclude that trade should be at the core of Pacific Asian development efforts.[11] What is relevant for these countries, he argues, is that a "vent-for-surplus" theory, rather than the more common "comparative-cost" trade doctrine, should be stressed. In developing this case, three critical assumptions central to the theory of comparative cost must be challenged and ultimately modified. First, Myint and others hold that many developing countries do possess significant and substantial surplus productive capacity. This is more than disguised unemployment. Unlike comparative-cost the vent-for-surplus model not only does not assume full employment, but it makes the further contention that exports (here of industrial raw materials) can be increased without lowering domestic consumption. Secondly, vent-for-surplus assumes that *domestic* demand for many of these potential exportables has been generally inelastic. Finally, vent-for-surplus proponents are generally dubious about internal factor mobility. Fairly rigid factor *immobility*, it would be argued, is a more reasonable supposition. Taken together, the threads of the vent-for-surplus model constitutes a powerful argument on behalf of international trade. Following this approach, subsequent chapters argue strongly that the general "vent-for-surplus" model has been, and is, highly plausible in explaining much of the Pacific Asian countries export patterns over the last two decades.[12]

How viable has this outward-looking trade strategy been? What relevance does it have vis-à-vis the region's Japanese trade? A central hypothesis of this study is that in line with the arguments outlined above, the sharp rise in international trade has been a major factor underlying the region's economic growth.[13] This means that the pro-trade arguments of Myint are supported more strongly than the more pessimistic conclusions of Myrdal.

In practice, rapid increases in Pacific Asian trade would require that exports be heavily concentrated around industrial raw materials and food products. To assert that the Pacific Asian countries should rely heavily upon this pattern of exports is to reverse the conventional arguments cited above with respect to the composition of trade, which contend that both low-demand elasticities and market instabilities accompany dependence upon exports of primary products and lightly processed commodities.

It is plausible to argue for an export-oriented strategy. What is needed, however, is to test this hypothesis against Pacific Asian data in recent years. Accordingly, the next section of this chapter attempts to analyze the key trends in Pacific Asian trade over the last fifteen years. With that analysis as a background, the remaining portions of the chapter endeavor to demonstrate that the region's trade patterns have corresponded to the outlines developed above before finally turning to an examination of Japan's impact upon Pacific Asian trade.

The Growth of Pacific Asian Trade

Every country in the world, whether developed or less-developed, engages in foreign trade. For centuries, the Pacific Asian countries have exported rubber, tin, rice, sugar, and other commodities to the rest of the world. No widespread, extensive coordination by government authorities or economic planners was needed to insure that some basic volume of trade would be carried out among those traditional commodities. What is principally at issue here, when differentiating among alternative economic strategies, is the extent to which foreign trade, and the entire foreign sector, are elevated to a high order of magnitude in the economic process.[14]

The basic aggregates and trends of Pacific Asia's exports and imports to the world are presented in Tables 3-1 and 3-2. Several different comparisons can be used to demonstrate that both Pacific Asian exports and imports have risen extraordinarily rapidly during the last ten or fifteen years. While the accuracy of some countries' individual trade returns may be open to some question, the broad trends discussed below in this chapter rest upon a relatively reliable foundation. In particular a strong argument can be made for relying with some confidence upon trend analysis. Many of the biases in the data are systematic and recurrent. Analysis of trends, accordingly, eliminates a major portion of the noncomparability in the trade returns.

The most striking finding in Table 3-1 was the magnitude of the increases in exports to the world that were recorded by ten of the twelve countries in Pacific

Table 3-1

The Growth of Pacific Asian Trade: Exports to the World, 1958-1972 (Millions of U.S. Dollars)

Country	1958	1962	1970	1971	1972
Australia	1,663	2,365	4,770	5,214	6,457
Burma	193	255	107	123	114
Mainland China	1,910	1,525	2,050	2,314	2,885
Hong Kong	568	766	2,514	2,871	3,478
Indonesia	755	682	1,009	1,247	1,548
Korea	16	55	835	1,068	1,624
Malaysia	616	856	1,686	1,637	1,721
New Zealand	700	789	1,225	1,362	1,766
Philippines	491	554	1,062	1,128	1,105
Singapore	1,025	1,116	1,554	1,755	2,181
Taiwan	148	213	1,428	1,998	2,916
Thailand	307	454	710	831	1,063
Total: Pacific Asia	8,392	9,630	18,950	21,534	26,858
World Exports	109,747	142,470	280,641	314,940	372,180
Pacific Asia as Percent of World	7.6	6.8	6.8	6.8	7.1

Source: Data for 1958 and 1962 for all countries but Mainland China taken from International Monetary Fund, *Direction of Trade: A Supplement to International Financial Statistics*, 1958-1962 (Washington, D.C. 1964). Data for 1970, 1971, and 1972 taken from I.M.F., *Direction of Trade, Annual, 1968-1972* (Washington, D.C.). Data was reported on an "IFS" basis whenever possible. The 1958 and 1962 Chinese data for 1958 and 1962 was taken from Robert L. Price, "International Trade of Communist China, 1950-1965," in U.S. Congress, Joint Economic Committee, *An Economic Profile of Mainland China*, Vol. II (Washington, 1967), p. 584. For 1970, Chinese data was taken from A.H. Usack and R.E. Batsavage, "The International Trade of the People's Republic of China" in U.S. Congress, *People's Republic of China: An Economic Assessment* (Washington, 1972), p. 349. For 1971 and 1972, Chinese data taken from *PRC, International Trade Handbook* (Washington, D.C., 1973).

Asia between 1958 and 1972. From the region as a whole, exports tripled between 1958 and 1972 in a rise from $8.4 billion in 1958 to $26.8 billion by 1972. Korean exports recorded the largest individual rate of growth, while only Burmese exports actually declined. By 1970, Australia, Hong Kong, and Taiwan, respectively, were the three largest exporters in the Pacific Asian region. The region's export growth rate is all the more impressive if the trade returns of Mainland China and Burma are eliminated. Since China was the region's largest exporter in the base year 1958 and accounted for nearly a quarter of the region's total sales, her relatively sluggish export performance depressed the region's growth rates considerably.

An examination of the data presented in Table 3-2 shows that imports of these twelve countries rose as rapidly as did exports. For Pacific Asia as a whole,

Table 3-2
The Growth of Pacific Asian Trade: Imports from the World, 1958-1972
(Millions of U.S. Dollars)

Country	1958	1962	1970	1971	1972
Australia	1,796	2,265	4,542	4,692	4,614
Burma	204	216	155	169	129
Mainland China	1,825	1,150	2,170	2,253	2,769
Hong Kong	849	1,163	2,905	3,387	3,902
Indonesia	513	647	893	1,174	1,452
Korea	378	421	1,894	2,394	2,522
Malaysia	541	797	1,413	1,435	1,643
New Zealand	707	1,162	1,156	1,248	1,445
Philippines	546	645	1,210	1,326	1,366
Singapore	1,221	1,317	2,461	2,828	3,383
Taiwan	222	297	1,524	1,844	2,524
Thailand	393	542	1,293	1,287	1,484
Total: Pacific Asia	9,195	10,622	21,616	23,984	27,233
World Imports	114,704	148,996	294,749	330,013	386,074
Pacific Asia as Percent of World	8.0	7.1	7.3	7.6	7.1

Source: Data for 1958 and 1962 for all countries but Mainland China taken from International Monetary Fund, *Direction of Trade: A Supplement to International Financial Statistics, Annual 1958-1962.* Data for 1970, 1971, and 1972 taken from I.M.F., *Direction of Trade: Annual 1968-1972.* Data was reported on an "IFS" basis whenever possible. The 1958 and 1963 Chinese data for 1958 and 1962 was taken from Robert L. Price, "International Trade of Communist China, 1950-1965," p. 584. For 1970, Chinese data was taken from A.H. Usack and R.E. Batsavage, "The International Trade of the People's Republic of China," p. 349. For 1971 and 1972, Chinese data taken from *PRC, International Trade Handbook* (Washington, D.C., 1973).

imports rose from $9.2 billion in 1958 to $27.2 billion by 1972. Taiwanese and Korean imports, which recorded the largest increases, rose by factors of 11 and 6, respectively. Again Burma lagged by being the only country whose imports actually declined between 1958 and 1972. Australia and Hong Kong were the region's largest importers and accounted for about one-third of the twelve-nation total. Furthermore, it should be noted that the region's gains are all the more striking when China's import returns are eliminated. In sum, the trends in these data reveals clearly that the absolute volume of Pacific Asian trade increased steadily and significantly over the period.

The summary national trade totals, however, obscure several additional findings that are highly relevant to the argument that Pacific Asian trade increased rapidly. How much, for example, did these twelve-nation totals rise in comparison to the world totals during the last two decades? Tables 3-1 and 3-2 also present data on world exports and imports over the same period. What is striking is that the region has succeeded in roughly maintaining its share of world trade, with the actual figure stabilizing around a 7 percent share of both imports and exports in recent years. If China is excluded from Pacific Asia, moreover, the data clearly shows upward trends in world shares. Viewed in terms of world totals as well as aggregate amounts, consequently, Pacific Asia gains in trade emerge as growing swiftly and in parallel with the rest of the world.

In some ways, simple world comparisons obscure the export-import perform- ance of the Pacific Asian countries. Since the twelve Pacific Asian countries are largely non-industrial in structure, and since ten of the twelve are less-developed countries, the relevant comparison is to set their trade against the data of other developing regions. This is done in Table 3-3 for exports. Two comparisons are made. The first, on line 1, aggregates the export returns for selected years for all twelve of the Pacific Asian countries that constitute the core of the study. The second eliminates Australia and New Zealand, which are hardly low-income countries, and China, which has often pursued autarkic policies. The results for the nine developing countries that remain are shown on line 2. Four other developing regions were selected for comparison, including Latin America, Africa, the Middle East, and the remaining countries in Asia not heretofore examined.

Comparisons of historical trends have traditionally offered a means of sustaining whatever point one wished to advance. This is because one could simply choose to examine whichever historical time frame provided the desired empirical support. Table 3-3 illustrates this dilemma. The central finding to

Table 3-3
Exports of the Developing Regions to the World, 1955-1972 (Millions of U.S. Dollars)

Region	1955	1960	1965	1970	1972
Pacific Asia	8,388	9,988	12,274	18,657	26,476
9 Developing Countries (Pacific Asia)[a]	4,541	5,235	6,308	10,686	15,754
Other Asia[b]	2,459	2,545	3,023	3,514	3,996
Latin America	7,365	7,959	10,100	13,840	16,200
Africa[c]	3,975	4,500	7,040	11,840	14,000
Middle East[d]	3,500	5,021	7,140	11,160	17,600

[a]Developing Pacific Asian countries include Burma, Hong Kong, Indonesia, Korea, Malaysia, Philippines, Singapore, Taiwan, Thailand.

[b]"Other Asia" included all the remaining Asian countries after the Pacific Asian countries were subtracted.

[c]Union of South Africa excluded from African totals.

[d]Northeast African countries were excluded from the reported Middle East totals and added to Africa in 1955 and 1960 to make the regional returns consistent with later breakdowns.

Source: International Monetary Fund, *International Financial Statistics*, selected issues. Totals were revised as noted above.

emerge from this data is that the Pacific Asia countries trade performance compares favorably when measured against other developing regions. From 1955 to 1972, Pacific Asian exports rose more slowly than those of Africa or the Middle East but more rapidly than Latin America and the remaining countries in Asia. For 1960-1972, these findings continue to hold. If one confines the examination to the most recent period from 1965 to 1972, however, it is apparent that Pacific Asian export gains were outstripped only by the petroleum-dominated Middle East countries. Parenthetically it should be noted that the "other" Asian countries had a much lower growth in exports than any other region.

The findings are more pronounced when Australia, New Zealand, and China are excluded from the totals. While the broad magnitudes retain the same patterns when compared from 1955 to 1960, Table 3-3 shows a sharp upsurge in 1965, when the nine developing countries in the region match or surpassed every other less-developed area in the world. Put somewhat differently, the *pace* of the region's export trends has accelerated sharply in recent years in both absolute and comparative terms.

The large and growing gaps between aggregate Pacific Asian exports and imports put an increasingly heavy strain on the region's overall balance of payments. Not only did the volume of trade rise, but there is considerable evidence to suggest that the region's increasing dependence on trade elevated its importance within their respective economies (see below). Imports, valued on a c.i.f. basis, are customarily greater than exports, valued f.o.b. The magnitude of these trade gaps, however, seem greater than transportation costs alone could account for. One way of explaining these divergencies is to argue that the reporting techniques were faulty. This does not seem wholly plausible. It seems more likely, moreover, that published trade returns would tend to understate *imports*, rather than exports. If so, the "true" trade gaps may have been even larger. Accordingly, it seems reasonable to attempt to explain the regional trade deficits by suggesting that the import-export totals were in fundamental disequilibrium. This enhanced burden was placed upon financial systems that were, even without any increased trade, already struggling to help provide the credits and capital formation required by domestic efforts to accelerate the growth of their respective economies. The international sector was not, of course, solely responsible for this overburdening, but it did make a significant contribution.

Capital inflows from abroad, it should be noted, can provide a means of reducing international demands for foreign exchange. The central theme of Chapter 7 is to discuss the specific ways in which these accommodating flows have been available to the Pacific Asian countries. Full discussion on this point, together with detailed evidence on all of the financial flows, will accordingly be delayed until then. Yet, the trade deficit question is an important one for the region, and no analysis of its past trade experience can be complete without considering carefully the constraints imposed by the continuing deficits.

With these rapidly growing Pacific Asian trade aggregates in mind, it is useful to begin to establish the impact of the foreign trade sector upon the respective national economies. No measure is unambiguously satisfactory. Employment and national accounts data for these countries are incomplete and not highly reliable. If one grants these limitations, however, it is still possible to establish plausible estimates of foreign trade's aggregate impact.

A principal measure of the magnitude of the foreign sector upon the domestic economy is to estimate trade dependency ratios. This approach requires that exports and imports be weighted as proportional shares of gross national product. In this context it is plausible to suggest that growing trade dependency ratios be taken as support for the hypothesis that many of the Pacific Asian countries have adopted outward-looking strategies.

The key data concerning trade dependencies is presented for Pacific Asian exports in Table 3-4 and for imports in Table 3-5. Three-year averages are used. In order to eliminate potential distortions caused by sharply divergent trends in a country's domestic and international price levels, data is presented in both nominal and real terms.

The basic results reveal several interesting findings. First, with the single exception of China, a country notable for its attempts at domestic self-reliance for most of the period since 1949,[15] the nominal export shares have been very substantial for most Pacific Asian countries. By 1969-71, the range of trade for these countries (excluding China) was between an eighth and a half of GNP, with an average of about 20 percent. Over time, moreover, most of the countries here

Table 3-4

Pacific Asian Export Dependency Ratios, 1957-1971 (In Percentage Terms)

Country	Exports/Gross National Product			Real Exports/Real Gross National Product		
	1957-59	1964-66	1969-71	1957-59	1964-66	1969-71
Australia	20	16	16	16	17	21
Burma	21	15	–	22	–	–
China	2.1	2.1	1.8	–	–	–
Indonesia	–	–	12.3	–	–	–
Malaysia	–	45	48	–	44	–
New Zealand	27	23	25	24	23	30
Philippines	12	18	17	11	19	22
S. Korea	3	9	15	–	10	31
Taiwan	12	19	32	12	28	44
Thailand	–	19	17	–	22	17

Source: Data for all countries except China was taken from various issues of the International Monetary Fund's *International Financial Statistics*, and United Nations, *Yearbook of International Trade Statistics* (New York). Data for Mainland China taken from Arthur G. Ashbrook, Jr., "China: Economic Policy and Economic Results, 1949-1971," and A.H. Usack and R.E. Batsavage, "The International Trade of the People's Republic of China," both in U.S. Congress, Joint Economic Committee, *People's Republic of China: An Economic Assessment* (Washington, D.C., May 18, 1972), pp. 3-51 and pp. 335-70.

Table 3-5
Pacific Asian Import Dependency Ratios, 1957-1971 (In Percentage Terms)

Country	Imports/Gross National Product			Real Imports/Real Gross National Product		
	1957-59	1964-66	1969-71	1957-59	1964-66	1969-71
Australia	21	17	16	18	18	18
Burma	25	16	–	–	–	–
China	2.0	1.8	1.7	–	–	–
Indonesia	–	–	16	–	–	–
Malaysia	–	42	44	–	43	–
New Zealand	28	24	24	28	26	24
Philippines	14	18	18	17	20	22
S. Korea	12	17	26	–	18	65
Taiwan	20	20	31	–	–	–
Thailand	–	20	21	–	23	22

Source: Data for all countries except China was taken from various issues of the International Monetary Fund, *International Financial Statistics* and United Nations, *Yearbook of International Trade Statistics*. Data for Mainland China taken from Arthur G. Ashbrook, Jr., "China: Economic Policy and Economic Results, 1949-1971," and A.H. Usack and R.E. Batsavage, "The International Trade of the People's Republic of China," pp. 3-51 and pp. 335-70.

did not experience large changes in their export shares, the two principal exceptions being South Korea and Taiwan.[a] The import dependency ratios in Table 3-5 reveal a set of broadly parallel findings. While the *average* proportion of imports in terms of GNP is noticeably higher—say, typically accounting for more than a quarter of marketed output—the lack of any pronounced *change* in the trends is readily apparent.[b]

There are several questions pertaining to this study that can be asked about trade dependency in Pacific Asia. The first is to question whether in fact there was little change in trade's proportion of marketed output over time. The second is to ask whether differential price effects can account for some distortion in the trends in nominal dependencies discussed above. The third and potentially the most interesting question is what happened to the growth of domestic output over these years, and what effect did that growth have on trade dependency and the international sector generally?

The first question can only be dealt with in cursory fashion here. At its heart is the comprehensiveness; and the quality, of the national income accounts statistics in some of the developing countries.[c] This study does not attempt to

[a]The low Korean results in 1957-59 are offset somewhat by the impact of her continuing postwar recovery efforts.

[b]These proportions could increase further as UNCTAD inspired special trade promoting measures are implemented. "Trade and Aid in Asia," in Far Eastern Economic Review, *1973 Far Eastern Economic Review Asia Yearbook* (Hong Kong, 1973), p. 55.

[c]See Appendix A for an expanded discussion of the reliability of Pacific Asian economic statistics with respect to international trade.

subject the region's national income statistics to a careful examination. Yet, the underlying quality of this data *is* important, and it would be good if other studies would begin to focus on ways to improve the quality and the comparability of the region's data. Here it is sufficient to note that over time more of a country's economic activity enters the market and is consequently included in its national accounts. This means that part of the increase in economic growth is due to more comprehensive data.[16] Trade returns, based frequently on customs information, is less subject to this upward bias. Taken together, there is evidence to suggest that the magnitudes of exports and imports in proportion to GNP *understate* the actual impact of the international sector on aggregate economic activity in recent years. Thus, in the context of this study, it is reasonable to argue that the trends in trade's proportion of marketed output have, contrary to Tables 3-4 and 3-5, risen over time.

What has happened to comparative price levels that would affect the findings above? Evidence of a very preliminary sort on the *real* magnitudes is available for six of the Pacific Asian countries. It must be stated clearly that there are major limitations to this data, and one should be extremely reluctant to place much confidence on these findings. From the point of view of this section, however, the key issue is whether real trade dependence has increased since the late 1950s. From what little data are available to answer that question, it would appear that the real proportions of trade to domestic output generally rose or, at the least, declined less than the comparable nominal figures. Since it follows that domestic prices rose more quickly than export/import prices, actual trade dependence may be further understated.

There are two principal reasons why the trade dependence of the Pacific Asian countries ostensibly was not larger. Both have as much to do with domestic economic gains as with foreign trade. First, the domestic economic performance of most Pacific Asian countries exhibited large, sustained increases during the last two decades. Table 3-6 presents data on GNP growth rates, in real terms, and for per capita income levels for a number of countries. While this data must be used with care, what is apparent is that with only a few exceptions the Pacific Asian region's domestic economic gains were considerable. Second, for eight of the eleven countries here, and in direct proportion to their per capita income levels, average real domestic growth rates accelerated during the last decade. If this data is regarded as fully plausible, the reason that the proportional share of foreign trade to total income rose slowly if at all was that *both* were increasing rapidly.

In low-income countries attempting to industrialize, a wide range of plant and machinery needs are required. Except for Australia and New Zealand, the capital-goods industries in much of Pacific Asia had neither the versatility nor the technological capacity to meet domestic industrial needs. For continuous changes in the productive structures to take place, it was necessary to import large and growing amounts of capital goods.

What is particularly relevant to the central theme of this chapter in this context is that it is difficult to imagine the broad economic growth outlined in

Table 3-6
Gross National Product Growth Rates, Pacific Asia, 1950-1970 (Real Terms)

Country	1969 G.N.P. (Per Capita)	Average Annual Rates of Growth, Real Gross National Product	
		1950-1960	1960-1970
Burma	$ 74	6.3	3.7[a]
Indonesia	104	3.8	3.3
Thailand	181	6.4	8.0
Philippines	219	6.5	5.7
Korea	228	5.0	9.2
Taiwan	346	8.1	9.9
Malaysia	351	4.0	6.0
Hong Kong	777	9.5	10.0
Singapore	844	5.4	6.9
New Zealand	1918	3.2	4.0
Australia	2660	4.3	5.3

[a]1960-1968.
Source: United Nations, *Handbook of International Trade and Development Statistics, 1972,* (New York: Conference on Trade and Development, 1972) compiled from Part VI, p. 239.

Table 3-6 taking place without the prior importation of a considerable volume of capital goods. Subsequent chapters fully explore the composition of Pacific Asia's imports with a view toward identifying the foreign capital goods components. Much of this discussion will accordingly be postponed. But a simpler, if more subtle, point is at issue here.

A major contention of this study is that Pacific Asian growth has been tied closely to trade. If one attempts to test that hypothesis against widely held notions of trade dependence, the findings and discussion above provide modest but not overwhelming support. But the argument here transcends nominal or real measures. For economic growth to be maintained, imported capital goods were required. Otherwise most of these economies would not have been able to sustain the pace of their industrialization. Whatever the data on trade proportions showed, Pacific Asia's *actual* dependence on trade as an engine of growth was significantly higher.

If imports are to be paid for, the foreign exchange can be provided by export earnings or foreign capital inflows. While both were important, what must be underscored here is Pacific Asia's ability to maintain large annual increases in exports. According to this argument, consequently, the region's actual export dependence was also high. That the export growth could be sustained while Pacific Asian exports continued for the most part to be concentrated among a few traditional primary products deserves separate and detailed treatment. Chapter 6 provides a more complete discussion of that trade composition.

Thus, for a variety of reasons, the region elevated trade to a high order of importance. Because export trade was concentrated among a small number of commodities, a final question must be raised. One can argue, for example, that if a sufficiently compelling reason exists, it would be theoretically possible for virtually any country to export something. According to this view, what is principally at issue are the *prices* the exported goods can command. Thus the question asked here is what happened to export prices, and to the terms of trade, during the period of greatly expand trade flows?

The basic data on overall export price indices are presented for seven countries in Table 3-7. What is immediately clear is that when 1958-1960 price levels are used as a base, the export indices rose for five of the seven countries between 1960 and 1970. (The two exceptions, Indonesia and Malaysia, are countries whose exports are largely dominated by natural resources.)

Data on the terms of trade for these countries are also shown in Table 3-7. The index numbers here refer to export price indices divided by the corresponding import price index. No attempt is made to reflect possible changes in productivity, in quality, or in technology. What results, therefore, allows one to make, at best, only preliminary judgments about relative price movements. Still the data do show that the same five countries achieved substantial gains in their terms of trade over the period in question. Put somewhat differently, these data provide statistical underpinning for hypotheses that the huge increases in foreign trade were not accompanied by clearly adverse movements in prices or terms of trade.

From this discussion and from the accompanying data, it is apparent that the impact of the foreign sector upon domestic employment and product markets throughout Pacific Asia has been great. In addition, subsequent chapters show that trade's impact upon certain key sectors was even larger than these findings would indicate. The potential stimulatory effects of trade have been large. An

Table 3-7
Pacific Asian Export Prices and Terms of Trade, 1960-1970 (1958-60 = 100)

Country	Export Prices				Terms of Trade		
	1960	1964	1967	1970	1960	1965	1970
Burma	97	110	129	111	97	115	105
Indonesia	104	90	87	93	104	92	85
Korea	111	104	122	138	111	115	131
Malaysia	109	90	78	83	108	95	75
Philippines	100	108	119	137	100	111	121
Taiwan	90	124	117	129	91	119	125
Thailand	91	108	112	108	90	117	100

Source: United Nations, *Handbook of International Trade and Development Statistics, 1972*, p. 295.

underlying theme of this section is that the contributions of exports and imports to the national economies have substantially increased, perhaps even more than these suggestive findings would indicate.

Pacific Asian exports and imports, in sum, rose considerably over the last decade and a half. In one sense, it can be argued that these twelve countries' foreign trade lagged somewhat behind the expansion of the world's imports and exports over the last fifteen years. But this represents too narrow a view. What is more relevant here is that not only did Pacific Asian exports and especially imports expand swiftly, but they accounted for stable and even rising shares of aggregate foreign trade when compared to other developing regions. In addition, the weight of the trade dependency evidence presented here tends to support the hypothesis that the foreign sector's role *within* these economies was likewise generally growing in importance.

Were it not for Japan, none of these findings would have been sustained. It is, therefore, highly instructive to begin to analyze the key role Japan has played within the Pacific Asian trade network.

Pacific Asia's Trade with Japan

Pacific Asian exports and imports grew steadily at rates fully comparable to world totals during the last fifteen years. Despite a continued concentration of exports among a few traditional commodities, terms of trade and the gains from trade seem to have held up well for the region as a whole. From 1958 to 1972, foreign trade tripled, and most of the Pacific Asian countries' foreign trade performance can be compared very favorably with that of countries in other developing regions around the world.

What is singularly striking is that one country, Japan, accounted for an enormous share of the increases in trade. As is argued more fully in subsequent chapters, Japan did so almost entirely by remaining within the context of the region's traditional, long-established commodity trade patterns. The purpose of this final section is to begin to place Pacific Asia's trade with Japan in perspective vis-à-vis the region's economic activity.

Both the growth rates and, especially by 1972, the magnitudes of Japanese trade flows with the Pacific Asian countries increased so rapidly as to be virtually unprecedented. The summary totals of the twelve countries' exports to and imports from Japan are presented in Tables 3-8 and 3-9. Where possible, these data were taken from the country trade reports. With some exceptions (Burma, Indonesia, and Mainland China are the most prominent examples), these data are generally viewed as reasonably reliable. In particular, the *trends* present a relatively high degree of internal consistency and are comparable with data reported by Japan. Some of the estimates for 1971 and 1972, however, are full of problems. As indicated in the tables, these figures were derived from

Table 3-8
Pacific Asian Exports to Japan, 1958-1972 (Millions of U.S. Dollars)

Country	1958	1962	1968	1971	1972
Australia	205.2	389.8	800.1	1454.1	1844.4
Burma	10.	12.8	9.9	12.5	13.3
China	51.6[a]	43.7[a]	203.8[a]	293.5[a]	441.0[a]
Hong Kong	21.0	38.5	96.4	186.2	235.6
Indonesia	27.4	86.6	172.2	529.5	746.1
Korea	9.8	23.5	99.7	262.0	409.7
Malaysia	57.9	118.9	253.7	296.1	294.8
New Zealand	15.4	26.1	85.9	117.3	195.4
Philippines	96.6	136.6	283.3	391.4	357.2[p]
Singapore	61.4	52.5	89.6	124.1	139.2
Taiwan	65.3	52.2	127.6	244.4	376.7
Thailand	23.3	63.8	138.2	205.7	224.0
Total−Pacific Asia	644.9	1,045.0	2,360.4	4,116.8	5,277.4

[a]Derived from Japanese import data.

[p]Preliminary.

Source: Data taken from International Monetary Fund, *Direction of Trade, Annual*, selected issues, including *1958-1962, 1968-1972*, and individual monthly numbers. All data is expressed in dollars.

published Japanese totals and, as such, they are not fully comparable with the trade returns for the earlier years. While the findings from the derived data should be treated with caution, the broad trends nonetheless emerge clearly from even the most casual examination.

The data in Table 3-8 show Pacific Asian exports to Japan for five selected years from 1958 to 1972. Few things point up the significance of Japan's expanded role in Pacific Asia's trade more clearly than data showing the rapid build-up in this trade that began in 1958. From 1958 to 1972, Pacific Asian exports to Japan rose from $644 million to well over $5 billion, which roughly represents an eight-fold increase. The trends were sustained through the years cited here, with total trade rising to over a billion dollars in 1962, more than doubling to $2.3 billion by 1968, and ultimately growing to more than $5.2 billion in the early 1970s. Put somewhat differently, by the start of the 1970s Pacific Asia *alone* was exporting more to Japan than had the entire world in 1958.

Further examination of these data reveals that the exports of virtually all twelve of the Pacific Asian countries to Japan rose steadily and by very large amounts. Both the aggregate totals and the annual growth rate trends for eleven of these countries show huge and sustained increases. Only Burma, whose world trade was also declining, failed to participate fully in these trends. Indonesia and Mainland China are perhaps the two exceptions to the pattern of unbroken

Table 3-9
Pacific Asian Imports from Japan, 1958-1972 (Millions of U.S. Dollars)

Country	1958	1962	1968	1971	1972
Australia	62.8	135.9	423.4	730.6	749.7
Burma	45.4	50.0	24.2	50.3	36.8
China	53.0[a]	40.4[a]	358.1[a]	635.8[a]	676.0[a]
Hong Kong	104.5	192.0	448.3	812.9	904.5
Indonesia	69.8	121.1	159.2	389.7	520.4
Korea	47.5	109.2	624.1	953.8	1,031.2
Malaysia	31.1	70.0	158.1	280.3	330.5
New Zealand	7.9	23.5	64.2	134.4	182.5
Philippines	81.1	106.4	351.7	389.6	422.9[p]
Singapore	87.8	119.8	226.2	555.3	664.9
Taiwan	89.5	103.9	361.6	827.1	1,048.6
Thailand	90.4	161.1	391.7	485.3	548.2
Total–Pacific Asia	770.8	1,233.3	3,591.8	6,245.1	7,096.2

[a]Derived from Japanese export data.
[p]Preliminary.
Source: Data taken from International Monetary Fund, *Direction of Trade, Annual*, selected issues, including *1958-1962, 1968-1972*, and individual monthly numbers. All data is expressed in dollars.

export increase, since the exports of both countries rose sharply in the late 1960s following the adoption of more outward-looking, trade-conscious policies on the part of their respective governments. By the start of the 1970s, moreover, Japan was accounting for nearly $2 billion of exports for Australia alone. Among the other major exporters Indonesia, China, Korea, the Philippines, and Taiwan were *each* exporting upwards of half a billion dollars or more to Japan.

If exports to Japan rose sixfold, what happened to Pacific Asian imports from Japan over the same period is even more striking. A basic question concerning imports is to ask whether these countries increasingly turned to Japan to supply their growing import demands. Data presented in Table 3-9 strongly supports the view that, if anything, Japan's impact upon Pacific Asian imports was even more significant than upon their export markets. Imports for eleven of the twelve countries rose enormously, and the upward trends were generally sustained throughout the entire period. Between 1958 and 1972, the twelve countries' imports from Japan rose from $770 million to well over $7 billion. The largest jump occurred between 1962 and 1968, when imports tripled by rising from $1.2 billion to $3.6 billion. The gains in these magnitudes are brought out more clearly when it is remembered that the Pacific Asian region's imports from Japan alone in the early 1970s approached their aggregate world import totals in 1958. Burma again was the single exception to these trends. The major importers from Japan include Taiwan, Korea, and Hong Kong, each of which purchased upwards of $1 billion of Japanese goods annually.

Further detailed breakdowns of this trade would add little of real importance to the general themes outlined above. The evidence presented in these tables points to the entire Pacific Asian region as, collectively and individually, looking increasingly to Japan as they expand their trade. By any measure of comparison, Japan's impact on the region's trade has expanded enormously since 1958.

Japan's performance within Pacific Asian markets as well as her role as a major customer for their exports will be analyzed in much fuller detail in the chapters that follow. Here it should simply be pointed out that the implications of the rapid Japanese trade build-up, even against a background of generally rising Pacific Asian imports to and exports from the world, were manifestly obvious. The corresponding trends in terms of the shares of these countries' markets for which she accounted are quite clear and can be readily documented. Market shares of foreign trade are not always a perfect measure of a partner country's impact or importance. Their respective rises here, however, are clearly noteworthy.

How great a factor had Japan become in terms of these twelve countries' trade shares? It is reasonably clear that, as the data in Tables 3-10 and 3-11 illustrate, Japan by the beginning of the 1970s had become a—if not *the*—major trading partner for much of the region. For this data too the customary warnings about the noncomparability of some of the trade returns must be acknowledged. Nonetheless, it is possible to highlight several broad trends. First, among the Pacific Asian export returns, the most striking finding is that by 1972 five of the twelve countries directed at least one-fourth of their total exports to Japan; in two additional countries, Japan accounted for one-sixth of total exports. These

Table 3-10
Pacific Asian Exports to Japan, Percent Shares, 1958-1972

Country	1958	1962	1968	1971	1972
Australia	12.6	16.7	22.7	27.8	28.3
Burma	5.1	5.9	8.9	10.1	13.2
China	7.2	5.7	13.8	16.1	19.1
Hong Kong	3.7	2.3	5.5	6.6	6.8
Indonesia	3.6	12.7	23.6	42.5	48.2
Korea	58.7	49.5	21.9	24.5	25.2
Malaysia	9.4	13.9	18.9	18.2	17.2
New Zealand	2.2	3.3	8.3	8.6	12.3
Philippines	19.7	24.7	33.0	34.7	32.7
Singapore	6.0	4.7	7.0	7.1	6.3
Taiwan	43.9	23.9	16.2	12.3	12.9
Thailand	7.6	14.4	21.0	24.7	23.7

Source: Data taken from country reports United Nations, Statistical Office, *Commodity Trade Statistics*, Series D, selected years, and International Monetary Fund, *Direction of Trade, Annual*, selected numbers.

Table 3-11
Pacific Asian Imports from Japan, Percent Shares, 1958-1972

Country	1958	1962	1968	1971	1972
Australia	3.4	6.0	10.8	15.6	16.3
Burma	22.2	25.6	13.4	29.7	28.7
China	6.6	5.7	25.1	35.9	32.8
Hong Kong	12.3	16.5	21.8	24.3	23.2
Indonesia	13.6	18.7	22.2	33.2	35.8
Korea	12.6	25.9	42.5	39.8	40.9
Malaysia	5.7	8.8	13.5	19.6	20.7
New Zealand	1.1	3.5	7.7	10.8	12.7
Philippines	14.8	18.1	27.5	29.4	30.9
Singapore	7.2	9.1	13.6	19.6	19.6
Taiwan	40.2	34.1	40.4	44.9	41.5
Thailand	23.0	29.6	34.1	37.7	40.2

Source: Data taken from country reports, United Nations, Statistical Office, *Commodity Trade Statistics, Series D*, selected years, and International Monetary Fund, *Direction of Trade, Annual*, selected numbers.

trends, secondly, were sustained throughout the period. Only two countries, Korea and Taiwan, exported *lower* shares of their exports to Japan in 1970 than in 1958. Australia, Indonesia, Malaysia, and Thailand, on the other hand, are conspicuous examples of countries where export *shares* have doubled or tripled (their export volumes, it was earlier shown, were also rising rapidly). Japan's share was the largest in Indonesia and accounted by 1972, for nearly 50 percent of her exports to the world.

If anything, Japanese shares of Pacific Asian imports represent an even broader, more far-reaching impact upon their economies. The core data on import shares from Japan is presented in Table 3-11. Few things underscore these trends more than the finding that for five of these countries, Japan, by 1972, provided more than one-third of their respective imports from the entire world. Japan's market penetration had come to account for 20 percent or more of the respective import totals for ten of the twelve Pacific Asian countries. The remaining two countries, New Zealand and Australia, recorded rapidly expanding import shares from Japan, though from a much lower base. Among all twelve Pacific Asian countries, only New Zealand purchased less than one-sixth of her imports from Japan by the end of the decade. Indeed, the most significant finding to emerge from this data may be the consistent pattern of uninterrupted growth in Japanese trade shares for all countries in the region. Put another way, the aggregate impact of Japan's market penetration of the region's imports was even more dominant and far-reaching within these economies than Pacific Asia's expanded export market shares for which growing Japanese import demands had accounted.

To state that Japanese trade shares have risen substantially may not be completely surprising in view of the evidence presented earlier that the developed countries generally were accounting for rising shares of world trade. In view of the heavy raw material concentration of Pacific Asian exports, furthermore, it may be entirely plausible to expect rather broadly based shifts in the direction of trade to have occurred steadily over the decade. How much of the growing imports and exports, accordingly, can be explained by an overall shift in the direction of Pacific Asian trade, in favor of developed countries and at the expense of the developing regions?

The data in Table 3-12 does offer some support for that hypothesis, though the evidence is at best mixed. Several countries, including Korea, New Zealand, and the Philippines, were directing very high shares of their exports to developed countries at the start of the period, and by 1972, the developed countries' shares had declined slightly. Other countries, including Indonesia, Hong Kong, and China, did redirect their trade shares significantly towards the developed areas. For Pacific Asia as a whole, however, the findings in Table 3-12 suggest that the shifts in overall trade direction were not in themselves nearly sufficient to account for the growing relative exports to Japan. What has happened is that there has been a shift in the direction of trade among the developed countries. In particular, as Japan's share of the region's trade has increased, traditional markets in Western Europe have declined in importance. Partly this may be due to faster Japanese growth, partly to Europe's increased tendency to look to Africa and Latin America, and partly, perhaps, to the disappearance of colonialist-inspired trade ties.

Table 3-12
Pacific Asian Exports to Developed Countries, in Percentage Terms, 1958-1972

Country	1958	1962	1968	1971	1972
Australia	69.0	66.4	73.3	71.7	74.1
Burma	16.6	25.0	42.3	36.6	40.9
China	12.1	19.1	40.5	41.4	45.9
Hong Kong	33.5	53.8	72.3	74.8	75.7
Indonesia	46.0	65.3[a]	65.3	72.1	78.7
Korea	89.8	76.0	85.4	85.5	85.9
Malaysia	54.4	56.1	55.5	53.3	62.5
New Zealand	89.0	88.0	84.5	80.8	82.9
Philippines	94.4	92.1	89.6	90.1	92.5
Singapore	32.8	56.6[a]	31.9	33.9	54.7
Taiwan	54.6	58.8	67.2	73.7	73.9
Thailand	40.3	42.9	55.1	57.8	51.9

[a]Derived data, may not be fully comparable with other years.

Source: Data calculated from International Monetary Fund, *Direction of Trade, Annual*, selected years.

It is important to be very clear about this shift in the direction of trade. The findings in this section show how swiftly Japan's share of the region's trade has increased. It is an easy step to suggest that Japan is building up a position of such economic importance that she threatens to dominate the region's foreign trade markets. Certainly any projection of the trends over the last decade, coupled with the underlying dynamism of Japan's domestic economy, does little to downplay such concerns.

Is this hypothesis correct? In large part, it is very misleading. The evidence presented above can also be used to support another, more far-reaching implication. As Pacific Asia's traditional markets in Europe have declined in growth as well as in order of magnitude, what has happened is that Japan has moved in to fill what would otherwise have been a vacuum. Who else would have purchased the Pacific Asian exports of raw materials and agricultural crops? Would the gains from trade noted above have been otherwise sustained? From this perspective, it is plausible to argue that in the *absence* of Japanese trade, the region would have had few alternative markets capable of supporting large trade flows. What has been commonly stressed in the literature are the problems stemming from Japan's huge participation in Pacific Asian trade. The purpose of these comments is to underscore precisely how much good Japan's trade has done for the region. *Without* Japan, it is plausible to suggest that the entire pattern of Pacific Asian development would have been sharply, and adversely, affected.

Conclusion

The analysis in this chapter has dealt with two kinds of Pacific Asian trade: trends in summary exports and imports with the world, and trends in the region's trade with Japan. This distinction is meaningful chiefly because of the huge, growing role Japan has come to occupy in much of the region's trade.

During the decade of the 1960s a number of Pacific Asian countries moved towards a development strategy that elevated foreign trade to a high order of importance. The appeals that imported machinery, capital goods, and consumer products can offer to developing countries are well known and need little comment here.

Less clear, perhaps, is how those imports are to be paid for. Partly that turns on exports. Accordingly, a major theme of this chapter has been to look at what has happened with respect to Pacific Asian's export experience during the last fifteen years. It was shown that both the absolute and the relative size of foreign trade has grown sharply for many of these countries. Between 1958 and 1972, Pacific Asia's exports tripled, and during the 1960s, real GNP grew sharply for virtually every country in the region. More surprising was that the terms of trade generally held their own throughout this trade expansion.

The major change was the steadily rising importance of Japan in both import and export trade flows. In some ways this could be viewed as a resumption of trade patterns that held during the 1920s and 1930s but were interrupted by the massive economic dislocations surrounding the Second World War. (Chapter 7 provides a more complete discussion of the restoration of normal economic relations between Japan and the Pacific Asian countries.) Yet, for Pacific Asia, there is a singularly major difference in that the two-way trade has in recent years centered around supporting the individual countries sustained and successful achievements in domestic economic growth. Without this trade with Japan, the region's development would have been very different, and it is hard to imagine that it would be operating at anything like its current levels of economic performance.

The effects of this trade on the countries' economies has been discussed only in rather general terms. It can be argued that this trade, especially with Japan, did allow continuing specialization along traditional product lines that would not otherwise have been possible. Following Myint's vent-for-surplus hypothesis, this trade expansion often came in precisely the sectors of these economies that could be most readily expanded. The marginal domestic demand for these products, it should be noted, was also slight. In sum, this is read in support of the notion that an outward-looking, trade-conscious strategy for the region has proven viable over the last decade.

A major theme of these two chapters has been that the Pacific Asian countries' trade flows to Japan, individually and collectively, have been considerably more important to them than the corresponding impact of the region upon Japan. During the 1960s Japan was able to expand her trade enormously with a wide range of countries. Much of Pacific Asia's trade gains, on the other hand, were found to have been attributable directly to Japan.

These two chapters have attempted to present the broad magnitudes of trade and economic activity for both the countries of Pacific Asia and Japan. This discussion was necessary to set the scene for an examination of the trends in the detailed trade flows between the two regions. An attempt has been made to place each area within the context of the other's trade network.

With this background, the next three chapters explain the trends in the Japanese-Pacific Asian trade over the last fifteen years. A key question, which is central to the remainder of the study, to be asked is what factors have accounted for the rapidly growing Japanese trade dominance within Pacific Asia. Essentially, have Japanese demand patterns been more important than Pacific Asian supply considerations? Has the reverse also held true, for Pacific Asian demand patterns?

Chapter 4 presents both the rationale and the framework of the model that will be used to identify these factors. Although the model is primarily directed toward analyzing import flows, some interesting data concerning export trends can be calculated within its general analytic framework. Chapters 5 and 6 then present the empirical findings from the model and attempt to explain and interpret these trends. Each Pacific Asian country will be examined vis-à-vis Japan by using both export and import data. While we know, or can accurately estimate, some of the answers to these questions from the broad aggregates presented in these two chapters, the detailed trends in this trade must be carefully examined.

4   A Method for Analyzing Trade Flows

In the previous two chapters the role and importance of trade in Japan and the Pacific Asian economies was briefly outlined. A principal theme of those chapters was to show how trade between Japan and the countries of Pacific Asia could be placed within the context of their respective world trade networks. The broad outlines of direction and magnitude of trade was established for Japan in Chapter 2 and for Pacific Asia in Chapter 3. How can this trade be explained? What factors accounted for the sharp rates of increase in these trade flows? How can the gains from trade be evaluated?

Why does a given country export—or import—some commodities but not others? The conventional trade literature argues that the fundamental causes of international specialization and trade turn upon differences between nations in factor endowments, or in technology, or in tastes, or the like. A large literature has been developed by economists in recent decades that identifies and then empirically tests the results of these differences upon the structure and composition of trade.

The central purpose of this chapter is to develop a methodology that examines changes in the volume, direction, and composition of a country's foreign trade with a view toward using that methodology to investigate and analyze Japanese and Pacific Asian trade flows. The chapter first considers several of the principal theoretical approaches that have attempted to explain international specialization. Since we are here interested in theoretical constructs largely for their ability to help us explain the real-world phenomena underlying Japanese-Pacific Asian trade, the core consideration in these sections constitutes an attempt to examine these hypotheses with respect to the degree of empirical evidence that can be mounted in support of them. What explanatory power can they offer? How readily can each of these major approaches be empirically tested for the principal trade with which this study is concerned?

The first several sections of this chapter attempt to answer these and related questions. It is argued that data limitations preclude a serious, careful investigation of many of the theoretical approaches that dominate much of the trade literature. Even leaving aside such details as the accuracy of the basic data against which these theories can be tested, the application of direct approaches are largely ruled out. The next part of the chapter, consequently, is devoted to developing a rationale for the use of indirect analytical methods. It also explores some of the literature that uses these methods.

The final portion of the chapter contains the specification of the trade model

62

that has been developed for use in this study to answer the questions posed above. The theoretical properties and the implicit hypotheses of the approach, including a brief discussion of its strengths and weaknesses, are then presented. In addition, the final section also frames a hypothesis for testing changes in a country's factor proportions as embodied in trade.

The Methodological Background

The theory of international trade has in recent years developed in a highly significant fashion. By beginning with the standard two-country, two-commodity, and two-factor model with identical production functions, where the factors of production are perfectly mobile within a region and completely immobile between regions, it is at least theoretically possible to determine the effects of foreign trade on the levels of domestic incomes and prices among countries for any given (fixed) set of utility functions, resources, and levels of technology. From this it can be shown that any given country can establish a level and composition of international trade that maximizes their utility function. Trade specialization, in turn, leads directly to a determination of factor prices, incomes, final commodity prices, and the gains from trade.[1] Each of these assumptions can subsequently be relaxed to reflect more countries, more commodities, joint utility functions, and the like, without disturbing the essential nature of the conclusions. At the heart of this theoretical analysis, however, is the assertion that gains from trade can be identified and specified over time. Once the gains from trade have been established, the strategy for maximizing comparative advantage clearly emerges. As Haberler has demonstrated, application of the doctrine of comparative cost enables domestic production to be coordinated with foreign trade so that a country can move onto its highest "domestic production-cum-trade" frontier of production possibilities.[2]

What is needed by any country attempting to optimize the employment of its resources is that the comparative costs for its potential exportables and importables be determinant. In practice, this would require that substantial cross-national data on production, technology, and factor endowment be available for a large number of countries. Unfortunately, little fully adequate data of this type exists, even among mature, industrial, high-income countries. For Japan, and especially for the Pacific Asian nations that comprise this study, the obstacles blocking an empirical study of "real" production functions for a number of industries in order to facilitate cross-national comparisons are enormous. Even then, however, what is really wanted is more difficult—a measure of the cross-national changes in production functions over time, so that, within the Japanese and Pacific Asian context, countries could construct a dynamic model of resource allocation-cum-trade that would reflect their experience as per capita income grew and their economic structure expanded and changed. Ideally the Southeast Asian nations would not want to maximize comparative cost advantages at one point in time; rather they would want to construct an infrastructure and employ their factors in a way that would maximize their gains over time. In so doing, of course, it would be good to reflect the experiences of earlier developed countries at their equivalent stage of development.[3] Except for Japan, the practical difficulties involved essentially limits this approach to merely a theoretical possibility. Even the few studies for developed countries that have been conducted suffer from methodological shortcomings, which makes their data less than ideal for answering the questions posed above.[4]

An alternative source of international cost comparison data—at least for industrial products—is to rely on the studies of manufacturing cost estimates done by one or more countries for firms that have both domestic and foreign branches. Two major difficulties limit this approach. First, while this work may be potentially interesting, one limitation is that it commonly focuses attention on the cost structure of domestic companies vis-à-vis their foreign branches. Studies with this focus do not measure or compare—or even attempt to reflect—the indigenous, locally owned manufacturing facilities that are in direct competition with both the exporter and his foreign branches. Since it is precisely this nation-by-nation comparative cost structure whose determination lies at the heart of the questions considered here, this work in its current state cannot be very regarded as being very illuminating.[5]

A second limitation stems from the composition of Pacific Asian-Japanese trade. Since much of this trade is concentrated among industrial goods and foodstuffs, any methodology focusing chiefly upon industrial cost comparisons would be inappropriate in that it simply wouldn't reflect the realities underlying much of the region's trade flows.

Finally, the long lead time needed to collect, process, and analyze the vast data requirements required here points to the *timing* of the availability of this data as a potential obstacle. Even given that the countries and numerous private companies involved in such a study are willing to provide the necessary data,[a] and assuming they could accurately specify the information required here— either of which are probably heroic assumptions—the results would be suffi- ciently delayed so that any country would be basing a given year's (optimal) trade patterns on cross-national comparative cost data that held several years earlier. Countries would be continuously adjusting their trade flows after the

[a]There is little reason to assume anything resembling full voluntary disclosure. Companies may not be willing to reveal this information for a variety of reasons, including a desire to maintain any hard-won competitive advantage, concern over attracting new entrants that would be potential rivals, worry that high profits or indeed full revelation of their financial data would make them subject to more taxation and/or government control, and the unwillingness that companies with a comparative disadvantage would have in making such information public.

fact, and perhaps in response to conditions that were no longer operative. In sum, it is plausible to call into question the usefulness of several of the methods of analysis in examining Japan's trade with Pacific Asia.

Other Approaches to the Problem

What other approaches to analyzing trade data exist? The literature abounds with parallel attempts by economists to measure comparative advantage and estimate the gains from trade. A number of these efforts were developed with a view toward identifying optimal patterns of factor employment and trade vis-à-vis the relative factor endowments of two or more countries. The next section of this chapter considers several of these hypotheses in order to assess their relevance for use in analyzing the Japanese-Pacific Asian trade flows.[6]

One central approach begins by modifying the neoclassical model in assuming that while national production *functions* are identical, the factors of production may not be qualitatively comparable. Wassily Leontief is associated with much of this work.[7] At the heart of this research are attempts to measure factor productivity on an efficiency-unit basis. When disaggregated findings for a large number of interindustry classifications are attempted for the Pacific Asian region, however, major difficulties exist. Taken together they make it virtually impossible to calculate a unique set of rank order industrial coefficients for each country that would reflect both the necessary factor distinctions and the cross-national differences in efficiency and factor quality that would be required to adequately represent the varied national productive experiences.[8]

Another approach used to measure comparative advantage by relying on a reformulation of earlier theory is found in some of the recent work of Belassa.[9] The central theme of this work is an attempt to empirically determine the validity of the classical model of comparative cost. Following lines of research originally suggested by MacDougall,[10] Belassa formulates the hypothesis that relative (cross-national) productivity differentials determine international specialization. Using 1950 and 1951 data for the United States and Britain for productivity, wages, unit production costs, and profits, he asserts that the impact of productivity differences between two countries can be identified by measuring the two countries' export shares in third markets.[11] Belassa attempts to correlate the export ratio variance between countries with their relative productivity differences, by commodity, over time.[12] One aspect of his research, which is interesting, provides a test of the hypothesis that relative (e.g., cheap) wages have important explanatory power in determining export patterns, at least in manufacturing industries. The hypothesis is not supported by the findings.[13]

A variant in comparing cross-national productivity levels in order to analyze trade patterns is to compare the relative levels of R & D (Research and

Development) spending in a country with its patterns of trade specialization. At the heart of this approach is a hypothesis by Keesing that there is a strong correlation between the extent to which any given industry engages in R & D spending, on the one hand, and the industry's degree of export competitiveness vis-à-vis other potential industries' exports.[14] R & D expenditures are a proxy representing innovation and the introduction of attractive new products. While Kessing's findings provide very plausible support of his hypothesis, this approach would seem to be most useful in analyzing trade patterns among labor- and capital-intensive industrial products and of considerably less relevance among the resource-intensive commodities that dominate Pacific Asian exports.[15]

Following one of the authors' earlier work on wage differentials in trade, Irving Kravis and Robert Lipsey have begun related experiments to estimate and compare price levels in different countries.[16] The work is an outgrowth of related efforts to study comparative prices and price trends, particularly as they bear upon efforts to develop new measures for price competitiveness in international trade. Recognizing shortcomings in earlier literature, they attempt to derive price changes in terms of index numbers by using fairly sophisticated multiple regression techniques. It has long been thought that two particular shortcomings of such price indices in the past have been the enormous differences in product specifications and commodity characteristics among countries, on the one hand, and the suspected upward bias of price indices due to inadequately reflecting quality improvements. Kravis and Lipsey suggest that at least some of the bias can be compensated for by interpreting the individual regression coefficients as proxies for "prices" for different quality characteristics between products and between countries.[17]

In terms of the questions asked in this study, Kravis and Lipsey have been less interested in analyzing the specific economic factors that underly price changes or that account for different cross-national price levels. Instead, they have chosen to focus their attention chiefly upon identifying changes in prices among machinery, transport equipment, and manufactured metal products. This work is useful to the degree that it is successful in highlighting price indices more explicitly. By reflecting more detailed information in the regression equations, it illuminates the nature inter-national price measurement procedures. The immediate application of this work may be limited, however, to the small number of products and countries for which detailed, information is currently available. The applicability of these regression techniques to the Pacific Asian countries' available data base is clearly open to question.

A Significant Omission:
The Non-Price Variables

A significant omission shared by virtually all of the theoretical constructs discussed here is any significant reflection, or even awareness, of the non-price

variables underlying trade. The approaches discussed above could be characterized as emphasizing "direct" variables in assessing trade—direct, because they
rely on factor endowments, productions costs, relative and absolute prices to
determine the comparative cost structure of trade, employment, and income
differentials. Common to all of the measures discussed above is that they are
"real," quantifiable, and at least theoretically capable of precise measurement.
Common to all, too, is that the need to reflect non-price variables in assessing
specialization and estimating the gains from trade is largely unmet.

The non-price variables come into play particularly when evaluating the
actual or potential trade between developed and less-developed countries that
this study attempts. Several can be briefly specified.[18] Quality differences of a
sort not adequately represented by the 3- or 4-digit SITC commodity breakdowns are perhaps the most prominent of the non-price variables. Sometimes
this may be due to differences in product specifications between countries. It
may also be due to differences in the type or style of products produced by
different countries, each of the slightly different products serving the same
general purpose in the respective country of production. There are also an
important set of characteristics associated with particular exporting companies
(or even countries), including the reliability of delivery dates, the existence and
availability of repair parts and technicians, the willingness to provide regular
service and maintenance activities, and the like. All of these bear upon the
conditions related to, or following, the initial sale. For some countries, different
weights and measures introduce a "common standards" factor that may pose
trade problems. Policies with regard to returned merchandise, for isolated cases
of quality defects, for example, could serve as an illustration of the general
categorical variable "good will."

A second set of non-price variables, functionally unrelated to the above, turns
on the general question of "credit." What payment terms are afforded to
importers? What currencies are acceptable? Related to this, will a given currency
be accepted only at a discount? How much grace is allowed before penalties
begin to accrue? What sort of long-term accommodations accompany large
purchases, especially of capital goods? The terms of sale and the variables
associated with credit, collectively exert a major influence upon the size,
direction, and commodity mix of exports, yet in common with the other
non-price variables, the conventional theoretical approaches have not explicitly
reflected any of these variables.

A third significant defect in the more traditional empirical tests should be
noted. It is sometimes difficult to decide whether a given purchase by one
country from another can properly be categorized as an "import." The question
that extends the rubric of non-price factors in yet another direction is especially
relevant for those countries whose foreign investment is at least in part directed
toward the extraction and processing of minerals and raw materials whose
ultimate destination lies in the country from which the investment originated.

Motives in foreign investment are in any case mixed and seldom singular.[19] Foreign investment designated under this category does, however, owe much of its impetus to the internal demand for the products as industrial inputs in the nation's domestic industry, rather than motivation generated principally by owners of capital simply seeking a greater return abroad. Chapter 7 treats foreign investment in much greater detail. What is relevant here is that these transactions are recorded in national accounts statistics as a capital outflow for the investing country, subsequently followed by increased exports from the capital recipient nation to the investing country. The anomaly is clear: what ostensibly resembles an increase in exports from second countries, which in turn might be explained by a variety of "real" changes in cross-national variables, in fact results from the earlier capital export. Depending on ownership and foreign nationals involved in the labor force, the activity represents as much an extension of domestic production as an increase in imports.[20] Simple and undifferentiated treatment of such goods flows in unwarranted and apt to be misleading.[b]

The relevance of the discussion of non-price variables to this chapter is straightforward. It seems plausible that while the non-price variables may be elevated to a higher order of importance for some commodities (e.g., machinery and transport equipment) than for others (industrial raw materials, for example), potential importers weigh them carefully, at least implicitly, before determining the composition and direction of trade. Yet a consideration of non-price variables is missing in the empirical tests discussed above. This is an omission whose consequence is very troubling. It causes conventional findings to be treated with even more caution, especially when it is likely that cross-national disparities among the non-price variables are sometimes wider than the variances in the more direct measures of inter-industry national productivity, wages, prices, and the like.

Some Preliminary Conclusions

The findings of the studies surveyed here could easily be enlarged by extending the discussion to related approaches along the same general methodological lines

[b]While this argument has traditionally held largely for mineral resources, there are indications that in response to rising labor costs in Japan, manufacturing is being carried out in Asia, especially in S. Korea and Taiwan, for re-export to Japan. Substitution of low-wage labor by high-wage countries should occasion little surprise. Rather, the point that is stressed here is that it may be difficult to separate national production and cost functions, and what they imply about the gains from trade, from domestic production and cost. An international "putting-out" system of this kind parallels the long-standing domestic Japanese industrial patterns of production "dualism," characterized by a few major industrial companies serviced by a larger number of very small, highly specialized companies that are highly complementary to, and often highly dependent upon, the major industrial concern. For a discussion of dualism in terms of the domestic Japanese economy, see Seymour Broadbridge, *Industrial Dualism in Japan: A Problem of Economic Growth and Structural Change* (Chicago: Aldine-Atherton, 1964).

as those noted above. Such a discussion would not, however, introduce any fundamentally new themes to the main questions that center upon the optimal determination of trade and employment patterns and upon which this section has focused.

What does all of this mean? It is possible to suggest several preliminary conclusions, which in turn have greatly influenced the direction of the remainder of this study. First, it is plausible to conclude that the straightforward attempts to measure "comparative advantage" are conceptually and empirically lacking, especially with respect to data, for use by Pacific Asian countries. On the one hand, any broadly inclusive hypothesized explanations for trade would be difficult to assert. On the other hand, such attempts as have been made to test these hypotheses have largely utilized data from the high-income, developed countries. In particular much empirical material has been drawn from the North Atlantic countries that most frequently include, but are not confined to, the United States and the United Kingdom. The focus of the present study is on intra-Pacific Asian trade, particularly vis-à-vis Japan. It follows that if comprehensive data for Western developed countries are not sufficiently available for the requirements stated above, it is hard to reasonably expect that accurate and detailed data for many of the developing countries in the Pacific region will be available.

Secondly, it has been argued that a methodological shortcoming common to most of these empirical attempts to test various trade theories preclude an adequate consideration of several non-price variables that are thought to constitute an important influence on trade flows. The ambiguity of the non-price variables makes them more difficult to quantify and probably insures that any resulting estimates of explanatory variables should therefore be advanced more hesitantly. The difficulty of dealing with these factors probably goes far in explaining their infrequent inclusion in trade constructs. Yet economists interested in international trade and economic development ignore them at the expense of comprehensiveness and realism. Their exclusion in the studies above constitutes a fundamental weakness common to all such efforts that is no less real despite its difficulty to overcome.

At present, then, these direct hypotheses have not been, and in some cases cannot be, tested with sufficient rigor to make one confident that the findings would be either supportable or operable. There is a need to find a method of analysis subject to the data limitations of the Pacific developing countries that will allow questions to be posed in a conceptual framework that permits careful investigation. Direct testing of the trade specialization hypotheses is ruled out. What must be done, consequently, is to develop "indirect" methods that would serve as proxies for the real variables that are not available. This chapter briefly considers several alternative "indirect" measures before turning to a specification of the methodology used in this study.

Theoretical "Indirect" Methods

Conventional "direct" econometric analysis of trade flows begins by attempting to measure the impact of such major variables as income, prices, and productivity changes directly upon the partner country trade flows. Yet we have argued earlier in this chapter that it may not be possible to specify and quantify all the relevant variables needed in order to utilize the direct techniques. What we now need to ask is whether it is *necessary* to do so. The answer is no, not surprisingly, since it follows from the relatively recent advent of "indirect" estimates of comparative advantage that have been developed as an alternative to empirically answering questions about factor use and the gains from trade.

The central hypothesis lying at the heart of all the indirect approaches is that the complex data requirements economists need in order to employ "direct" measures of the levels of trade specialization and the gains from trade (including comparative wage levels, industrial productivity, domestic factor endowment, and the like) are implicitly reflected in a country's trade returns. Accordingly there is no need to *separately* identify and calculate the effects of these variables. In this view, they are already contained in the actual trade returns.

Bela Belassa put forward the general case for "indirect" estimates when he asked:

> . . . is it necessary to explicitly take account of all the influences that determine comparative advantage? This would be a rather laborious exercise and, in view of the difficulties of assigning numerical values to these variables, it might bring disappointing results. Instead, for purposes of indicating the possible consequences of trade liberalization, it appears sufficient to provide information on "revealed" comparative advantage.[21]

How can indirect measures be used to answer the trade questions that have been posed in this chapter? What empirical precedents for these techniques have been advanced in the literature? One of the first attempts to employ indirect procedures was made by H. Tysznski in 1956.[22] Concentrating chiefly on manufactures in the first half of the twentieth century, he attempted to investigate the effects of changes in world demand for exports and the accompanying shifts in the competitive demand for exports and the accompanying shifts in the competitive position of several leading manufacturing nations in the world. Tysznski calculated the trade shares of each of fifteen classifications of industrial products. A country's trade shares subsequently increased or decreased in the future, he asserted, due to changes in the structure of foreign trade or to changes in the competitiveness of the country vis-à-vis a number of other countries. Other studies, emphasizing primarily exports, have adopted this method in more recent years.[23]

Following this general theme, Belassa has developed another indirect measure of comparative advantage.[24] He also focuses on manufactured products among largely developed countries. Belassa's methodology ultimately seeks to determine a country's ratio of exports to imports. Cross-sectional comparisons of these ratios over time for a given commodity group exhibit what he calls "revealed" comparative advantage. For example, if a country was successful in steadily increasing the ratio of exports of that commodity as a share of the total exports in terms of the ratio of imports of that commodity as a share of total imports, the likely explanation, according to Belassa, is that such results identify or point to likely changes in demand and supply conditions. Rather than look at productivity and wage-level data to see what commodities ought to be exchanged, says Belassa, one determines from the data what has been traded and essentially asserts that productivity and comparative wages are already reflected in the goods flow. There is an implicit presumption that trade patterns are rational. Indeed, a weakness of this approach is that *any* trade pattern is assumed "correct." Explanations of that pattern are then attached to it, after the fact.[c]

The work of Belassa, together with the empirical demonstrations by several associates for the countries in which they specialize, is promising especially as it points to commodity areas that may be profitably explored. The drawbacks to this approach, however, include the following points: (1) it lumps all the competitive and structural factors together into one overall category and thus cannot differentiate between even major factors, and (2) it can give potentially misleading answers for products that are either not imported, or not exported, in sizable quantity. Indeed, in analyzing the results one must guard against interpreting the absolute size of the ratios as an implicitly strict and rigid "ranking" of revealed comparative advantage opportunities.

There is, finally, a variant on the relationship between competitiveness and export shares that should be noted. Fleming and Tsiang, in a paper that again concentrates on the experiences of developed countries, have attempted to correlate export changes between a given pair of years with price changes for those same years.[25] Over time, it is expected that this approach would lead to something resembling an "average" elasticity of substitution in demand between different countries' exports. It could, that is, approximate the long-run reactions of potential buyers to alternative suppliers.[26] Fleming and Tsiang follow the practice of the model used in this paper by attempting to allow for the demand factors that are capable of being quantitatively reflected. They in turn attempt to correlate changes in cross-national export shares to changes in the commodity composition and geographic distribution of world demand in preparing their estimates. They also attempt to reflect changes in "competitiveness," especially in terms of prices, in assessing the changing export shares of the major industrial

---

[c]Belassa would probably argue that since economists are seeking to determine both the critical factors influencing trade, and their magnitudes, for specific countries, "revealed" comparative advantage is useful in that it points to the commodities, and in turn the factors, that should be explored.

countries they considered. This work, if extended to the developing countries they considered. This work, if extended to the developing countries in the Pacific region, is promising in that the overall supply parameters (trade "acceptance") are estimated. In its present form, however, the data is so limited (and relatively old, since 1954 is the most recent year reflected) that its chief interest lies in the theoretical model, rather than the empirical results.

The Suggested Approach

Following a line of inquiry originally suggested by Deutsch and others,[27] the core methodology of this study utilizes a variant of persistence forecasting. What is wanted, of course, is a way to identify both structural (demand) and competitive (supply) factors in explaining changes in international trade flows of any given country vis-à-vis the rest of the world. Following Belassa, a central contention underlying the methodological procedures of this study is that indirect measures can be usefully employed in order to measure and explain changes in the trade patterns between Japan and the Pacific Asian countries over time as well as to measure, as he does, the impact of various trade liberalization methods.[28]

Rather than attempting to measure changes in Japan's or the Pacific Asian region's trade patterns with the *world*, we are principally concerned here with measuring changes in the direction, volume, and composition of trade between Japan and a number of neighboring countries in Pacific Asia vis-à-vis the world. In the chapters that follow, two principal questions are raised: (1) what has been the effect of Japan's exports within the trade networks of the respective Pacific Asian countries, and (2) what can be said about the effect of the Pacific Asian region's exports, singly and as a group, upon Japan's aggregate imports?

The impact of Japan's exports to Pacific Asia, and *vice versa*, will accordingly be measured not so much in terms of the composition and magnitudes of the export flows themselves but in terms of the relative import acceptance by the recipient country. In the methodology outlined below, it is hypothesized that the import returns of the partner countries can be taken as the measure of import acceptance. The import data are then hypothetically divided into three conceptual components: (1) the demand prediction, (2) the structural demand prediction, and (3) the competitive effect.

The underlying reasoning is easy to document. For example, the explanations for changes in Japan's exports to any given country j (which, subject to transportation costs, should be equal to j's imports[d]) depend in part on the

---

[d]They may not be, due to differences in commodity classification procedures, variances in timing that render a given calendar period's returns not strictly comparable, and, potentially the biggest and most mischievous factor, statistical errors and omissions, among other things. For a useful discussion of the limitations in this data, see, for example, Seiji Naya and Theodore Morgan, "The Accuracy of International Trade Data: The Case of the Southeast Asian Countries," *Journal of the American Statistical Association* 64, no. 326 (1969), pp. 452-67.

import capacity of *i*. By how much, it is first asked, have *j*'s total imports from all sources grown over any specific period? What is wanted here is a compound import growth rate for any given period in question. Since overall import demand rose sharply for Japan as well as most of the Pacific Asian countries discussed below during the decade of the 1960s, the compounded growth rates for these countries were generally positive.

How much did any given Pacific Asian country's import demand rise? In the following, let

M_{1j} = country *j*'s imports in the base year, year 1;

M_{nj} = country *j*'s imports in the end year, year *n*, where *n* = the number of years $(1,2, \ldots n)$ between the base and end years;

R_j = overall compounded rate of growth for country *j*'s aggregate imports for any *n*-year period.

Thus

$$M_{nj} = (M_{1j})(1 + R_j)^n. \tag{1}$$

If, instead of examining the total volume of imports, one presents disaggregated data in terms of individual commodities, (1) can be written as follows:

Given that

$$M_{1j} = \sum_{x=1}^{z} (M_{1jx})$$

where $x = 1, 2, \ldots z$ individual commodity categories, then

$$\sum_{x=1}^{z} (M_{njx}) = \sum_{x=1}^{z} [(M_{1jx})(1 + R_j)^n]. \tag{2}$$

Furthermore, using lower case symbols to denote any country *j*'s imports in a given year from a single partner country *i*, we see that country *j*'s total imports from any partner country *i* can be expressed as

$$m_{1ji} = \sum_{x=1}^{z} [(m_{1jix})]. \tag{3}$$

It follows that the first hypothetical value, the Demand Prediction coefficients (D.P.), can be readily calculated as follows:

$$\text{D.P.} = (m_{nji})^* = (m_{1ji})(1 + R_j)^n \tag{4}$$

$$= \sum_{x=1}^{z} [(m_{1jix})(1 + R_j)^n],$$

where the hypothetical or postulated D.P. values of j's imports from i in year n are denoted by an asterisk. The Demand Prediction values are thus a function of

The Demand Prediction values are thus a function of the growth in country j's import demand together with an extrapolation of i's share of j's aggregate market in the base year. It follows that i's predicted of hypothetical sales to j in some end year n would equal country j's *actual* imports from country i provided it simply maintained its base year market share of j's imports. During periods in which j's import demand grows, of course, the signs on the D.P. coefficients would always be positive.

But simple persistence forecasting of foreign trade shares is not apt to be very illuminating. In analyzing the structural changes embodied in trade patterns over time, it is quite likely that the commodity composition of a given country's imports will shift over time. Such shifts in trade composition would be particularly apparent as and if the underlying structure of the country's domestic economy was simultaneously undergoing a rapid transformation. (In the context of this study, of course, a principal theme of Chapters 2 and 3 was to illustrate some of the rapid economic transformations that were taking place during the past two decades in Japan and the Pacific Asian countries.)

In assessing the overall changes in country i's exports to j, therefore, it is useful to ask how, if at all, the commodity composition of country j's import demands has itself changed over time—that is, have the commodity *supply* patterns of i's exports corresponded to the commodity demand patterns for imports that j had developed by the end of any given period? Put somewhat differently, in analyzing the role of i's exports into j's total import network, could a significant part of i's success be explained by the fact that it happened—or was able—to "specialize" in a particular mix of commodities for which j's import demand grew the most rapidly—weighted, of course, by the respective shares of those commodities in j's base year import mix?

The key question here clearly turns on the *structure* of j's import demands. How can the degree to which j's import demands fit the particular pattern of i's exports be satisfactorily assessed? Several alternative explanations for this structural "specialization" phenomena can be offered. On the one hand, such specialization could have resulted from a determined marketing strategy on the part of country i. It is plausible to speculate that their exporters would have attempted to formulate forecasts aimed at identifying the import needs of country j that offered the greatest promise of rapid growth in subsequent years. As a part of that strategy country i would then attempt to stake out sizeable market shares in those commodities. At the heart of this approach is that the potential exporter must attempt to project the relevant income elasticities of demand and prospective domestic import-substituting production capabilities in country j for several of its respective potential export commodities and commodity groups. At the opposite end of the continent from the active marketing strategy outlined above, on the other hand, an essentially passive explanation could result from an exporter finding itself, essentially by accident, specializing in a mix of exportables for which foreign demand happened—to its virtual surprise—to be rapidly growing. The same pattern of commodity demand and foreign supply would hold in either case. What is different in the explanations is the extent to which the exporting country used sophisticated procedures (or shrewd guesses) to establish the commodity patterns of its principal exports to any partner country j.

It follows that a procedure for estimating the impact of the structure of j's import demands upon the degree of success of i's exports are straightforward. The procedure will be called the Structural Demand Prediction (hereafter S.D.P.). It can be readily calculated as follows, if

r_{jx} = the compounded growth rate for any n-year period for each of the z individual commodities or commodity categories country j imports from the world.

It follows that j's Structural Demand Prediction (S.D.P.) for some country's can be readily calculated as follows:

$$\text{S.D.P.} = \sum_{x=1}^{z} [(m_{1jix})(1+r_{jx})^{n}] - \sum_{x=1}^{z} [(m_{1jix})(1+R_{j})^{n}] \quad (5)$$

$$= \sum_{x=1}^{z} (m_{njix})^{**},$$

where the two asterisks denote the predicted, hypothetical values of each of the z products j imported from any country i after the trend influence of j's overall import patterns from years 1 to n have been removed.

It can be shown that the Structural Demand Prediction (S.D.P.) coefficients will accordingly be positive for commodity categories for which a country's import demand has increased faster than its overall aggregate import demand and negative for those importables for which the importing country's demand has lagged behind its overall growth in aggregate imports. The *sign* on each individual S.D.P. commodity category coefficient may thus be positive or negative. The *magnitudes* on each S.D.P. coefficient, however, are directly related to the relative importance the exporting country i had occupied within j's import network during the start of any given period. The more important a supplier country i was in the base year, the larger the absolute value of their respective S.D.P. coefficients in some future year n would be.

The final set of coefficients attempts to identify and account for changes in competitive strength among competing trade partners within the context of country j's imports. It was shown above that for any exporting country i, both the Demand Prediction and the Structural Demand Prediction coefficients turn largely upon external (demand) factors, chiefly if not wholly outside the control of potential exporters.[e] The focus of the remaining coefficient, the Competitive Effect (C.E.), on the other hand, lies principally upon the exporter's side. It turns largely upon *internal* (supply) factors, over which a potential exporter is thought to be able to exercise some control. In this approach the C.E. is used residually to account for departures from the sum of the two demand predictions. The C.E. coefficient helps to explain, for any potential exporter i, such things as the differences in international marketing and export promotion, changes in cross-national productivity levels, and relative changes in international price levels and/or exchange rates.[29]

Specification and measurement of the Competitive Effect is straightforward and can be calculated as follows:

$$\text{C.E.} = \sum_{x=1}^{z} [(m_{njix}) - [(m_{njix})^* + (m_{njix})^{**}]] \tag{6}$$

$$= \sum_{x=1}^{z} (M_{njix})^{***}$$

where three asterisks denote the predicted, hypothetical gains (or losses) any country i achieved resulting from changes in its competitive position in j's market vis-à-vis the rest of the world, positive coefficients indicating competitive gains and negative coefficients competitive losses.

It should be emphasized that all three of the coefficients measure one country's performance only in the context of its impact upon another country. Any trade flows are thus susceptible to being explained by some combination of the D.P., S.D.P., and C.E. values. While the imposition or modification of trade barriers facing actual or potential exporters (whether trade-creating or trade-

[e]One major exception here would be in the case of bilateral barter trade agreements. At issue here is whether foreign demand vis-à-vis another country is in fact independent of exports sales to that country. Of the countries examined in this study, however, the concept of barter is probably of possible relevance only—if at all—to Mainland China.

diverting) would affect the magnitude of the resulting trade flows, most such barriers should not disturb an exporter's *relative* competitive position, especially insofar as the trade barriers imposed are common to all actual or potential exporters. To the considerable extent that the Competitive Effect results rely on relative cross-national comparisons rather than absolute advantages, it is clear that significant elements of the *competitive* trade components also lie outside the sole control of any given exporting country.

An Overview of the Methodology

There are several distinct advantages to this method of analysis. While it may be argued that under the rubric of the "competition" category, many varied influences are working, so that the effect of any given factor is suppressed or hidden, a key advantage of this format is that for the Pacific region as a whole, as well as for individual countries, it is possible to know which countries are developing competitive and/or structural demand advantages in which key commodities or commodity groups. Even more, it is possible to compute which countries have, absolutely and dynamically, enjoyed the largest (and the smallest) advantages, and which have lost the most ground. In practice, this study compares Japanese imports and exports with world trade for the Pacific Asian countries, a comparison that can be justified on grounds of the exceedingly dominant role Japan has come to play within the economies of these countries.

A related advantage is that it is possible to regroup the commodities into larger category groups that are suggested by other criteria. One such division might emphasize the dominant factors used in the production of goods, so that categories could be established for capital-intensive, labor-intensive, as well as agricultural and natural resource-intensive goods.[f] Such groupings would permit, at least inferentially, the testing of a whole range of hypotheses concerning Japanese or Southeast Asian comparative advantage in given products, based on production inputs, vis-à-vis partner countries over time. It might be interesting to determine the extent to which the Japanese response fit the patterns traditionally predicted by trade theory based on factor endowment and the like.

Before considering the findings, the limitations of this methodology ought to be noted. Since the selection of the base year must be somewhat arbitrary, one weakness is simply that the structural and competitive effects cannot be unambiguously determined; this follows from the differences between Paasche and Laspreyre index numbers.[30] (The suggested correction has been noted.) This limitation is not insurmountable. Even if precision must suffer, the signs and general magnitude of the competitive effect will be clear. Greater potential

---

[f]Using SITC 2- and 3-digit categories, all goods would be force-fit into one or another grouping.

difficulty, however, lies in the many factors that are loaded under the broad component of competition, including both the price and non-price factors. While elements of all of these are at least potentially present, taken together they tend to blur the analysis and make it difficult to isolate and examine any given factor—something that it is in any case extremely difficult to do.[31] Such limitations point clearly to the need for economists to assemble the data[g] and develop the tools of measurement that would enable these limits to be overcome. In the absence of such data, however, and because this methodology does permit several very useful questions about both the patterns and the composition of trade to be answered, the above trade methodology has been adopted. It offers the opportunity of obtaining potentially useful answers to questions concerning current and dynamic trade patterns in the Pacific region.

This discussion provides the background for testing the model against Japanese-Pacific Asian trade flows for a twelve-year period. Chapter 5 examines Japanese exports to Pacific Asia, both in terms of Japanese exports to the world and in terms of Pacific Asian import trends; Chapter 6 does the same thing for Japanese imports. Thus, it is to the empirical results of the study that we now turn.

---

[g]See, for example the dispute on the accuracy of intercountry *trade* flows in Southeast Asia. That these data are closely questioned only emphasizes further the limitations of working with published data on wage rates, productivity, and input and output prices, to say nothing of non-price variables.

5

Japanese Exports to Pacific Asia: Empirical Results and Future Prospects

Up to this point in the book, Japanese foreign trade—and especially Japanese exports—have been treated in a highly aggregated, summary fashion. The principal distinction heretofore has been between Japan's exports to the Pacific Asian region as compared to the rest of the world. Little apart from the gross volume of trade has been emphasized.

To be sure, Japanese exports to the Pacific Asian region have risen steadily and enormously since the late 1950s. Partly this can be explained by rising import demand within these countries. To the extent that their outward-looking development strategies were successful, of course, imports from industrial countries like Japan would be expected to play a key role in their subsequent development. But much more remains to be said before the entire story of why Japan occupied such a large role in this trade is more clearly understood.

Trade can be a key vehicle for spreading improvements in technology to developing countries, although there is little of a summary nature that one can usefully say about technological transfer to a dozen countries that differ in a number of significant ways. The discussion in this chapter, therefore, focuses chiefly upon asking what products or commodity patterns were actually involved in the trade? What special role did Japan assume, both in terms of commodity structure and in terms of growing competitive strength? How, that is, can the rapid Japanese gains within the context of this rising trade be explained?

Prior to World War II, the bulk of Japanese exports were directed towards the Pacific Asian community, which in this study is defined as a somewhat broader geographic area than the principal areas in which prewar Japanese trade centered. From the point of view of Japanese exporters, Pacific Asia's purchases rose sharply in absolute terms throughout the last two decades, though the region's relative role declined substantially. From Japan's perspective, the question is how did Pacific Asia fit into the overall Japanese export market? What can be said about the region's contribution to Japanese exports?

The factors analyzed in this chapter follow directly from the analytical approaches developed in Chapter 4. Pacific Asian imports from Japan, on a highly disaggregated basis, are analyzed in terms of the three coefficients developed in Chapter 4. Underlying this discussion, of course, is a continual attempt to explain the Japanese trade gains both in the aggregate and in terms of individual commodities. The emphasis rests primarily upon analyzing the region's actual import patterns over these years.

The central theme of this chapter is that Japanese exports benefited from both structural and competitive gains but that, especially during the late 1960s, the competitive factors were much more significant. So long as the region's imports were increasing, Japanese exports continued to grow sharply. A principal finding from these data, however, is that by the start of the 1970s Japanese exports were already accounting for major, and even dominant, shares of many important products in most Pacific Asian countries.

The role of Pacific Asia within Japan's export market is dealt with in the first part of this chapter. The core section then examines and analyzes Pacific Asian imports from Japan with a view towards differentiating between gains in the principal types of products imported. The final section briefly examines the trade prospects for the coming years. In past years, it will be argued, Japanese competitive gains were a considerable factor in the expanded trade. Because in a number of cases the potential for future competitive gains is limited, the principal argument advanced here is that Japan's future exports will be considerably more closely tied to the region's overall import capacity than had been true in the past.

Pacific Asia's Role in
Japanese Exports

Japanese exports to the world rose at exceptionally rapid rates in recent years. This data is well known, and little comment is required here. From 1958 to 1970, her exports increased at a compounded annual rate of 17.4 percent. During the 1962-1970 period, the comparable rate of increase accelerated further, to 20.5 percent. In quantitative terms, exports nearly quadrupled during the decade of the 1960s. By any standard, Japanese sales abroad were massive, and the pace of this expansion showed little sign of diminishing.

Yet, this virtually unprecedented export performance masked fundamental shifts in the commodity composition of Japanese sales abroad. That this is so is hardly surprising. It would be more remarkable in many ways if the commodity composition of exports had *not* shifted to meet the changing needs of foreign buyers. For that matter, it is not easy to see how any nation could steadily and disproportionately expand its foreign trade without being able to identify and respond to demand patterns abroad. The chief point to be made here is that Japan has consistently been able to shift the structure of her exports to meet foreign needs.

The argument that the commodity concentration of Japan's exports has shifted dramatically can be demonstrated by an examination of her trade data for several different years. The principal findings are shown in Table 5-1. The data presented uses the 10 SITC 1-digit commodity classifications, and it is taken from two standard trade sources.

Table 5-1
The Commodity Breakdown of Japan's Exports to the World, 1958-1972 (Thousands of U.S. Dollars)

SITC No.	Commodity Group	1958	1962	1970	1972
0	Food	235,828	330,316	632,106	647,000
1	Beverages & Tobacco	—a	9,317	15,689	19,000
2	Crude Materials	75,559	159,144	326,582	447,000
3	Fuels	12,440	19,497	47,567	74,000
4	Fats & Oils	30,828	24,315	25,665	27,000
5	Chemicals	137,789	261,962	1,264,561	1,784,000
6	Basic Manufactures	1,745,220	2,072,835	6,475,957	8,264,000
7	Machinery, Transportation Equipment	627,407	1,252,868	7,833,824	13,654,000
8	Miscellaneous Manufactures	—b	786,267	2,572,718	3,388,000
9	Other	0	0	154,562	258,000
	Total	2,865,779	4,916,552	19,719,232	28,591,000

aFor 1958, Japanese exports of Beverages and Tobacco are included in Foods (SITC Group 0).

bFor 1958, Japanese exports of Miscellaneous Manufactures are included in Manufactures (SITC Group 6).

Source: Data for 1958, 1962, 1970 taken from Japan's export returns in United Nations, *Commodity Trade Statistics, Series D*, Vols. VIII, XII, and XX (New York: Statistical Office), selected years. Data for 1972 taken from OECD *Economic Surveys: Japan* (Paris, 1973), statistical appendix, p. 87.

It is possible to highlight several broad summary trends from this data. First, while every category except Fats and Oils grew at extraordinarily rapid rates, there was a pronounced shift in Japan's world commodity mix between 1958 and 1972. This is so because the two Manufactures categories (6 and 8), which had accounted for more than 60 percent of Japanese exports in the late 1950s, rose considerably in absolute terms. Relatively speaking, however, the proportionate increases grew somewhat more slowly than total exports. By 1972, accordingly, those two manufacturing categories accounted for only about 40 percent of Japanese exports. This relative decline, parenthetically, can be explained largely by the drastic decline in importance of Japanese textile exports. Textile products' share of Japan's exports declined from nearly a quarter to about 7 to 8 percent by the start of the 1970s. Which categories achieved the largest rates of increase? Table 5-1 shows that the largest was recorded in the Machinery and Transport Equipment category, which rose more than twentyfold between 1958 and 1972. By 1972, moreover, this category accounted for nearly 50 percent of Japan's total exports, which easily made it the largest category. While the Chemicals category also rose with disproportionate swiftness, its aggregate importance continued to be minimal. What emerges, therefore, is a composite picture of Japanese exports that grew enormously while remaining highly concentrated among three or four categories.

Against this overall background, the importance of the Pacific Asian region can be more readily assessed. It was earlier shown that the region has accounted for a remarkably stable proportion of Japan's world exports. The questions are what particular products did Japan export to Pacific Asia, and what quantitative importance did the region, as a whole, account for within those product groups? Combining purchases from all twelve countries, Table 5-2 shows that Japan's exports to the region grew at an overall rate of 20.5 percent between 1962 and 1970.

The Japanese export data in Table 5-2 are shown divided into four categories: Agricultural Goods, Natural Resources, Labor-Intensive Manufactures, and Capital-Intensive Manufactures. The full list of SITC products placed in each category is shown below. This breakdown, like any other, is somewhat arbitrary. It is put forward here, however, because it provides a plausible basis for analyzing the trade flows, and it is not possible to derive an exact categorical breakdown reflecting factor proportions in any case.

The argument that the commodity shares of Japanese exports to Pacific Asia did not greatly change receives a good deal of support from the data presented in Table 5-2. When exports are divided into the four categories shown in the table (not including, for 1970, an insignificant amount of exports unclassified by kind), it is easy to see that the respective growth coefficients rose at comparable rates for every group except Labor-Intensive Manufactures. Not surprisingly, capital-intensive manufacturing exports to Pacific Asia rose the fastest, by some 23.4 percent at compounded annual rates, which rate was only slightly less than Japan's comparable world rate. It follows that the share of the Capital-Intensive

Table 5-2
The Commodity Breakdown of Japan's Exports to Pacific Asia, 1962-1970
(Thousands of U.S. Dollars)

Commodity Group	1962	1970	Compounded Annual Rate of Growth 1962-1970 (In Percent)
Agricultural Goods	57,935 (12.1)	246,502 (33.5)	19.84
Natural Resources	12,259 (51.2)	47,210 (71.3)	18.36
Labor-Intensive Manufactures	511,808 (22.6)	1,488,042 (25.2)	14.27
Capital-Intensive Manufactures	651,425 (30.4)	3,493,728 (28.1)	23.36
Total	1,233,944 (25.1)	5,278,430 (27.0)	20.03

Note: Pacific Asian countries include: Australia, Mainland China, Hong Kong, Indonesia, Republic of Korea, the Fed. of Malaysia, New Zealand, Philippines, Singapore, Thailand, and Taiwan. The individual commodity groups do not always add to the total, due to the exclusion of SITC 9 from the subtotals. The SITC commodity group classifications are:
Agricultural Goods: 0, 1, 2 (excluding 231.2, 251, 266, 267, 27, 28), 4.
Natural Resources: 27, 28, 3.
Labor-Intensive Manufactures: 6 (excluding 661-664, 67, 68), 8, 267, 541, 733.1.
Capital-Intensive Manufactures: 5 (excluding 541), 7 (excluding 773.1), 231.2, 251, 266, 661-664, 67, 68.
Source: Data for 1962 and 1970 taken from Japan's export returns in United Nations, *Commodity Trade Statistics, Series D.*

Manufactures group in Japan's exports to the region increased from slightly more than half in 1962 to two-thirds by 1970.

The major source of the relative decline in Japanese Labor-Intensive Manufactures to Pacific Asia was the textile industry. A considerable growth in textile-product exports did continue to occur, although within that industry the rapid growth was much more pronounced in synthetic fibers and products. Indeed, some idea of the magnitudes of Japanese exports can be obtained when one points out that textile exports rose by *only* 12 percent compounded annually, which rate constituted a relative drag on Japanese export growth.

How much exports to Pacific Asia in each of the principal classifications contributed to Japan exports is shown in parenthesis. What is striking here is the stability of the two manufacturing groups' shares between 1962 and 1970. Table 5-2 shows that the region accounted for a quarter of Japanese sales in each category. The considerably larger shares in the other two categories are made less meaningful by their relatively insignificant size.

Of much greater interest than the simple growth rates of Japan's exports to the Pacific region, however, is an analysis of her trade performance in the region as compared to exports to the rest of the world. By taking the twelve countries collectively, it can be shown that Japan's exports grew relatively in three of the four principal categories. The single exception was the heavy manufacturing category, which can be explained on the grounds that the region's industrial structure, even by 1970, was simply not sufficiently developed to provide any greater import demand from Japan.

What emerges clearly from this discussion is that Japanese exporters could and did sell their products throughout the region, even though what goods they sold were typically manufactures that were often fabricated from the region's raw materials. The distances involved were relatively short, and thus transportation costs were seldom of major importance. This was because value was high in terms of bulk—exactly the reverse of many of Japan's imported raw materials.

There is considerable evidence to suggest that one principal reason for Japan's success lay in the large number of highly specialized trading companies that had representatives throughout the region. These companies could and did perform a number of key functions, each of which contributed to Japan's export successes. Because of their detailed knowledge of economic demands in a particular region, the trading companies, which represent the products of many different firms, were able to identify and fill industrial needs quickly. Their integrated sales forces were able to provide credit, assure delivery dates, and provide a range of alternative products from which to choose. They also had access to technical expertise, repair and maintenance services, and even engineering and design advice. Japanese machinery and manufactures enjoyed a consistently high reputation for quality. JETRO (Japan External Trade Organization) also provided considerable assistance to potential exporters.

The relative backwardness of the industrial milieu in many of these countries, particularly in the rural areas, made the host of financial and technical services Japan provided a particularly appealing feature of trading with—or really buying from—Japanese exporters. These trading companies were at the same time buying massive quantities of raw materials from several of these countries, of course, so that intimate economic relationships were fostered. Other nations could have competed more successfully in these markets, but the point is that they didn't.

Japan's Impact upon Pacific Asian Imports

The economies of the twelve countries in the Pacific Asian region have much in common. While their respective levels of income and production per capita range over quite different levels of economic performance, their basic structural characteristics exhibit broadly similar patterns. The employment and productive structure of most countries relies heavily upon the agricultural sector, and to a lesser extent upon industrial raw materials. Common to most countries, in addition, have been development strategies substantially depending upon trade.

Japan has been the major—or at least a primary—trading partner for most of the Pacific Asian countries. The discussion in this section attempts to identify some of the principal factors that help explain how large Japan's exports to the region have become.

The findings, and the supporting discussion to answer these questions, could be presented in several ways. If one looks first at the commodity composition of each of the countries' imports from Japan, the most striking finding is that the import mix of the countries examined was broadly very similar for each country in the region. Table 5-3 presents data on the percentage shares of each of four main commodity groups, by country, for 1970. No argument that 1970 is more than a representative year will be made, although the consistency of these trade share patterns would not differ significantly if other years surrounding 1970 were examined.

What is clear from this data is that Japan exported only manufactures to every country in the region. To be sure, the proportion between light and heavy manufactures fluctuated considerably, as the data in Table 5-3 make clear. On that score, of course, it is possible to argue that different classification schemes would affect the percentage shares reported in light versus heavy manufactures— although again it is not likely that the broad patterns shown here would be significantly affected.

Given that Japanese exports to the region were heavily concentrated in manufactures, and given the data above with respect to Japan's rising shares of trade, the central purpose of this section is to put forward a rationale to explain Japan's extraordinary success among these products. When the detailed commodity patterns of trade are examined, the underlying explanations for Japan's growing penetration of the import markets of these countries begin to emerge. Since the detailed trade statistics, including the ten 1-digit SITC commodity classifications and the individual commodities in which Japan has been a significant supplier, are simply too unwieldy for presentation in this chapter,

Table 5-3
Pacific Asian Imports From Japan: Principal Commodity Groups, Percentage Terms, 1970

	Agricultural Goods	Natural Resources	Labor-Intensive Manufactures	Capital-Intensive Manufactures
Australia	3	1	37	58
Hong Kong	5	1	55	39
Korea	11	2	23	64
New Zealand	1	—	30	69
Philippines	5	2	12	81
Singapore	2	1	44	52
Taiwan	3	1	18	77
Thailand	1	1	22	75

Source: United Nations, *Commodity Trade Statistics, Series D.*

only the summary findings are presented. Table 5-4 displays, for the rapidly growing countries, the summary totals of their imports from Japan together with the breakdowns for the Demand Prediction, the Structural Demand Prediction, and Japan's Competitive Effect.

The Demand Predictions show what these countries' imports from Japan would have been if their respective base year (1962) import levels from Japan had risen at precisely their overall (world) import growth rates. The Demand Prediction simply projects what the proportional share of the respective countries' 1970 imports Japan would have been if she had succeeded in maintaining her 1962 overall shares. These totals are shown in Column 1 of Table 5-4.

Given the huge changes in Japan's trade shares, the Demand Prediction does little more than provide a static yardstick against which these gains can be measured. Of greater consequence, accordingly, are the countries' import demand projections for each of the two or three dozen principal import commodities. The Structural Demand Coefficients ask whether the overall weighted commodity composition of Japan's exports to a given country was biased in favor of commodities that grew relatively rapidly or slowly. A positive S.D.P. coefficient means that Japan was exporting a weighted mix of products whose import rates were growing disproportionately rapidly. The larger the positive (negative) coefficients, of course, the greater the advantage (handicap) Japanese exportables faced.

The data presented in Table 5-4 show that four countries, including Hong Kong, the Philippines, Singapore, and Taiwan, had positive S.D.P. coefficients with Japan, while the other four shown had negative coefficients. Of the eight

Table 5-4

Pacific Asian Import Coefficients from Japan, 1962-1970 (Thousands of U.S. Dollars)

Country	Demand Prediction	Structural Demand Prediction	Competitive Effect	Total Imports from Japan
Australia	323,367	−27,284	277,437	576,383
Hong Kong	478,810	71,125	141,160	691,090
Korea	772,548	−229,363	266,086	809,275
New Zealand	43,128	−4,389	83,701	122,504
Philippines	219,595	33,517	116,022	369,138
Singapore	223,485	179,428	73,377	476,294
Taiwan	521,686	92,436	40,249	654,415
Thailand	382,483	−37,439	140,843	485,931

Source: Data taken from the various country reports, United Nations, *Commodity Trade Statistics, Series D.*

countries, in fact, only Singapore's coefficient was large and positive. With this single exception, it therefore becomes difficult to explain the rapidly increasing Japanese market penetration by pointing to Japanese "good fortune" in that demand for the commodities in which her exports were concentrated was growing disproportionately rapidly. Her established market position among "favorable" products was clearly an advantage, but it was generally not of overwhelming importance.

The most striking, though hardly unexpected, result was that for trade as a whole Japan recorded sizeable gains in the Competitive Effect coefficient for all eight countries. This is shown in Column 3 of Table 5-4. This means that Japan had on balance increased its market share of many commodity groups, including products for which demand was growing both rapidly and relatively slowly. While the C.E. factor was the largest for Korea, Hong Kong and Taiwan also experienced greatly increased market penetration by the Japanese. The principal explanation for Japan's trade gains, accordingly, is that she achieved major competitive gains at the expense of third countries among the major commodity groups in which she had already been specializing. Further, while Japan on balance increased her overall market shares in these eight countries, it should be remembered that the aggregate import volumes within the region were rapidly expanding. Japan's export volume, and her expanding market shares, thus had scope to increase without necessarily affecting the absolute trade volumes of the Pacific Asian countries' other trade partners. "Relative displacement" is quite obviously much easier within the context of rapidly expanding imports. It can be accomplished simultaneously while trade with third countries is being maintained at established levels. Third country *totals* can even be allowed to increase somewhat.

More important than a simple discussion of the aggregate competitive effect coefficients is a breakdown of these returns by principal commodity groups. A rough picture of the competitive magnitudes involved for two of the most important major commodity groups is shown in Table 5-5. Two findings should be briefly underscored here. First, Japan's competitive gains were several times larger for heavy manufacturing than for light manufacturing–striking support to the argument that Japan has a strong comparative advantage in capital-intensive products. Second, it can be seen that Japan's C.E. coefficients were significantly greater for the Heavy Manufacturing category for each of the eight Pacific Asian countries shown.

Yet Japan's very success in increasing market shares carries with it a note of caution for the future. One country cannot continually gain market shares at the expense of other nations (the upper limit is obviously 100 percent). In evaluating the prospects for future trade, the detailed commodity trade patterns must reflect the likelihood that gains in the future must perforce be expected more from S.D.P. rather than from C.E. factors.

Table 5-5
Pacific Asian Competitive Effect Coefficients: Imports From Japan, 1962-1970

Country	Light Manufacturing	Heavy Manufacturing
Australia	38,872	253,893
Hong Kong	41,203	93,045
Korea	92,215	144,703
New Zealand	14,566	66,512
Philippines	8,828	111,866
Singapore	−25,132	90,704
Taiwan	11,278	39,444
Thailand	−10,720	123,816

Source: Data taken from the various country reports, United Nations, *Commodity Trade Statistics, Series D.*

The Detailed Commodity Patterns

Aggregate totals can obscure much that is interesting about changes in Japan's exports of individual product classifications. The question is what can be said about the principal commodity groups Japan has been exporting to Pacific Asia? Although some 25 to 35 industrial export categories were examined for each country, this section confines itself to discussing only the most significant of the individual findings relating to the major Japanese export products.

Textiles

Ten or fifteen years ago, cotton fabric was one of Japan's major exports to many countries in the region. Cotton textiles were key exports to Australia and New Zealand and also accounted for 15 to 20 percent of sales to several other countries including Hong Kong and Thailand. In more recent years, however, cotton textiles declined dramatically in importance with much of the drop being attributed to very unfavorable structural demand trends. Japan also suffered small competitive declines with several countries. These declines reflect the build-up of domestic textile industries in many of these countries, and they probably also reflect the sharp upsurge in export competitiveness in countries like Hong Kong, Korea, and Taiwan.

Synthetic textile products, yarn and thread, and related products, however, show quite different trends. Demand for Japanese synthetics grew rapidly in Korea, Taiwan and Hong Kong, and in general throughout the region. Japan's competitive gains were huge in Hong Kong, and very large in Korea and Australia. Pacific Asian demand for synthetic fabric grew rapidly, and Japan generally maintained her strong position as a synthetic fabrics supplier.

On balance, however, structural factors for textile imports in the Pacific Asian countries appeared far less favorable by 1970 than they had in 1955 or 1960. Japan's competitive position remained relatively strong, but those gains were highly concentrated among a very few countries. Textiles generally were becoming much less important in these trade flows.

Steel

The most striking finding for the eight countries' imports of steel and steel products (pig iron, sheets, plates, and the like) was that the S.D.P. coefficients were positive, though not typically large for six of the eight countries. Secondly, Japan's competitive position grew steadily, and often at large rates, especially in Australia (where steel imports from Japan climbed from $5.2 million in 1962 to $65.3 million in 1970), New Zealand, and Taiwan. This means that steel products, which figured importantly in Japan's exports at the start of the period, were clearly able to expand upon their earlier market shares in Japan's aggregate exports for most of these countries.

Motor Vehicles

This category, which includes cars, motorbikes, buses, trucks, and the like, has expanded rapidly over the last ten years. Most of Japan's gains can be explained by superior gains in competitive advantage. This finding is particularly true of Australia, Thailand, and the Philippines. On balance, however, vehicle imports supplied by Japan grew to assume major importance within most Pacific Asian markets.

Machinery

There are more than a dozen major commodity classifications within machinery. One possible division is between non-electric (SITC 71) and electric (SITC 72), although such broad groupings undoubtedly lump together a number of differentiable products somewhat arbitrarily. The machinery groups are large and highly important import categories for the Pacific Asian countries. The findings reveal that the appropriate S.D.P. coefficients were nearly always large and positive, which serves to emphasize the key role imported capital goods played within these economies. Japan's competitive position generally increased within most countries.

Within the machinery group, telecommunications equipment and textile machinery were among the principal categories. Here, too, Japan's competitive position was so large that extraordinary efforts will be required to simply maintain her current market shares, let alone increase them.

In sum, machinery imports from Japan moved to the first order of magnitude for Pacific Asian countries, and both structural and competitive coefficients were largely positive within these markets.

Chemicals

The chief chemical products imported by the countries in the region were plastics and chemical fertilizers. Industrial chemicals, however, were generally not significant. Generally, these products declined in importance in terms of Japanese total exports, even though they did account for about a tenth of total Pacific Asian imports. The most interesting finding revealed by the data is that the structural factors were almost universally negative. The findings were particularly adverse for Korea and Taiwan. The C.E. coefficients, on the other hand, were always positive, especially for plastics imports. Generally speaking, the Pacific Asian countries seemed to rely increasingly upon Japan to supply many of their chemical products' needs, though their demands here increased at a modest rate when compared to other major import commodity classifications.

Manufactures

This is really a residual manufactures category. Since such major commodity subgroups as textiles and steel were discussed earlier, those findings have been deleted from the manufactures data discussed here. What remains are such products as paper, instruments, clothing, watches and cameras, and the like. The C.E. coefficients were universally positive—enormous for Australia, and very large for the Philippines and Hong Kong. Yet the remaining manufactured import groups grew somewhat sluggishly when viewed against the background of the region's total trade.

Other Products

Pacific Asia imports important quantities of many other products from the world, including foods, petroleum, industrial raw materials, and fats and oils. Apart from a relatively small quantity of processed fish, however, Japan was never a factor in the region's imports of most of these products, and no further detailed commodity breakdowns will be put forward.

These findings point to the crucial role competitive factors played within the detailed commodity breakdowns. Within this context, furthermore, careful examination of the detailed trade returns show that more than half, and as much as 80 percent of Japan's competitive gains was contained within the machinery and transport goods sectors. By aggregate size as well as by relative shares, much of Japan's success during the 1960s in maintaining growing shares of these countries' markets was heavily dependent upon these product groups.

Import Commodity Concentration

This chapter has concerned itself primarily with questions concerning the magnitude and direction of Japanese-Pacific Asian trade flows. If a major share of Japan's increased market shares could be explained by gains in Japanese competitive strength among established commodity groups, this means that export deepening rather than export widening provides the more persuasive explanation of these trends.

But this raises the question of how concentrated Japan's exports were. If exports are highly concentrated among a small number of products, a country risks encountering at least two potentially major difficulties. First, highly concentrated export patterns (a few commodities accounting for, say, two-thirds or three-quarters of their total sales) are much more vulnerable to market fluctuations within the importing countries, over which exporters exercise very little control. The more specialized a country's exports have been, the greater the risks arising from actual or potential market instabilities.[1] The second problem relates concentration to existing market shares. It is clearly not possible to provide more than 100 percent of a country's imports of any given commodity. Furthermore, the greater the market share of a commodity a given country (e.g., Japan) provides to another country, the more its future trade gains in this commodity are forced to depend upon the rate at which the importer can increase its purchases of that commodity. The potential scope for an exporter to continually have competitive gains or to increase its market shares is consequently limited. In the extreme case, when the share of the market rises to 100 percent, all *further* trade gains become entirely dependent upon the growth of import capacity.

Within this perspective, two broad questions can now be asked to further assess the role that Japanese exports have played within the Pacific Asian trade network. First, how concentrated were these exports among a few key commodities? How much of the trade, for example, can be explained by Japanese specialization in a narrow range of products? Furthermore, did import concentration in a few commodity groups tend to increase or decrease over the last ten to twelve years? Secondly, what happened to the shares of world imports Japan provided to the Pacific Asian importers over those years? Especially for Japan's major export goods, is Japanese "displacement" now approaching upper limits? (Conversely, has Japan been unable to achieve or sustain high market shares even in the commodities in which she has specialized?)

Table 5-6 shows all the basic data needed to answer these questions. These data show, for each country, the four or five major commodity imports from Japan for both 1962 and 1970, together with the percentages of these imports Japan supplied. This data can also be related to the respective trade totals, which are also reproduced here.

How concentrated were Japanese exports to these countries? Japan's exports consisted almost wholly of manufactured products (iron and steel, including steel shapes and sheet steel), textiles (including synthetic fabrics, cotton goods, and yarns and thread), transportation equipment (motor vehicles and ships), machinery and telecommunications equipment, and some chemical products (notably chemical fertilizers and plastics). Within this range of products, as Table 5-6 clearly shows, one or a few individual products were seldom dominant. Few commodities account for as much as 25 percent of a given country's imports from Japan. When the examination is confined to the SITC 3-digit level, furthermore, the sum of Japan's largest four or five largest commodity exports to most of these countries does not account for major proportions of the countries' imports from Japan.

By either measure, consequently, a significant finding is that Japanese exports (at the 3-digit level) were not highly concentrated among a few individual commodities during the last decade, even though most exports were largely confined within the product groups noted above. There have been exceptions, but on balance, the Pacific Asian countries' imports were not highly concentrated.

Examining the data for 1970 also shows that import concentration declined in comparison with the 1962 returns. This means that the Pacific Asian countries' imports from Japan, never highly concentrated, became even less specialized during the course of the last decade. Seen from the Japanese perspective, her exports to each of the individual countries occupied a relatively small place within the Japanese trade network, which further lessened the possibility that demand instabilities for individual products abroad would result in adverse reverberations in Japan's domestic economy.

In response to the question of the market shares (measured against third country competitors) of these key imports that Japan provided, two broad findings emerge from the summary trade returns in Table 5-6. They are (1) the percentage share of a given country's imports supplied by Japan have risen substantially in a number of key products over the last several years, parallel to the rising total Japanese trade shares, and (2) Japan's percentage shares in several commodities for many of these countries have risen sufficiently high as to suggest that an upper limit on continued increases in market shares is rapidly being approached. Constraints on increasing market shares will limit the growth of the C.E. for Japan in these markets, which in turn would signal that a critical

Table 5-6
Market Shares and Concentration of Pacific Asian Key Imports from Japan, 1962 and 1970, by Country (Thousands of U.S. Dollars)

Commodity Classification	Imports from Japan	Imports from Japan as % of Imports from World	Commodity Classification	Imports from Japan	Imports from Japan as % of Imports from World
	1962			1970	
			AUSTRALIA		
650 Tex.	62,726	25.5	650 Tex.	99,466	30.5
652 Cotton Tex.	41,266	45.8	732 Vehicles	85,318	20.9
653 Syn. Tex.	9,480	21.4	670 Iron & Steel	65,272	48.5
670 Iron & Steel	5,206	11.2	720 Ele. Mach.	44,038	14.7
032 Fish	4,816	53.5			
Total	133,054	6.0	Total	576,383	12.9
			HONG KONG		
652 Cotton Tex.	30,648	55.2	653 Syn Tex.	124,328	63.4
653 Syn. Tex.	23,228	37.7	651 Tex. Yarn	63,597	42.0
670 Iron & Steel	14,105	38.5	724 Telecom.	42,640	50.7
651 Tex. Yarn	12,798	55.9	581 Plastic	37,636	54.1
724 Telecom.	12,761	64.0	670 Iron & Steel	36,897	48.2
Total	192,020	16.4	Total	691,090	23.8
			REPUBLIC OF KOREA		
670 Iron & Steel	16,471	75.5	719 Non-Elc. Mach.	67,400	55.9
561 Chem. Fert.	15,818	25.3	651 Tex. Yarn	61,923	96.9

Table 5-6 (cont.)

Commodity Classification	Imports from Japan	Imports from Japan as % of Imports from World	Commodity Classification	Imports from Japan	Imports from Japan as % of Imports from World
REPUBLIC OF KOREA (cont.)					
651 Tex. Yarn	6,944	25.6	735 Ships & Boats	42,468	64.4
717 Tex. Leather Mach.	5,810	72.1	653 Syn. Tex.	35,077	96.3
			512 Organic Chem.	37,137	80.9
Total	109,231	25.9	Total	809,275	27.1
	1962			1970	
NEW ZEALAND					
650 Tex.	11,366	14.8	670 Iron & Steel	33,971	31.7
670 Iron & Steel	4,011	6.6	700 Machinery	31,513	7.6
700 Machinery	2,897	1.4	653 Syn. Tex.	12,714	30.0
Total	23,686	3.5	Total	122,504	9.9
	1962			1970	
PHILIPPINES					
674 Steel Sheets	16,182	66.9	672 Iron & Steel	34,080	57.1
719 Msc. Non-Elc. Mach.	9,603	24.1	719 Misc. Non-Elc. Mach.	30,900	30.8
835 Ships & Boats	6,311	73.2	674 Steel Sheets	28,878	91.8
732 Vehicles	5,077	10.6	732 Vehicles	24,722	26.6
561 Chem. Fer.	5,071	35.5	266 Syn. Fiber	19,174	86.7
Total	106,354	18.1	Total	369,138	30.5

SINGAPORE

	1962		1970		
650 Tex.	43,342	52.3	653 Syn. Tex.	106,671	75.3
700 Machinery	19,000	14.2	674 Steel Shapes	40,729	83.6
670 Iron & Steel	13,738	45.3	732 Vehicles	24,627	27.2
Total	119,803	9.1	Total	476,924	19.4

TAIWAN

	1962		1970		
561 Chem. Fer.	13,494	82.8	724 Elecm. Equip.	63,327	68.4
674 Steel Sheets	9,514	76.2	674 Steel Sheets	55,066	89.9
719 Mis. N-Elc. Mach.	44,403	61.4	719 Mis. N-Elc. Mach.	44,403	61.4
266 Syn. Fibers	4,475	97.2	717 Tex. Lea. Mach.	30,421	41.7
			651 Tex. Yarn	27,956	86.1
			266 Syn. Fiber	26,685	90.1
Total	103,863	34.1	Total	654,415	42.8

THAILAND

	1962		1970		
652 Cotton Tex.	23,613	75.1	732 Vehicles	70,108	60.8
732 Vehicles	18,813	45.0	674 Steel Sheets	37,030	89.7
653 Syn. Tex.	14,167	86.6	717 Tex. Mach.	33,757	72.2
674 Steel Sheets	11,228	78.4	653 Syn. Tex.	25,434	77.7
673 Steel Shapes	7,000	57.6	581 Plastics	21,242	72.4
Total	161,386	29.5	Total	485,931	37.6

Source: Data taken from United Nations, *Commodity Trade Statistics, Series D.*

factor contributing to the gains in Japanese exports was being lessened, if not eliminated. For example, Japan supplied more than 80 percent of steel sheet imports for Taiwan, Thailand, Singapore, and the Philippines; merely *maintaining* those market shares in the future may prove to be as difficult as *attaining* them was in the past.

The Economic Rationale for
Japanese Exports

Japanese exports to the Pacific Asian countries, which increased very substantially between 1958 and the 1970s, were analyzed by using the methodology presented in Chapter 4. The results reported in this chapter provide a set of quantitative coefficients that help make the Japanese export performance better understood. In one sense, therefore, it may be argued that the demand, structural demand, and competitive effect coefficients fully explain the ever-increasing Japanese export dominance within these countries.

Yet it is interesting to speculate further on the underlying reasons that were the result as well as the cause of this trade performance. The demand and structural demand coefficients are in this context relatively unambiguous. Developing Pacific Asian countries clearly required machinery, industrial products, and perhaps above all, the technology embodied within them. These demand patterns have been widely reported in the literature,[2] and there is consequently little that is surprising about these results.

The same conclusion is not as true about the competitive effect coefficients. Both in terms of their size and their rates of growth, Japan simply was much more successful in the Pacific Asian export markets than most every other country in the world, even given that the influence of the "favorable" structure of demand could be (and was) removed. The most interesting question here is to attempt to account for the strong Japanese competitive showing. Accordingly, it will be asserted that at least four factors have been influential in terms of the Japanese export performance.

Perhaps the most salient factor is the multifaceted roles played by Japan's huge general trading companies. The role trading companies have played in the expanded trade was alluded to in an earlier section. Operating on a very small profit margin, these companies each deal in thousands of commodities. A key element in their success is their access to massive amounts of credit and financing, both long-term and short-term. Their trade volumes are enormous, and the major trading companies dominate this trade. Morishisa Emori has shown that the ten largest firms have in recent years accounted for 50 percent of Japan's total exports and 60 percent of her imports.[3] These general trading companies also provide a number of added services, including inventory supplements, insurance, warehousing, and transportation. Most importantly, their widespread representation throughout the region provides them with a detailed knowledge of local needs. These companies, working closely with domestic Japanese producers, can employ a wide variety of marketing strategies. By virtue of their widely diversified commodity structure, they can sell or even barter almost any product, often on very short notice. Overall, the comprehensive nature of the many services they provide enables these companies to continually expand their shares of the Pacific Asian market. Their unique form of organization, which is peculiar to Japan, probably accounts for a major share of the explanation for Japan's overall competitive gains.[4]

A comparable, related organization that offers some of the same competitive advantages of the private Japanese general trading firms is the non-profit, semi-governmental agency JETRO (Japan External Trade Organization). With offices throughout the Pacific Asian region, JETRO is the public counterpart to the privately organized trading companies. It actively promotes two-way trade, offers market research and trade information, and sponsors many trade fairs and exhibitions.[5]

A second explanation for Japanese competitive strength in Pacific Asia is her highly coordinated, informed, and continually active drive to export.[6] This export drive is a chief illustration of the result of most industry being tied directly to the cause of export expansion. Japanese industry is well organized to quickly supply products that may be in demand, and most firms offer good quality, swift delivery, and, where needed, financing or promotional assistance. The stimulus to export can no longer be explained away by saying that Japan "must" export because she "needs" imports, since recent balance of trade surpluses have removed much of the immediate pressure. The underlying rationale for the impetus behind this strong export drive is clearly beyond the scope of this study. Many other observers have noted,[7] however, and it is plausible to argue that it has some significance in accounting for the Japanese export expansion.

Relative price differentials potentially provide a third way of explaining Japanese competitive strength. Japan's exceptional labor productivity gains have been a key stimulus to enhance price competition. The hypothesis to be tested would likely be whether Japanese export prices held steady or declined relative to a given country's other exporters. Such a hypothesis is exceptionally difficult to test.[a] The data limitations of most of these countries are exceedingly severe. For some countries, furthermore, few sources of import price series exist. For such series as are available, problems of comparability and reliability interpose themselves very quickly.[b] It would be a bold economist who relied heavily upon inferences supported by the kind of aggregate data that are generally available.

---

[a]This is a prime reason why the methodology in Chapter 4 was adopted. By its nature, the model gave few demands for any sort of disaggregated cross-national foreign trade price information.

[b]What price evidence is available generally consists of import price indices. Little information is provided on either the comparability of the commodity weights in the index vis-à-vis the Japanese commodity mix, or on quality changes.

An obvious alternative is to calculate the unit value prices. Since most of Japan's exports are composed of machinery and capital goods, neither the technology or the quality changes in the "units" can be at all taken for granted as constant. While unit value indices may yield some potentially useful information for certain kinds of products (some industrial raw materials whose characteristics are carefully specified and graded, for example), such procedures have largely ruled out the type of commodities Japan has been principally exporting. There is also the danger that such an approach will eliminate some of the very differences it was ostensibly trying to measure.

With this large caveat firmly in mind, it may still be asked how the relative import price levels compare with aggregated Japanese export prices. Upon examining data for several Pacific Asian countries, including Australia, Malaysia, Singapore, Korea, New Zealand, the Philippines, Taiwan, and Thailand, the principal finding is that Japanese export prices moved with or lagged these countries' import prices.[c] New Zealand and the Philippines are the clearest examples of countries whose import price indices rose much faster than Japanese export prices. A presumption that Japanese competitiveness owed something to relative price margins thus receives some support from this data, but the caution with which these findings should be treated cannot be too highly emphasized.

A final point should also be mentioned. Japan was found to have recorded major competitive gains in several machinery categories in Pacific Asia. Some would argue that Japan, being herself somewhat more labor-intensive than other industrial countries, emphasizes a technology that reflects these relative factor proportions. Part of Japan's competitive strength in machinery, so this argument goes, thus can be accounted for by the somewhat greater labor-intensive blend of her technology, particularly for the machinery she exports. When coupled with Japanese exports of repair parts and maintenance requirements, it does have an intuitive appeal. In fact, there is little direct evidence in support of this point, and it may owe much of its appeal precisely to the fact that it *sounds* plausible.[d]

Japan's Export Prospects
in Pacific Asia

What can be said about the prospects for Japan's exports to the Pacific Asian countries in the future.[8] This question can immediately be divided into two

[c]The basic data used here is contained in the International Monetary Fund, *International Financial Statistics* (Washington, D.C.) various monthly numbers in recent years.

[d]A typical example is that "technical know-how and productive techniques nurtured from within Japanese agriculture and small scale business are more utilitarian in Asian countries than the multra-modern, capital-intensive production methods in the West." MITI, *Tsusho-Sorn (Foreign Trade White Paper–General Survey)* (Tokyo, 1965), pp. 333-5, taken from Robert Ozaki, "Japan's Role in Asian Development," *Asian Survey* 8, no. 4 (1967), pp. 327-44.

parts: (1) how fast are the import capacities of these countries projected to grow in the 1970s, and (2) how much of a share of those imports can Japan be expected to supply? First, in regard to the import capacity question, the consensus of several published estimates points toward an expected increase in GNP approaching an upper limit of 6 to 9 percent, compounded annually.[9] Given this rate of growth, however, there is a surprising divergence on Japan's prospects. Hollerman, on the pessimistic side, argues that Japan's trade prospects "do not seem particularly bright"; he suggests Pacific Asia's import capacity from Japan would grow rapidly only with a much greater volume of Japanese economic aid.[10] The Japan Economic Research Center's forecast is not sufficiently disaggregated for a careful comparison, although it does predict that Asia will account for a decreasing percentage of Japanese exports.[11] Kahn, projecting an average 7 to 8 percent growth rate for the regions' economies (Hong Kong, Taiwan, South Korea, and Thailand would grow faster, at 10 percent or better annually), remains much more optimistic about future trade prospects. For a region he designates as non-Communist Pacific Asia (NOCPA),[e] Kahn confidently predicts that by 1980 40 percent to 50 percent of Japanese exports will, by 1980, be directed to those countries. The greatly increased volume of exports will be accompanied, it should be added, by enormous Japanese capital flows to the area, estimated at $5 to $10 billion. The result would be a virtual commercial dominance by Japan's large trading companies.[12] Still other observers would concur with Kahn and emphasize the ever-deepening economic interdependence in the region organized and coordinated by Japan's major international trading companies as a key element in the projected expansion of Japan's market penetration.[13]

What do the findings of this study suggest about Japan's export prospects to the Pacific Asian countries? Any explanation for the enormous rise in Japanese exports to many of these countries must include both structural and competitive factors. Japan's commodity export structure has been built around such long-standing exports as machinery, transportation equipment, and steel—key products for developing countries in Pacific Asia, and products for which import demand was growing rapidly. Japan's ability to expand her market shares of these products, however, was found to have considerably greater explanatory power in accounting for her gains during the last decade.

If rising competitiveness in Pacific Asian markets accounted for much of Japan's past success, it also signals a potentially major constraint upon her future prospects. This data points to the conclusion that Japan is approaching an upper limit on the extent to which it can achieve competitive gains among its key, established export products. Japan is neither unwilling nor unable to further

[e]NOCPA includes eleven of the twelve Pacific Asian countries (the exception being "Communist" China) together with Cambodia and South Vietnam. Herman Kahn, *The Emerging Japanese Superstate: Challenge and Response* (Englewood Cliffs: Prentice-Hall, 1970), p. 134.

diversify her exports. Continued Pacific Asian economic growth will, of course, require expanded imports of machinery, chemicals, and the like. Consequently any approaching upper limit would not *end* Japan's trade expansion. It would, however, tend to *limit* her export prospects. This means that the gains for Japanese exports in the 1970s will accordingly be more closely tied to the Pacific Asian countries' future structural demands and absorptive capacity. Just as Japan switched from a heavy dependence on textile products in the late 1950s to a broader emphasis on steels, ships, vehicles, and largely non-electric machinery and capital goods, so the 1970s may call for a further export transformation, perhaps centered more upon manufacturing and agricultural capital goods, power machinery, and the like.

Putting all these factors together, these findings raise the clear possibility that Japan's *future* exports to Pacific Asia may be reasonably expected to expand at rates somewhat slower than those to which Japan has become accustomed. Since the region has accounted for more than a quarter of Japan's total world exports and provided a major and critically important source of foreign exchange, these findings suggest that it may be difficult for Japan either to maintain her recent world export expansion rates or to continue to pile up foreign exchange surpluses. These trends, if realized, can be expected to adversely affect the entire Japanese economy—although clearly they are likely to have a smaller impact in the 1970s than the same constraints would have imposed in 1960 or even 1965.[14]

Seen from Pacific Asia's perspective, many of the same factors are found to be applicable. The already dominant position Japan has achieved in many key industrial and capital goods products means that Pacific Asia's import growth in demand from Japan will be increasingly limited to the rate at which they will be able to increase their overall purchases of each of those given commodities—that is, continuation of Japan's past trends within Pacific Asia would in a very few years make the question of Japanese competitive advantage a moot point. Import capacity also turns upon the Pacific Asian countries' export prospects (discussed in Chapter 6) and possible accommodating public and/or private capital flows (discussed in Chapter 7), among other factors. Their long-standing and rising trade deficits vis-à-vis Japan will also be expected to influence their capacity for increasing purchases from Japan.

Any rise in trade restrictions in the rest of the world, and especially from other industrial countries, will of course limit the export prospects of both Japan and the Pacific Asian region. Such a conclusion is hardly surprising. Yet any loss in third country export markets will reverberate into the domestic economies of the Pacific Asian countries with great effect, by lowering their import capacities and consequently threatening their ability to purchase imports from Japan.[15] Paradoxically, however, Pacific Asia's longer-term reaction to increased protectionism throughout the world may well be to turn *more* to Japanese and Asian markets. It is reasonable to hypothesize that these nations will seek increased regional cooperation as both a reaction to and a safeguard against the external restrictive actions of economic blocs in European and North American markets.[16] While the *level* of trade might decline in the short run, it is interesting to speculate whether *shares*, and the accompanying interdependence may be further stimulated over the intermediate term.

Another threat to continuous expansion of these trends in Japanese-Pacific Asian trade would come if nationalistic pressures were exacerbated by the growing, and highly visible, role that Japanese economic interests were playing in the domestic economies of these countries. Any such pressures are conjectural, and speculations on them lie far outside the scope of this study. If these pressures were to succeed in blunting or depressing the trade flows, moreover, it is hard not to imagine that the economic aspirations of the region would be adversely affected. Japan must be sensitive to these nationalistically inspired pressures if she and the countries in the region are to prosper together.

In sum, a "naive" trade forecast might well point to the trade prospects being less attractive than they were a decade ago. There is little doubt that the *absolute* magnitudes of exports will not continue to expand. The question is how fast. As and if the region's growth continues, and if one or more of the special factors noted above become manifest, however, Japanese exports to Pacific Asia could further expand relatively as well as absolutely, from her current dominant position. In any case, Japan's continuing importance to the Pacific Asian region does not appear to be threatened.

Conclusion

Japanese exports to the world increased at an annual compounded growth rate of more than 15 percent during the 1960s. While exports continued to play a significant part in Japanese industrial production, however, the composition of her exports was undergoing a fairly far-reaching transformation. Machinery, transportation equipment, and chemicals were rapidly outstripping manufactures as textile exports in particular declined in relative importance. Within this context Pacific Asia was found to increase in importance to Japan, as both the structural and intercountry coefficients were found to be favorable. Broadly speaking, the commodity flows to Pacific Asia paralleled her world export flows, and in recent years Japan's exports grew by nearly 20 percent a year. Both the trade magnitudes and the continuing foreign exchange surpluses that resulted from the export-import residuals provided clear signals that Pacific Asia would continue to be a key area for Japan in the future.

If the Pacific Asian countries individually provided small markets for Japan, their imports from Japan nonetheless grew much faster than from the rest of the world. It was found that the chief explanation for the increased Japanese shares of the Pacific Asian import markets was Japan's consistent—and growing—

competitive advantage with respect to third countries in these markets. The structural characteristics of Pacific Asian imports, on the other hand, often were nearly neutral with respect to the commodities Japan had been supplying. While Pacific Asian imports from Japan were not especially highly concentrated among individual commodities, by 1970 it could be seen that Japan was supplying high proportions of many key imported products for these countries. It was suggested that Japan would consequently have difficulty in the future in maintaining the competitive *gains* that had in the past accounted for much of their market gains, though *maintaining* their established competitive position does not seem overly ambitious. Japan gives every indication of continuing to be a (even *the*) major supplier in the future. In the absence of major transformation of Japan's domestic economy, or of more rapid import growth capabilities on the part of these countries, however, their rates of imports from Japan could be expected to more closely approximate their comparable rates of increase from the rest of the world.

Pacific Asian Exports to Japan: New Gains for Traditional Commodities

During the last fifteen years the rapid growth of Japanese exports to the Pacific Asian region tended to obscure the almost equally large rises in Japanese *imports* from Pacific Asia. The chief purpose of this chapter is to raise several key questions about the impact of Pacific Asian exports upon Japan. Chapters 2 and 3 showed that Japan was (and has been) a major buyer from many of these countries. What follows here is an analysis of the trends in Pacific Asian exports to the world and to Japan. How important a role, quantitatively, did Japan occupy within Pacific Asia's world export network? How fast have these countries' exports to Japan grown? Both the structural and the intercountry market growth coefficients for Pacific Asian exports will be analyzed to help assess the contribution Japan has made to the region's exports.

In a fundamental sense, of course, it was the sustained rapid growth in Japanese demand for many traditional industrial products that so greatly influenced the scope and magnitude of this trade. The major portion of this chapter is devoted to explaining the rapid increase in Japan's imports from each of the Pacific Asian countries during the last decade. The methodology developed in Chapter 4 is used here, and Japanese import returns form the basic source of data. How fast, accordingly, did Japan's import capacity grow? How much of Pacific Asia's gains can be attributed to good fortune or to skillful marketing strategy, in that Japanese traditional demand for Pacific Asia's principal commodity groups increased at more rapid rates than Japan's overall import demands? The chapter also asks how much of these gains can be attributed to superior Pacific Asian competitive strength within the Japanese market? Finally, how (if at all) did the commodity concentration ratios change in this trade? How broadly based were Japanese imports from the region? Put another way, can much of these countries' success be attributed to dominant structural or competitive effects in just a few key commodities, which in turn might endanger further export expansion by tying it to increases in demand in those few commodities? Alternatively, has Pacific Asia made widespread commercial inroads in many commodity groups?

In the discussion that follows, it should be noted that the findings and the data were in most cases confined to the 1962-1970 period. This period is long enough to provide a meaningful test for these questions. Clearly, however, Japanese imports have been growing so rapidly that these findings should be updated and tested every few years.

The Pacific Asian Export Market

There are several reasons why most of the Pacific Asian countries preferred in the past to trade with Japan. Most such reasons are strongly related to economics. Japan, poorly endowed with natural resources, was a prime market for the region's industrial raw material exports. More importantly, the Japanese import capacity was growing rapidly. Japan was geographically nearby, which meant low transportation costs. Long-established commercial patterns and Japanese trading companies greatly facilitated the two-way flow of goods. Cultural and social similarities in these societies also promoted a favorable economic climate.

Many of these Pacific Asian countries had historically experienced long-standing colonial relationships that significantly influenced both the direction (towards Atlantic countries) and the composition (industrial raw materials and foods and consequently relatively little manufacturing) of their trade. Most of the impetus for these politically inspired relationships, however, had disappeared by 1950 or 1955. Chapter 3 attempted to demonstrate that Japan had become the major trading partner for many of the Pacific Asian countries during the 1960s. Of the twelve countries included in this study, for example, it was found that five directed between 20 and 40 percent of their total exports to Japan, while another three sent more than 10 percent of their exports to Japan.

The central purpose of this section is to analyze the importance of the Japanese trade within the context of Pacific Asian export flows. The growing Japanese shares of Pacific Asian trade were, at least to some extent, widely expected. Studies by the United Nations Economic Commission for Asia and the Far East and the Japanese Economic Planning Agency both forecast that Japan would become a more important market for Pacific Asia during the 1960s.[1] Two key themes run through these studies. First, for most Pacific Asian countries, exports to Japan were expected to grow significantly faster than their exports to the rest of the world. As seen from the Pacific Asian perspective, therefore, Japan had been expected to become an even larger factor in the countries' exports. Given that the region's exports were likely to be heavily concentrated in primary products, however, the second principal finding was that the *rate* of export growth to Japan would be quite low. This meant that the Pacific Asian region's share of the aggregate Japanese *import* market would be likely to decline steadily. Both the relative and absolute growth potential of Pacific Asian exports was thought to be fairly modest, probably averaging around 4 percent.[2]

With this discussion as a background, how did Pacific Asian exports to Japan actually grow during the 1960s? What trends began to emerge? How did export rates to Japan actually grow when measured in terms of worldwide trends? Finally, this section asks how the export trends can be explained in light both of Japan's needs and the region's supply capability.

Japan's growing importance as a buyer of Pacific Asian exports is in actual fact underscored by the region's export growth rates to Japan in recent years. Table 6-1 presents summary data on the region's exports to Japan in recent years. For comparability with the detailed, 4-digit trade returns analyzed later in this chapter, virtually all data in this chapter is taken from the U.N. *Commodity Trade Statistics* volume. Not surprisingly, for all but two countries, Pacific Asian export growth rates to Japan have grown at rates that were at least double their compounded growth rates of exports to the world. Even the two exceptions, Korea and Taiwan, recorded compound export growth rates to Japan of 30.6 percent and 19.4 percent, respectively. Those export gains could be considered small only in the context of their virtually unprecedented export growth rates to the world during these years.

Overall, the most interesting finding in Table 6-1 is that Pacific Asian exports to Japan grew at compounded annual rates of more than 10 percent for every country except Malaysia. The individual growth rates were highest for Korea, Indonesia, and Hong Kong, respectively, but the broader finding pointed up by Table 6-1 is that virtually every country's exports to Japan rose sharply.

This is reinforced by the rising percentages of Pacific Asian exports Japan accounted for in 1970. Lines 3 and 4 of Table 6-1 show in quantitative terms the principal role Japan occupied as a customer for most of these countries. Viewed somewhat differently, in the absence of expanded exports to Japan, the export performance of most countries in the region would have been very different.

By any measure, accordingly, earlier pessimistic predictions concerning the export potential for the Pacific Asian region to Japan can generally be found not to have held. With the exceptions noted above, exports to Japan from the region rose steadily and rapidly. Japan's expanding purchases from and impact upon Pacific Asian exporters had by the 1970s made her a prime market for the entire region.[3] The question is, what made these earlier trade projections fall so far short of the actual trade levels?

Analysis of the Commodity Trends:
Pacific Asian Exports to Japan

The discussion in the last section demonstrated that the Pacific Asian region's exports to Japan grew much more rapidly than its exports to the rest of the world. The major purpose of this section is to explain this growth within the context of the commodity composition of Pacific Asia's world exports. To do so, the study must carefully analyze the detailed commodity flows. How much, for example, has the commodity composition of the region's exports to Japan moved in parallel with their exports to the rest of the world? Put another way, has the region's exports to Japan broadly reflected its evolving commodity trade specialization patterns? Alternatively, are those countries now exporting a distinctly different pattern of goods to Japan than they are to the rest of the world?

Table 6-1
Pacific Asian Exports to Japan, 1962-1970 (Millions of U.S. Dollars)

	Australia	Hong Kong	Indonesia	Korea	Malaysia	New Zealand	Philippines	Singapore	Taiwan	Thailand
Total										
1962	389	13	41	27	119	26	137	52	52	64
1970	919	81	179[a]	230	136[b]	120	419	118	216	180
Percent Share										
1962	16.7	2.3	6.0	49.5	13.9	3.3	24.7	4.7	23.9	14.1
1970	27.4	4.0	24.6[a]	27.7	15.[b]	10.	39.6	7.6	15.1	26.3
Annual Compounded Growth Rate, 1962-1970	11.3	25.2	27.9[a]	30.6	2.7[b]	20.9	15.1	10.7	19.4	13.8

[a]1968.
[b]1967.

Source: United Nations, *Commodity Trade Statistics, Series D*, Vols. XII-XX, (New York: Statistical Office).

The summary findings for a number of commodity groups are presented in Table 6-2. Basically these commodity groups follow the composition aggregation discussed in Chapter 5, in which a country's exports are grouped into agricultural products, natural resource-intensive commodities, labor-intensive manufactures, and capital-intensive products. The same caveats expressed in Chapter 5 are relevant to these groupings, which are meant to be illustrative rather than rigorously precise. In particular, it is likely that considerable intercountry factor proportion differentials exist within some individual commodities. Furthermore, this data has been compiled from the export country sources. As such, these returns may sometimes differ significantly from the comparable import totals reported by Japan. As Chapter 4 stressed, however, the key factor to keep in mind when discussing either the methodology or the accuracy of the raw data is that consistency by the reporting country is an essential criterion for the data. While detailed commodity breakdowns (typically 29 commodity classifications per country) were used to calculate these coefficients, most of the discussion on the detailed commodity flows is presented in the next section.

With these limitations in mind, it is useful to turn to the findings presented in Table 6-2. Pacific Asian exports to Japan in each of the four summary commodity groups are shown for 1962 and 1970. Apart from relatively insignificant entries for armaments and for unclassified goods, which have been excluded from these subtotals, and apart from errors and omissions, virtually all the countries' exports should be reflected in one or another of these categories.

These data go far in explaining the trends in Pacific Asian exports to Japan. The most striking overall finding is the extent to which Pacific Asian exports were concentrated among agricultural and natural resource products. This is shown clearly in Columns 1 and 2. With only a few exceptions, including Hong Kong, Korea, and Taiwan, the commodity concentration among non-manufactured products changed little over the last decade. (The sizeable entries for Malaysia in 1962 and 1967 in capital-intensive manufactures are due largely to her exports of tin to Japan.) Whatever is said about the size of exports, consequently, the evidence here suggests that the *pattern* of exports did not evolve greatly from traditional patterns. The principal change is that some increase in manufactures was recorded by a few countries in the region; in no sense was the export diversity widely shared throughout all the countries of Pacific Asia. Even for these countries, moreover, their manufactured goods exports to Japan simply did not account for major market shares.

In this context, it is interesting to speculate upon some of the factors underlying these exports. Partly, of course, they could come from, for example, the plants of successful Korean or Taiwanese entrepreneurs, as an outgrowth of domestic industrial expansion. Yet it is known that there began to be considerable private Japanese investment in manufacturing plants in Pacific Asia beginning in the late 1960s. These data are also consistent with a hypothesis that the rising Pacific Asian manufactures exports resulted from overseas private

108

Table 6-2
Pacific Asian Exports to Japan Summary Commodity Groups, 1962-1970 (Millions of U.S. Dollars)

Country		Agricultural Goods	Natural Resources	Labor-Intensive Manufactures	Capital-Intensive Manufactures
Australia	1962	305	59	5	20
	1970	374	450	9	67
Hong Kong	1962	2	7	4	0
	1970	12	13	44	11
Indonesia	1962	10	31	0	0
	1968	37	137	—	5
Korea	1962	20	5	1	—
	1970	85	38	84	23
Malaysia	1962	36	57	—	26
	1967	25	47	—	63
New Zealand	1962	23	—	0	3
	1970	108	1	3	8
Philippines	1962	103	32	0	1
	1970	229	185	3	3
Singapore	1962	32	19	—	0
	1970	42	69	2	2
Taiwan	1962	49	1	1	1
	1970	124	8	57	25
Thailand	1962	62	2	0	0
	1970	155	12	3	3

Source: United Nations *Commodity Trade Statistics, Series D.*

Japanese investment and, ultimately, from Japanese-owned plants located in Pacific Asia. Little direct evidence is available to test this hypothesis, but a full discussion of Japanese public and private capital flows is offered in Chapter 7. (And this investment, it will be argued, was by no means confined to industrial plants.) Yet what is relevant to the argument put foward here is that domestically owned Pacific Asian exports may not be as diversified as the data in Table 6-2 seemingly indicates. If this is so, the region's self-generated exports may continue to be heavily concentrated within the resource-intensive commodities.[4]

If the principal dynamic force underlying the region's expanded exports to Japan was the ability of the several countries to increase sales of agricultural and natural resource-intensive products to Japan, the question is how important a market was Japan for these commodities? Also, how did the region's commodity exports to Japan compare with their export patterns to the rest of the world?

The data in Table 6-3 show the percentage shares of agricultural and natural resource exports for which Japan accounted, together with the compounded growth rates of each country's exports to Japan during the last decade. These findings go far in explaining the underlying trends in the region's exports to Japan. By looking first at the annual compound rates of growth, it can be seen that these growth rates were maintained at exceptionally high levels for virtually every country in the region. This is particularly true for natural resource exports. The data in Column 2 shows that the annual rates of increase approached 30 percent *per year* for six of the ten countries. These rates of growth follow directly from the magnitudes put forward in Table 6-2; what is principally underscored here is the extent to which the earlier pessimistic forecasts of Pacific Asian export prospects so greatly *underestimated* the actual trade levels.

If the commodity export growth rates to Japan were significantly larger than the comparable data for the rest of the world, it follows that the commodity shares for which Japan accounted would rise commensurately. What Table 6-3 also shows is the dominant position Japan occupied in the region's exports of agricultural goods and, even more, of national resources. Japan was not only the most important single customer, but she was also, in many cases, a customer that purchased more than the rest of the world taken together. More important for this discussion, it is clear that in the absence of Japan, Pacific Asia's export earnings in these commodity groups would have been reduced by a major degree, which result, to a greater or lesser degree, would affect every country in Pacific Asia.

The rapid growth in *commodity* exports should not be allowed to turn attention away from the relative *absence* of Pacific Asian exports of manufactured products to Japan. The effect of this commodity disparity is seen most clearly when Pacific Asia's exports to Japan are compared directly with its exports to the world. The chief finding here is that Pacific Asian exports to Japan were concentrated disproportionately upon commodities in which aggre-

Table 6-3
Pacific Asian Exports to Japan, Percentage Shares and Compound Growth Rates, 1962-70

		Agricultural Goods	Natural Resources
Australia	1962 %	16.6	40.6
	1970 %	20.9	66.3
Ave. Annual Growth Rate		2.6	29.0
Hong Kong	1962 %	5.6	86.5
	1970 %	29.0	53.3
Ave. Annual Growth Rate		25.2	8.3
Indonesia	1962 %	2.3	12.3
	1970 %	9.8	41.6
Ave. Annual Growth Rate		25.1	28.0
Korea	1962 %	58.6	60.2
	1970 %	62.7	75.5
Ave. Annual Growth Rate		20.0	26.7
Malaysia	1962 %	6.4	87.8
	1970 %	4.8	60.7
Ave. Annual Growth Rate		−6.7	3.8
New Zealand	1962 %	3.0	15.6
	1970 %	10.3	14.4
Ave. Annual Growth Rate		21.3	33.7
Philippines	1962 %	21.8	60.4
	1970 %	30.9	77.5
Ave. Annual Growth Rate		10.4	24.4
Singapore	1962 %	5.5	9.8
	1970 %	6.0	18.1
Ave. Annual Growth Rate		3.6	17.2
Taiwan	1962 %	43.9	23.5
	1970 %	40.4	45.6
Ave. Annual Growth Rate		12.3	28.1
Thailand	1962 %	15.7	4.6
	1970 %	29.3	51.2
Ave. Annual Growth Rate		12.1	29.2

Source: United Nations, *Commodity Trade Statistics, Series D.*

gate exports were growing relatively slowly. In view of the world export data shown above, what results is the finding that the region's exports to Japan centered around a set of commodities that when taken together formed a pattern that differed significantly from these countries exports to the rest of the world. In addition, the comparable world export growth rates for those commodities were on balance rising sluggishly.

This means that the principal explanation for the rising proportion of Pacific Asian exports to Japan falls largely upon Japanese demand for a fairly narrow array of industrial raw materials and food products. These were resource-intensive commodities, for which export demand was growing *slowly* for the region, as opposed to demand shifts in favor of the textiles, clothing, and light manufactures that these countries had begun increasingly to export. Japanese demand alone provided a considerable impetus for these traditional exports. The chief effect of Japan, consequently, was to bolster export earnings among traditional commodities for which few alternative markets existed, rather than to allow Pacific Asia to *diversify* her exports or to facilitate the region's attempts to gain commercial footholds in a number of manufacturing exports. Yet Japan, as the first or second largest customer for virtually all of the Pacific Asian countries, was clearly a major source of foreign exchange for the entire region.

The evidence cited above makes it clear that the gloomy, pessimistic predictions of fairly static or slowly growing Pacific Asian exports were generally not realized, at least in terms of Japan.[5] A real question for future export prospects, however, is the place of these countries within Japanese import trade patterns. The next section of this chapter asks how these countries did within the context of the Japanese import market. How competitive were these countries? What can be shown about the growth in Japanese structural demand for the major products they exported? How concentrated were their exports to Japan? It is to these questions that we now turn.

Japanese Imports from Pacific Asia

The central purpose of this section is to analyze and assess the trade gains of the Pacific Asian countries within the context of Japan's overall imports. The last section suggested that in terms of the Pacific Asian export sectors, most of these gains could be attributed to rapidly increasing Japanese market growth for what were largely primary products. A key question here will be to explore the nature of the structural import demand changes within the Japanese economy. How much export penetration have the Pacific Asian countries, individually and collectively, achieved within the Japanese market? How much can be attributed to their ability, or willingness, to export a mix of commodities for which Japanese demand had been rapidly growing? How much, for that matter, can be attributed to rising competitive gains by these countries?

The principal data used in this section has been taken from the United Nations *Commodity Trade Statistics, Series D.* Only Japanese import returns have been used. In terms of comparing this data to the Pacific Asian exports discussed in the last section, it is plausible to expect that Japanese imports from Korea would be larger than the comparable Korean exports to Japan. One difference is that exports are recorded f.o.b., imports c.i.f. A number of other factors may affect discrepancies between the two sets of data.

The summary trade findings are presented in Table 6-4. This data includes, typically for the 1962-1970 period, Japan's imports from the respective countries' (and from the world) for some 29 commodity classifications,

Table 6-4
Japanese Import Coefficients from Pacific Asia, 1962-1970 (Thousands of U.S. Dollars)

Country	Base Year Imports	Demand Prediction	Structural Demand Prediction	Competitive Effect	End Year Imports
Australia	435,565	1,458,998	-115,329	164,075	1,507,816
Burma	16,290	54,421	3,366	-45,340	12,570
China	46,023	154,134	3,322	96,383	253,838
Hong Kong	18,938	63,231	7,032	21,455	91,810
Indonesia	91,156	304,965	23,240	208,456	636,604
Korea	28,506	95,060	415	133,434	228,989
Malaysia	186,255	623,875	139,344	-565,508	226,944
New Zealand	34,026	113,638	19,511	24,463	157,662
Philippines	183,960	615,963	-111,836	29,381	535,508
Singapore	22,701	75,544	6,781	4,261	86,546
Taiwan	61,379	205,392	37,504	7,823	250,785
Thailand	71,679	235,570	-54,623	4,661	189,614
Twelve Country Totals	1,196,478	4,004,791	-41,274	212,543	4,176,656

Source: United Nations, *Commodity Trade Statistics, Series D*; United Nations, *Yearbook of International Trade* (New York); Department of State, *Battle Act*, Annual Reports, various years (Washington, D.C.).

including the "residual" calculations for the ten basic SITC 1-digit categories. Both base year and end (1970) year data are provided. The basic calculations include Demand Prediction, Structural Demand Prediction, and Competitive Effect Coefficients in an attempt to explain the subsequent growth (or decline) in this trade over the period in question.

The summary findings concerning the Pacific Asian countries' imports to Japan illustrate why the region as a whole barely held its earlier place within the overall Japanese world import market. A key finding is that eight of the twelve countries have increased their market shares of Japanese imports. As shown in Table 6-4, however, with the exception of Australia, most of the eight had previously been marginal suppliers to Japan (although several of the countries *did* provide significant shares of important individual commodities). Indeed, Japanese imports from Australia were much larger than from the other seven countries combined.

What has happened to Japan's demands for the Pacific Asian countries' exports? The key results are contained in the Structural Demand Prediction import coefficients. Table 6-4 shows that although the S.D.P. coefficients for only three of the twelve countries were negative, those three (Australia, the Philippines, and Thailand) were together so large that the Summary S.D.P. coefficient for the twelve countries was negative. Negative S.D.P. coefficients suggest that the imports from a given country are on balance composed of a commodity mix for which import demand is growing slowly. The −$41,274 coefficient here, measured in terms of the size of the trade, is not significantly different than zero, which means that Japan's import mix from Pacific Asia, as a composite, roughly kept pace with her total import mix—neither better nor worse.

The negative coefficients can be explained by the slow growth of Japanese import demand for the key imports from Australia (very predominantly wool, and then wheat, sugar, and other crude materials), from the Philippines (crude materials), and from Thailand (rice and other food crops). These imports increased substantially less rapidly than Japan's overall import rates.

The remainder of these countries did record positive S.D.P. values, with Malaysia's clearly being the largest. The principal finding, common to all the countries, that emerges from this data is the extent to which a very few industrial raw materials or food products (seldom more than three) dominated the S.D.P. coefficient totals. Put another way, the S.D.P. returns are characterized by just a few commodities whose growth rates, appropriately weighted for their size distribution, have deviated sharply from the overall Japanese import pattern. Such a finding, of course, contrasts sharply with these countries' *imports* from Japan. Pacific Asian import S.D.P.s were much more widely distributed among a number of commodity products, as Chapter 5 repeatedly showed.

What can be said about the competitive edge Pacific Asian countries have achieved? As Column 4 of Table 6-4 indicates, a major finding is that ten of the twelve Pacific Asian countries were able to attain a positive competitive performance. For some of these countries (Indonesia, Australia, and Korea), furthermore, the C.E. coefficients were quite large—though the *negative* C.E. of Malaysia dwarfed any individual positive coefficient. Line 13 reveals that the summary coefficient for the region, collectively, was significantly positive, which suggests that the countries' net ability to maintain export growth and market shares to Japan in the commodities in which they were specializing was affected.

If the positive aggregate C.E. coefficients Pacific Asia was able to achieve more than made up for its negative S.D.P. values when measured for some thirty commodities, the reasons it did so turn largely upon the demand for key commodity groups. In Table 6-5, the results of a breakdown of Japanese imports into four commodity groups are presented, along with Japan's compounded import growth rate from Pacific Asia in each group. The major findings are unmistakable. The S.D.P. and C.E. coefficients for three of the four groups were positive, as were the aggregate results. In Column 3, furthermore, it can be seen that Japanese imports rose by more than 20 percent annually in three of the four groups, and by 12 percent for agriculture. In this context it should simply be pointed out that the light manufactures imports in 1962 were sufficiently small that the 47 percent annual increase in imports recorded is due partly to the low initial base.

The paradoxical nature of these findings highlights a fundamental anomaly with respect to Japanese import growth from the Pacific Asian countries. A widely advanced hypothesis throughout the development literature is that non-industrial countries face myriad difficulties when they attempt to sharply expand their traditional exports of primary products. A parallel theme is that less-developed countries' exports are highly concentrated. It is then typically

Table 6-5
Summary Commodity Coefficients, Japanese Imports from Pacific Asia, 1962-1970 (Thousands of U.S. Dollars)

Commodity Group	Structural Demand Prediction	Competitive Effect	Compound Growth Rate, Imports from P.A.
Agriculture	−494,808	−202,579	11.8
Natural Resources	124,610	420,429	22.1
Light Manufactures	23,466	201,195	47.2
Heavy Manufactures	7,538	67,266	20.5

Source: United Nations, Statistical Office, *Commodity Trade Statistics, Series D*; United Nations, *Yearbook of International Trade*; U.S. Department of State, *Battle Act*.

asserted that the growth in demand for their export commodities, which often consist of a few raw materials and food crops, has been sluggish in their major (developed country) export markets. Furthermore, with certain obvious exceptions (petroleum, for example), the projected income elasticities of demand for these commodities have generally been small. All of this points to uncertain, and even pessimistic, export prospects for many less-developed countries.

Japan has been a major exception to the model sketched above. The summary findings concerning Japan's import growth from the Pacific Asia show that Japan's ever-growing need for raw materials reversed the customary pessimism associated with low-demand elasticities facing many of these raw materials. Even Japan's increases in agricultural imports, despite a number of domestic protectionist measures, rose at rates that regularly exceeded 10 percent a year.

What these findings suggest, of course, is that the Pacific Asian countries' exports to Japan differed significantly from the pattern of their exports to the rest of the world. *Apart* from this Japanese demand, accordingly, their trade structures would have been even more sharply altered, and their trade levels reduced, especially since Japan alone had come to account for large shares of many of their traditional industrial raw material exports. Thus in terms of composition as well as aggregate magnitude Japanese markets have to an important degree permitted many of these countries to maintain a more balanced export demand structure than what would have been otherwise possible. Far from centering trade upon rapidly growing and often more technologically advanced products, Japanese demand has been heavily concentrated along the traditional lines of Pacific Asia's long-standing export products, which sectors would suffer severe dislocations in the absence of this demand pattern. It is true that Japan's actual import patterns did not provide a great stimulus to Pacific Asian export diversification. Instead, Japanese demand has been a key element in maintaining and strengthening the established primary production sectors in these countries.

The Detailed Commodity Patterns:
Japanese Imports from Pacific Asia

During the 1960s imports from the Pacific Asian region generally followed the same rates of growth as Japanese imports generally. If Pacific Asian exports consisted largely of industrial raw materials and food products, the key question here is to establish the detailed nature of the trade's commodity composition, as well as to point out any possible changes in Japanese import patterns. What specific commodities did Japan import from the Pacific Asian countries, and how fast was Japan's import demand increasing for these key commodities?

The detailed commodity breakdowns for Japanese imports from the Pacific Asian region are highlighted below. What follows here are the summary findings for the key commodities Japan imported from the region as a whole.

Cereals

Wheat and maize comprised Japan's major imports in the cereal category. By 1970, Australia had become a major supplier of wheat, as Japan purchased about a fifth ($57 million) of her total imported wheat there.

Maize was imported in much smaller quantities from the Pacific Asian countries. Thailand was Japan's principal supplier of maize, but the 1970 amount ($37 million) made it a small item within Japanese imports from Thailand.

Small amounts of oats, rye, and other cereals were also imported. Japanese imports of rice were generally insignificant. The major overall observation here, accordingly, is that Japan has not relied heavily upon the Pacific Asian region to supply key amounts of her cereal imports at any recent time. Even more, the region generally supplied somewhat smaller shares of Japan's various cereal products at the end of the 1960s decade than at the start.

Other Foods

Japan also imported relatively modest quantities of meat, fish, dairy products, sugar, and fresh and processed fruits and vegetables from the region. Except for sugar, the increases in Japanese demand for most of these products grew considerably faster than her demand for cereals, and the Pacific Asian countries participated in most of the increases.

Generally, the sharp upward movements in demand for meat, fish, vegetables, fruit, and the like can be plausibly explained by the rising standards of living in Japan that has resulted in more variety being introduced into the Japanese diet. Such trends may be expected to continue, even though their overall impact upon trade will probably not be sizable. What is again more striking, however, is that the region as a whole did not maintain its earlier shares of these Japanese food imports. Pacific Asian sales did rise steadily, and by very large amounts. What happened nonetheless was that the region's summary C.E. coefficients were negative for everything èxcept meat. This means that Japan's imports from other regions rose even more rapidly than did those from Pacific Asia.

Textile Fibers

Japan imported significant quantitites of two textile fibers—wool and cotton. Australian trade dominated Japan's wool supply throughout the last decade. New Zealand was also an important supplier. None of the twelve Pacific Asian countries were able to supply significant amounts of cotton.

For wool, the most noticeable factor emerging from a study of the detailed trade returns is that the structural component was both very large and negative. Australia's competitive gains were very small. New Zealand, whose exports of wool were concentrated relatively much more heavily upon processed, degreased wool, achieved sharper competitive gains. Generally speaking, Japanese demands for imported wool has grown very slowly over these years. However, as much as 90 percent of her wool did come from Pacific Asia.

By the end of the decade, silk had become a moderately important imported fiber. China and Korea together accounted for about 80 percent of the total Japanese silk imports. Silk's extremely rapid import growth rates did insure that the structural factors would be very favorable.

Overall, Japanese import demand for most textile fibers grew at only moderate rates throughout the 1960s. Much of this can probably be explained by the shift in Japan's industrial structure, away from what had been a high export concentration on textile products. Much of Japan's current textile exports, it should be noted, are built around synthetic fabrics, which have a somewhat smaller import content.

Fuels

Japanese import demand for fuel grew rapidly throughout the decade. This demand was centered around two commodities, coal and petroleum. Only two countries in the region, Australia and Indonesia, participated in these imports to any appreciable degree. Australia as a major supplier of coal to the Japanese. Coal imports from Australia approached $250 million in 1970, as Australia increased her share of Japanese coal imports from 6 percent in 1958 to more than 25 percent by the start of the 1970s. Several other Pacific Asian countries, including Korea and China, also exported relatively insignificant amounts of coal.

The other key fuel import was petroleum. The importance of oil to Japanese industry is widely known, and little comment is required here. Basically Japan, with limited domestic oil reserves, must rely upon foreign oil for virtually all her needs. Japan has been importing most of her petroleum from the Middle East, and in Pacific Asia, Indonesia was her only major source of crude petroleum. From 1958 to 1970, Japanese purchases of Indonesia petroleum rose from $18 million to more than $366 million. At its peak, however, Indonesia accounted for only about 10 percent of Japan's imported oil needs. The real importance of Indonesia, however, is twofold. First, its huge untapped oil reserves make its potential for the future unlimited, and, secondly, its oil supply allows Japan to diversify her imports from an exclusive dependence upon Middle East sources. Both of these roles sharply enhance Indonesia's future role.

Pacific Asia supplied important quantities of petroleum products, including gasoline and particularly residual fuel oils. Indonesia and Singapore accounted for more than a third of Japan's imports of residual fuel oils.

In sum, while two or three Pacific Asian countries were important factors in coal or oil markets, the aggregate quantities of imported fuels from the region as a whole were only moderately important to Japan throughout the decade.

Metals

Japan imported substantial quantities of several metals and ores from the Pacific Asian region. For iron ore, the most striking finding is that Australia had become a major supplier of iron ores by the early 1970s. Japan imported $421 million of iron ore from Australia in 1970, which represented more than a third of her total imports. This is in sharp contrast with the late 1950s when Australia did not ship any ore to Japan. Malaysia had been Japan's leading source of iron ore at the start of the decade, but by 1970 the absolute totals of this trade fell by 20 percent to $46 million in 1970. Imports from the Philippines showed a flat trend over the decade, as she too suffered relative displacement. Pacific Asia also supplied smaller amounts of iron and steel scrap, but these totals remained at relatively insignificant levels throughout the period.

Japan also imported a wide variety of non-ferrous ores, including copper, nickel, bauxite, lead, and manganese. Several countries, and particularly Australia, accounted for significant shares of one or more of these ores. The Philippines and, to a lesser extent Australia, supplied between a third and a half of Japan's copper imports, and Australia and Indonesia were important suppliers of nickel.

Other Industrial Raw Materials

There were several other major industrial raw materials that Japan imported from Pacific Asia. Wood and lumber products were imported in substantial quantities from the Philippines and, to a lesser extent, from Indonesia and New Zealand. Some measure of this growth is apparent from the fact that Japan's wood imports from the Philippines alone were $262 million in 1970, which was only slightly less than the world imports in 1962.

Japanese imports of natural rubber rose slowly over the decade. Malaysia had been Japan's principal Pacific Asian supplier of rubber, but Japanese imports declined slowly over the decade. Thailand had assumed greater importance by the 1970s, and Indonesia was becoming a factor.

The final commodity consists of oil seeds, nuts, and the like. China's exports of soya beans accounted for the largest single trade flow, and imports of copra from Indonesia and the Philippines was significant.

What common elements run through the summary trends of the major commodity groups? Two observations seem to stand out. First, the Pacific Asian region as a whole, let alone the individual countries, supplied the dominant, preponderant share of Japan's imports for few if any of the major industrial raw material commodity categories. The single exception is natural rubber, and that was hardly a key commodity import for Japan in 1970. Of the food products, the region did supply important shares of some imported fish and vegetables categories, but even in these, the question of market dominance should be raised with extreme caution. Second, whatever share of these ten to fifteen major commodity imports the region accounted for in 1960 and 1962, there was a strong likelihood that that share had not been increased materially in 1970. There were some exceptions among individual countries and within individual commodities. Yet the Pacific Asian region was not, particularly after 1966, fully participating in the gains in Japan's imports.

Why not? What factors can help explain these declines? The next section examines the data and assesses the implications of the twelve countries' import commodity concentration over time. Once that is completed, the chapter then attempts to explain the seeming inability of the Pacific Asian region to fully participate in the rapidly growing Japanese import market.

Japanese Import Commodity Concentration

A key question for assessing the impact of and gains from trade turns upon the extent to which trade has been highly concentrated among a few commodities. This section asks what happened to the commodity concentration of Japanese imports from the Pacific Asian countries. Given that total imports have risen substantially, how dependent was that rise, for most Pacific Asian countries, upon just a few commodities? (The alternative hypothesis, of course, would be that the trade patterns were characterized by a widely distributed mix of imports.) A second question that is relevant here is to examine the extent that these countries supplied significant parts of Japan's imports, especially in the major items in which trade has been concentrated. How much of Japan's total imports of each of these major commodities have the respective Pacific Asian countries accounted for? For that matter, have some of these countries become the dominant supplier for important individual commodities? If so, how does that market dominance affect their future prospects? The empirical support for many of the findings discussed below as taken directly from the summary trade data shown in Table 6-6, to which frequent reference will be made.

Despite the very rapidly growing Japanese imports from ten of these twelve countries, a major finding from the table on key imports and import concentration is that for every country in Pacific Asia, Japanese import concentration declined somewhat and, in a few cases, sharply during the last decade. One simple measure of trade concentration is the shares of a country's total imports

Table 6-6
Market Shares and Import Concentration of Japan's Key Imports from the World and from Pacific Asian Countries, 1962-1970, by Country (Millions of U.S. Dollars)

Commodity Class	1962			Commodity Class	1970		
	Imports from Australia	Imports from Australia as % of Imports from World	Percent of Japan's Imports from Australia in this Category		Imports from Australia	Imports from Australia as % of Imports from World	Percent of Japan's Imports from Australia in this Category
AUSTRALIA							
262 Wool	254,865	81.0	58.5	281 Iron Ore	421,657	34.9	28.0
321 Coal	41,003	20.1	9.4	262 Wool	276,786	76.1	18.4
041 Wheat	28,988	16.0	6.7	321 Coal	248,847	24.5	16.5
Total	435,565	7.73	100.	Total	1,507,816	7.99	100.
BURMA							
054 Vegetables	8,683	50.2	53.3	054 Vegetables	5,802	10.6	46.2
042 Rice	2,631	11.0	16.2	667 Pearls	2,386	2.0	14.2
263 Cotton	2,254	0.6	13.8	242 Wool	1,791	0.1	19.0
Total	16,290	0.29	100.	Total	12,570	0.07	100.
CHINA							
221 Oil Seeds	17,551	8.5	38.1	221 Oil Seeds	41,872	7.7	16.5
276 Crude Mat.	4,151	6.6	9.0	276 Crude Mat.	19,006	9.9	7.5
031 Fish	3,204	24.1	7.0	031 Fish	21,679	8.6	8.5
				261 Silk	27,104	32.2	10.7
Total	46,023	0.82	100.	Total	253,838	1.34	100.
HONG KONG							
282 Iron and St. Scrap	4,256	2.4	22.5	841 Clothing	18,661	20.9	20.3
284 Metal Scrap	3,291	6.3	17.4	284 Metal Scrap	7,104	8.6	7.7
				031 Fish	10,513	4.2	11.5

Commodity	Value	%	%	Commodity	Value	%	%
				729 Elec. Mach.	6,963	2.4	7.6
Total	18,938	.34	100.	Total	91,810	0.49	100.
INDONESIA							
331 Crude Pet.	67,270	10.8	73.8	331 Crude Pet.	318,116	14.2	50.0
283.3 Bauxite	4,962	37.5	5.4	242 Wood	176,222	12.7	27.7
221 Oil Seed	4,931	2.4	5.4	332 Pet. Prod.	48,243	8.8	7.6
Total	91,156	1.62	100.	Total	636,604	3.37	100.
KOREA							
042 Rice	6,287	26.4	22.1	650 Textiles	42,558	19.0	18.6
031 Fish	5,576	41.9	19.6	031 Fish	23,358	9.3	10.2
281 Iron Ore	4,783	1.5	16.8	261 Silk	37,188	44.1	16.2
				283 Metal Ores	14,823	14.6	6.5
Total	28,506	.51	100.	Total	228,989	1.21	100.
MALAYSIA							
281 Iron Ore	84,794	20.7	33.6	281 Iron Ore	46,152	3.8	20.3
231 Rubber	62,615	44.4	45.5	231 Rubber	44,997	29.9	19.8
687 Tin	27,732	92.2	14.9	687 Tin	92,213	90.3	40.6
Total	186,255	3.30	100.	Total	226,914	1.20	100.
NEW ZEALAND							
262 Wool	12,753	3.9	37.5	262 Wool	30,496	8.4	19.3
242 Wood	6,659	2.3	19.6	242 Wood	46,863	3.4	29.7
Oil Meat	6,453	45.1	19.0	Oil Meat	31,956	24.1	21.6
Total	34,026	0.60	100.	Total	157,662	0.84	100.
PHILIPPINES							
242 Wood	120,864	42.2	66.1	242 Wood	262,443	18.8	49.3
283 Metal Ores	24,675	15.2	13.4	283 Metal Ores	173,946	16.4	32.6
281 Iron Ore	17,468	5.5	9.5	281 Iron Ore	23,035	1.9	4.3
				061 Sugar	17,181	5.0	3.2

Table 6-6 (cont.)

122

Commodity Class	Imports from Australia	Imports from Australia as % of Imports from World	Percent of Japan's Imports from Australia in this Category	Commodity Class	Imports from Australia	Imports from Australia as % of Imports from World	Percent of Japan's Imports from Australia in this Category
				HONG KONG (cont.)			
Total	183,960	3.26	100.	Total	533,508	2.83	100.
				SINGAPORE			
332 Pet. Prod.	18,915	8.9	83.3	332 Pet. Prod	70,651	12.8	81.5
				284 Metal Scrap	3,611	4.4	4.2
Total	22,701	0.40	100.	Total	86,546	0.46	100.
				TAIWAN			
051 Fruit	7,584	40.6	12.4	051 Fruit	41,632	21.1	16.6
061 Sugar	31,091	23.1	50.7	031 Fish	24,133	9.6	9.6
				243 Wood	21,723	12.1	8.7
				841 Clothing	16,964	20.2	6.8
Total	61,379	1.09	100.				
				THAILAND			
231 Rubber	27,459	25.2	38.3	231 Rubber	56,408	35.1	29.7
040 Cereals	21,294	5.7	29.7	040 Cereals	41,112	3.9	21.7
221 Oil Seeds	7,567	3.7	10.6	031 Fish	15,099	6.0	8.0
Total	71,679	1.27	100.	Total	250,785	1.33	100.

Source: Data taken from United Nations, *Commodity Trade Statistics, Series D.*

for which the top three or four products accounted. By this standard, an interesting point is that not one of the twelve countries examined experienced an increase in commodity concentration. Comparing import concentration with trade shares during the decade also supports the assertion that countries from which Japan's imports declined, relatively, were typically countries whose import concentration was the highest. This measure of concentration is arbitrary, but the fact remains that in these cases, at least, "excessive" concentration has hardly been an advantage. (In this regard it would be interesting to compare relative *price* trends with the degree of import concentration.)

No unambiguous measure of excessive import concentration exists. When three commodities comprise at least 80 percent of Japan's total imports from a country, however, it can be asserted that the import composition has been very highly concentrated. Accordingly, Table 6-6 shows that five countries, including Indonesia, Singapore, the Philippines, Malaysia, and Burma, all had highly concentrated import patterns in terms of Japan.[6] Furthermore, Australia, New Zealand, and Thailand's three largest commodity exports totaled more than 60 percent of their total exports to Japan in 1970. Relative import concentration did decline somewhat for these countries between 1962 and 1970. Nonetheless, this trade continues to be characterized by Japan's purchasing large amounts of a few key commodities from each of these countries (and they become "key" commodities precisely because Japanese purchases have been major and very narrowly centered).

The pattern of Japanese imports is thus seen to be broadly unchanged: a very narrow range of raw materials and foodstuffs, among which Japanese purchases were heavy and rapidly growing. What is striking is that apart from some textiles and clothing in 1970, her key imports are concentrated almost exclusively outside of manufactures. This import pattern can be contrasted against a more extensive, widely distributed range of imports. Japan's consistency in selectively purchasing these few commodities over time, it should be noted, might well have provided Japanese importers with added market power to demand preferential treatment in terms of prices, quality control, prompt delivery dates, and the like. More importantly, it also subjected the Pacific Asian exporters to potentially volatile trade pressures emanating from such consistently high concentration.

It is fundamental to an understanding of this trade that Japanese imports did grow. Seen from Pacific Asia's perspective, the experience of the 1960s was clearly that Japanese commodity demands for these traditional commodities were growing so rapidly that the risks attendant upon very high degrees of concentration were simply not realized. (Continued high concentration rates among commodity imports for which entry is not easily limited does not, however, guarantee against such risks subsequently being realized.)

Seen from Japan's perspective, on the other hand, these high import concentrations were regarded without any great alarm. This was especially true since most of the Pacific Asian countries were not only marginal suppliers overall but seldom had achieved dominant market power within even a single 3-digit commodity. In 1970, Australia supplied 8 percent of Japan's imports; Indonesia and the Philippines, 3 percent; and none of the other countries provided as much as 2 percent. Japanese import demands were so large, and the needs for raw materials growing so rapidly, that high import concentration ratios were viewed as neither particularly threatening nor unusual.

By the beginning of the 1970s, furthermore, there were very few cases of Pacific Asia being the dominant supplier of any major individual commodities. Malaysia supplied 90 percent of Japan's tin; Australia, 76 percent of her wool; and Thailand, more than half of her imported jute. No other country accounted for more than 50 percent of any given commodity, which finding is in contrast with the more numerous dominant suppliers in 1962.

An additional consequence of Pacific Asia's lack of dominance in many of these key commodity imports is that further competitive gains are generally not constrained by current market position. There is ample scope for virtually any of these exporters to increase their sales, and their share of the market, to Japan during the next few years. This finding differs markedly, it will be remembered, from Japan's export position in the Pacific Asian import markets. A principal finding in Chapter 5 was that Japanese dominance in many commodities was already so high as to essentially limit future gains to the growth in these countries' respective markets.

One cautionary note is in order. All of these key imports consisted of industrial raw materials and foodstuffs. As and if Pacific Asia is able to diversify her exports to Japan—especially in such labor-intensive light manufactures as textiles and clothing—the trends in commodity concentration highlighted above will be modified further.[7] On the other hand, if Japan instead elects to relax her import barriers in favor of *more* food, Pacific Asian trade could increase without any commensurate change in its commodity concentration patterns.[a]

A further, and final, point deserves to be made. Contrasting the above findings with those on Japan's export concentration (a proxy for import concentration of these twelve Pacific Asian countries) discussed earlier in Chapter 5 demonstrates quite convincingly that Pacific Asia's exports were much more concentrated than were her imports vis-à-vis Japan. In both directions, moreover, the degree of concentration typically declined over the period studied. Trade diversification does seem to have been occurring, although it has so far been confined within fairly narrow limits.

---

[a]Indeed, there have been many proposals to deliberately favor additional food and raw materials imports from Pacific Asia as part of regional trade realignment schemes; trade preferences or "administrative guidance" would insure that Japanese importers would divert agricultural purchases from Europe to Pacific Asian suppliers. See Kiyoshi Kojima, "A Pacific Economic Community and Asian Developing Countries," *Hitotsubashi Journal of Economics*, 7, no. 1 (1966).

The Economic Rationale
for These Trends

From the data presented above, it seems reasonable to conclude that Pacific Asia, as a whole, was successful in at least maintaining its share of Japan's imports throughout the last decade. To be sure, Japan's place within Pacific Asia's export markets showed much more rapid relative increases. In absolute terms, of course, Pacific Asian exports to Japan accelerated markedly. Even allowing for slight relative declines in some individual products, the data here confirms both the rapidly growing magnitudes of this trade and its increasing importance within the export structure of these twelve countries.

It is interesting to speculate on the reasons that Pacific Asian exporters were able to maintain their relative position among suppliers of Japanese imports. In the brief discussion that follows, three hypotheses are put forward with a view toward accounting for these trends. This discussion is confined to economic influences; no consideration of political, cultural, or other phenomena is attempted.

The initial major consideration, viewed from the Japanese side, stems from constraints imposed by her balance of payments. Chapter 7 explores this question in some detail. Here it is sufficient to remember that Japan's balance of payments was in deficit until the mid-1960s and that Japan did not begin to record really sizeable trade surpluses until 1968 and 1969.[8] While imports were keenly important to Japan,[9] she had to earn the foreign exchange to pay for them. Especially during the late 1950s and early 1960s, import decisions could not be divorced from export prospects. Consequently, Japanese import flows were strongly affected by the overall trends in the *bilateral* trade between other countries or regions. Pacific Asia had been a long-standing, well-established export market for the Japanese, as the discussion in Chapter 5 clearly showed. This means, in the context of the argument put forward here, that part of the rationale for Japanese imports from Pacific Asia stemmed from the fact that offsetting *export* sales to the region were relatively easily achieved. In the extreme, this view asserts that the continued ability of Pacific Asia to increase her exports to Japan had little to do with the region's possible price or quality advantages. It was instead derived from *Japanese* export competitiveness in Pacific Asian markets. Japan bought imports so that Pacific Asia could earn some foreign exchange—which in turn would be used to purchase Japanese exports.[10]

These bilateral considerations were probably more important when Japan's overall balance of trade was in deficit. Data in Chapter 7 shows that throughout these years Pacific Asia has been the major source of surplus foreign exchange to Japan. Beginning in 1965, Japanese trade balances moved from deficit to surplus.[b] This is relevant in the context of this argument because it signalled a decline in her paramount need to earn foreign exchange in Pacific Asia. Consequently the Japanese emphasis on *two-way* trade flows has to some extent been mitigated in recent years.

A second principal reason why this trade grew to its current levels is that Japanese demand for industrial raw material imports held up much better than had been expected. Even given the massive structural shifts in Japan's economy, her resource-using patterns were sustained at the high levels reported above. This means that concentrating upon raw material exports, especially for such countries as Australia and Indonesia, proved to be an excellent strategy for the region.[11]

The final reason turns upon Japanese ownership or participation in industrial enterprises and resource exportation in the region. Production by Japanese subsidiaries abroad that is destined for ultimate sale in Japan is often recorded as an export from the producing country to Japan. By the beginning of the 1970s, consequently, Pacific Asian total export receipts were probably greater than domestically owned export production.

Unfortunately too little work has been done on the sales of Japanese subsidiaries abroad to enable this study to estimate this component of Japan's import flows. Partly this is due to the extreme sensitivity of the Pacific Asian region, especially the Philippines and Thailand, to perceptions of a steadily enlarged Japanese role in their economies. Yet it is plausible to speculate that this component of Pacific Asian exports is significant now and will probably increase in the years ahead.

The thrust of the arguments above point toward reasons why Pacific Asia was able to maintain its earlier share of Japanese imports. Yet it is also plausible to speculate in the other direction about why their trade didn't increase by *more* than it did. Why weren't Pacific Asia's exports to Japan *larger*? Little direct evidence is available to answer that question, though it would be interesting to speculate upon the role played by supply rigidities among Pacific Asian exporters. As Kitamura has shown, however, what may have happened was that Japanese import demands were simply growing faster than Pacific Asian countries' export capacities could grow.[12] Put another way, Pacific Asian exports to Japan were much more impressive when examined in the perspective of Pacific Asian exports than within Japanese imports. In the absence of supply rigidities, it is interesting to conjecture whether this trade could not have been larger than it in fact was.

If export capacity is the key, Japanese participation and investment in exploiting these industrial raw materials would presumably eliminate many of

[b]By the 1970s these concerns had been largely eliminated. For example, a recent MITI White Paper on Trade urged that "Apprehension over Japan's balance of payments which was once a keynote of Japan's import policy has become a thing of the past." see JETRO, *Foreign Trade of Japan, 1971* (Tokyo, 1971), p. 29.

the actual or potential capacity-oriented obstacles.[13] If it did so, how much would the region's exports rise, particularly from countries like Indonesia, Malaysia, and the Philippines?[14] Also, some newly opened sources of industrial raw materials may offer some advantageous product characteristics not now available from alternative sources. (Oil with a low sulphur content is one case in point.)

Another factor that may have limited Pacific Asia's export shares may be due to a basic, fundamental Japanese desire to geographically diversify her import sources of industrial raw materials more fully than she had in the past.[15] Earlier examination of the period beginning in the 1930s or even the immediate postwar years, showed that Japan's dependence upon the twelve countries for many imports had been exceptionally high. The earlier section of this chapter dealing with commodity concentration showed that Japan had achieved a significant increase in her geographic diversification, at least in terms of the Pacific Asian region. Any loosening of Japan's balance-of-payments constraints meant that a major obstacle to a long-term diversification policy would be removed. Import diversification may also improve Japan's chance to import raw materials increasingly from sources of supply in which production is being undertaken with Japanese capital and management participation.[16]

All of these factors are attempts to explain the past trends in Pacific Asian exports to Japan. What of the future? What are the competitive prospects for the Pacific Asian countries within the Japanese market? What structural demand changes will occur, and how are they likely to affect the Pacific Asian export commodity mix? The next section of the study attempts to answer these questions.

Pacific Asian Export Prospects:
Future Trends in Japanese Imports

What are the future prospects for a further expansion of Japan's imports from the Pacific Asian countries? Rather bleak trade forecasts are often encountered in the literature. A major part of the problem to some is the existing pattern of this trade. Kitamura notes that the current structure of domestic output and foreign trade is such that even the lifting of all regional trade barriers would not greatly increase overall regional trade flows. Domestic supply rigidities in these countries would also constrain trade growth.[17] In fact, argues Kitamura:

The primary task of economic policy will not be so much to expand commodity exchange along traditional lines as to create a new complementary system of production which would open up improved prospects for accelerated growth.[18]

An uncritical assembly of these factors would point to expectations of rather modest, if not disappointing, trade prospects in the future.

Such a view, upon examination, appears unduly pessimistic, and perhaps even untenable. Whatever the case may be for Pacific Asian exports generally, Japan appears to be a significant exception. At least four broad factors appear operative here, and they will be discussed in turn. Each tends to suggest somewhat enhanced prospects for Japanese trade for these countries. If all factors were to be realized, the prospects for Pacific Asian trade would seem to be bright.

First, a major attraction of Japan's domestic market to Pacific Asia generally is that it is already huge, it continues to grow rapidly, and it is expected to increase substantially in the years to come.[19] How fast will Japanese trade grow? Forecasting future trade levels is clearly a speculative undertaking, and any such long-term forecasts ought to be treated with caution. With that caveat in mind, however, it is significant to note that one major study has estimated that Japanese imports will increase at an average annual rate of 17 percent for the decade of the 1970s—just slightly faster than the comparable rates in the 1960s.[20] While the *share* of the Pacific Asian countries of Japanese imports is forecast to decline slightly, the enormous magnitudes of those imports will insure that Japan's importance among Pacific Asian exporters will continue to increase sharply in the years to come. Indeed, it is plausible to speculate that the growth in Japan's import demands will enable Pacific Asian exports to rise by the more than a factor of four times 1970 levels.[21] In this first view, then, Asian export prospects will continue to be attractive so long as Japanese domestic growth and import capacity continues to expand rapidly.

Although some Pacific Asian export dispersion has occurred, Japanese imports from the region nonetheless continued to be concentrated among industrial raw materials (ores, petroleum, coal, wool, and the like) and some foodstuffs. Japanese demand for these key imports from Pacific Asia is expected to continue to be relatively strong.[22] Of the principal commodities in this trade, Japan's range of substitutability within her current industrial structure may not be very great.[23] Few countries were dominant suppliers in any single commodity. The region's potential for continuing to export these commodities remains high. To the extent that Pacific Asian countries compete against each other in some commodity groups (rubber, ores, rice), of course, gains for the region as a whole may be limited. Some countries may be partially displaced as others achieve competitive gains, with the overall gains limited to Japan's import growth in the given commodity.[c]

The third factor that bears upon Pacific Asian export prospects is the continuing transformation of the Japanese agricultural sector. By way of background, the rapid Japanese industrial growth in the 1950s and 1960s was

[c]The annual increase in demand for overseas natural resources is expected to be at least 11 percent a year through 1975. If those trends continue, Japan by 1980 will import more than 30 percent of the world total resource trade. See "Outlook on Natural Resources Problems," *Japan Industrial World* 4, no. 1 (January 1972), p. 22.

clearly facilitated by the sharp increases in her industrial labor force. In large part this gain was attributed to shifts of labor from the agricultural sector to manufacturing and construction. From 1955 to 1968, for example, employment in agriculture declined from 16 million to 9.3 million workers. In addition, by 1968 many of those workers were part-time. Including increased population, this meant that the share of Japanese workers in agriculture dropped from 39 percent to 18.6 percent.[24] The non-agricultural labor force rose by nearly 4 percent annually. Since average hours worked by employees rose slightly, a principal finding is that both non-agricultural employment and the rise in employee hours worked in the manufacturing sectors rose at rates that were virtually unprecedented for major industrial country cross-national comparisons during such a relatively short period of time.[d]

The Japanese agricultural sector that remains is highly capital-intensive, and Japanese output per hectare is the highest in the world.[25] Yet farm relative income differentials continue to lag industrial wage levels, even though the agricultural sector is heavily protected against foreign competition. Short of major, unforeseen changes in technology, it is not easy to see how current land and labor endowments can be reduced further without affecting output. Facing domestic political pressures to limit inflation and curtail rising Japanese food prices, on the one side, and facing growing foreign pressures to relax import barriers against foodstuffs, on the other, it is possible to conjecture that Japan will further lower import barriers to unprocessed agricultural products. Adoption of such a policy measure could mean that Japan would turn first to Pacific Asia to satisfy many of these food needs.[26] The need to liberalize import controls, especially on agricultural products, is widely recognized in Japan.[27] If such measures begin to be adopted, the prospects for these countries *extending* their exports of a number of commodities would then appear bright.[e]

Increases in Pacific Asian agricultural exports to Japan fall generally within the existing structure of trade. The fourth possibility is for the region to follow traditional comparative cost doctrines and expand its exports of labor-intensive manufactures to Japan.[28] The key obstacle to this trade lies in Pacific Asia's ability to compete with Japanese labor-intensive industry than in the extensive network of Japanese import restrictions. The need for liberalizing imports to facilitate labor-intensive imports is widely recognized, and Japan has begun to do so.[29] There are indications that some small commodity shifts have begun to take

---

[d]From 1953 to 1965, Japan's increase in non-agricultural employment was 56 percent, more than any other major industrial nation (and more than triple the United States growth of 18.6 percent). For a comparison of twelve mature industrial countries together with a more extended discussion of these matters, see Angus Maddison, *Economic Growth in Japan and the U.S.S.R.* (New York: W.W. Norton, 1969), pp. 50-72, especially p. 53.

[e]The Japanese government has already agreed to provide marketing experts to help the Thai government study and plan agricultural production for export to Japan over the next five years. See *Bangkok Post*, October 15, 1971, taken from International Monetary Fund, *International Financial News Survey* 23, no. 48 (December 8, 1971), p. 407.

place. The most conspicuous examples are textiles (synthetics and cotton goods), paper, and miscellaneous electric machinery.

Conclusion

There is little reason to believe that Pacific Asian export prospects will be anything but attractive in the years to come. Seen from the Pacific Asian countries' perspective, the Japanese market has been enormous. If not widely accessible in terms of manufactured products, it has nonetheless provided a key, rapidly rising market for the region's traditional commodity exports. Little stands in the way of such trends being continued, so long as Japan remains prosperous and continues to grow.

Within the context of the Japanese import market, many of the same factors appear to be operable. Japanese economic growth, favorable structural demand coefficients for key exports, and some competitive gains all contributed to sharply rising Pacific Asian exports to Japan. In terms of the relative trade magnitudes involved, Japan was found to have been far more important to the Asian countries than they were, individually and sometimes collectively, to her.

All the countries in the region except Burma increased their exports to Japan enormously, and by 1970 or 1972, Japan had become the single largest customer for most of these countries. A major finding was that Pacific Asian exports to Japan were directed more to Japan's customary needs than to the new export products these countries had begun to develop. The negative S.D.P. coefficients for many of these countries reflected the somewhat "backward" nature of their Japanese trade. These exports continued to be narrowly centered among just a few raw material commodities for each country, though commodity concentration had declined during the last decade for all twelve countries. The potential threats inherent in heavy export concentration were not realized, though it must quickly be added that Japanese growth was expanding so consistently that virtually every country did well. A real test of the pitfalls contained in concentration must wait for a sharp contraction in Japan's domestic economy.

Some of the findings yield at least potentially ominous signs for the future. When the Pacific Asian countries were measured against the rest of the world among Japanese imports, they were found to have just maintained their earlier shares over the decade. Looking ahead, Japanese desires for geographical diversification and resource-saving industrial patterns might dim the growth of this trade somewhat.

In sum, the region's future prospects are seen as depending chiefly upon continued Japanese prosperity and growth. Japan's willingness to further transform her economy, depart from her long-standing import patterns, and begin to accept expanded quantities of labor-intensive manufactures and agricultural products would further stimulate the region's future exports to Japan.

7

The Balance of Trade and Financial Flows

The previous two chapters discussed in detail the rapid growth of trade between Japan and Pacific Asia. A simple comparison of Japan's exports to and imports from the Pacific Asian region, whether on a country-by-country or a regional basis, revealed clearly that during the entire period under examination here, Japan was able to record large, and even growing, trade balances with the Pacific Asian countries. This was particularly true for the less-developed countries in the region. Most of this time, on the other hand, Japanese trade with the rest of the world was in deficit.

As a result, Pacific Asia was also important to Japan in that it was a net supplier of foreign exchange for much of the postwar period. The first section of this chapter attempts to quantify the size of that outflow during the last decade or so. Japan could, and did, use this foreign exchange to buy imports from other regions. As seen from Pacific Asia's perspective, on the other hand, many countries in the region experienced a net outflow of foreign exchange to Japan. Their interest in maintaining the export and especially the import patterns discussed above can be taken for granted. Otherwise, there would have been little point in developing the two-way trade flows they did.

The fundamental issue that concerns us in this chapter is whether, during all or part of this period, Japan was contributing financial resources to the Pacific Asian region in return. This is relevant both to provide a more complete picture of Japan's economic relationship with Pacific Asia and to understand how the region was able to finance continuous trade deficits with Japan. It is, of course, far beyond the scope of this study to offer a detailed analysis of these countries' complete international financial positions. Based on the findings here, however, it is not difficult to speculate that in the absence of net accommodating capital inflows from one source to another, Pacific Asia's ability to finance ever larger future trade deficits is very much called into question.

A principal finding of the chapter is that Japan has been directing very substantial amounts of financial assistance to many of the less-developed Pacific Asian countries. The next several sections, accordingly, are devoted to a discussion and analysis of these capital flows. Counting direct and indirect economic assistance, export credits, private investment, and official lending, Chapter 7 asserts that Japanese economic assistance of all types grew rapidly during the last decade. Although recent, detailed data is very limited, it can be argued that much of this Japanese capital has been directed to the Pacific Asian region.

131

The present trends are uncertain enough to make forecasting the future a bold enterprise. Nonetheless there are many indications that Japanese direct private investment to the region, at least insofar as political interferences from the recipient countries abroad do not manifest themselves, will expand enormously during the remainder of the 1970s. Thus, it is plausible to argue that at least for the next few years, rapidly growing Japanese capital inflows will substantially offset the trade imbalances that resulted in net regional capital outflows to Japan. This would remove a principle obstacle threatening a continuation and further extension of the two-way trade flows.

Put another way, however, it may equally be argued that much of Japan's ability to finance these capital inflows follows directly from her past trade successes, both in the world and in Pacific Asia. Viewed in this perspective, Pacific Asia's need for accommodating flows was not unrelated to Japan's capacity to provide those capital flows. It is interesting to speculate on the extent to which the trade deficits and capital inflows will be allowed to grow in the future. Particularly when seen from the perspective of five or six Pacific Asian countries, several potential difficulties concerning the growth of the future magnitudes will subsequently be raised.

Japan's Balance of Trade
with Pacific Asia

From the data on the two-way trade flows presented in earlier chapters, it is possible to infer that Japan's balance of trade was favorable for most years in terms of many of the Pacific Asian countries. Since exports generally grew somewhat faster than imports in the region, it may also be inferred that the Japanese trade surpluses were probably increasing over time. The explanations for these changes were presented in Chapters 5 and 6. Accordingly, the principal task of this section is to present and analyze the actual Japanese balance of trade with each of the twelve Pacific Asian countries between 1958 to 1972. How large were these magnitudes? More importantly, how can the surpluses and deficits in Japan's Pacific Asian balance of trade be related to Japan's overall (world) trade balances? Put another way, how important were these surpluses within the context of Japan's overall trade balances? How much, that is, did the Pacific Asian region compensate for, or offset, trade deficits with other regions?

In the discussion that follows, much of the data is taken from Japanese sources. The accuracy and comparability of this data is subject to many of the same limitations discussed in earlier chapters. Exports will be reported f.o.b. from Japanese ports, and imports c.i.f. The trade balances that result, however, hold true for only Japan. The partner country returns, to be fully comparable, must add c.i.f. costs from Japanese imports. Any modifications for differences in recording, classification, or timing procedures would lead to greater differences.

This means that if, for example, Japan had recorded a $100 million trade surplus with country X in a given year, the corresponding totals for country X, using Japanese data, would result in a deficit of *more* than $100 million. Depending upon which country's data is used, the balance of trade calculations would consequently result in an upward bias for deficits and a downward bias for surpluses.

With these limitations in mind, we can begin to examine the actual Japanese balances of trade for Pacific Asia. The basic findings, rounded to millions of U.S. dollars, are presented in Table 7-1. From the summary data presented in the table, it would appear that the Japanese trade balances with the Pacific Asian region can be divided into three fairly distinct periods. From 1958 to 1964, the two-way trade flows were roughly in balance, and the resulting surpluses or deficits moved within a fairly narrow band. Japanese surpluses in 1958, 1960, 1962, and 1963, for that matter, were slightly surpassed by her deficits in 1959, 1961, and 1964. From an examination of all twelve Pacific Asian countries together, a picture emerges of a net balance of two-way trade that was spread fairly evenly between Japan and the region.

Between 1965 and 1967, the picture changed noticeably. During those years the Japanese net trade balance with the region rose to considerable surplus. The

Table 7-1
Japan's Balance of Trade with Pacific Asia, 1958-1972 (Millions of U.S. Dollars)

Country	1958	1962	1966	1968	1970	1972
Australia	−163	−297	−388	−504	−918	−1,474
Burma	34	37	31	26	26	20
China	−3	−7	9	101	315	118
Hong Kong	88	173	322	413	608	792
Indonesia	12	24	−56	−105	−302	−584
Korea	45	109	262	501	589	554
Malaysia	−101	−146	−206	−238	−252	−31
New Zealand	−11	−7	−46	−32	−43	−83
Philippines	−10	−63	−46	13	−79	−12
Singapore	64	82	86	147	336	585
Taiwan	14	57	108	321	450	670
Thailand	62	76	159	218	259	270
Pacific Asian Totals	32	38	236	841	970	825

Note: Balance of Trade equals exports minus imports. Totals may not add due to rounding.
Source: International Monetary Fund, *Direction of Trade, Annual, 1958-1962, 1962-1966, 1964-1968, and 1968-1972* (Washington, D.C., selected years). All data was taken and computed from Japanese sources.

magnitudes were striking. They averaged about $275 million, or more than three times the peak of the preceding period. During these years Japan consolidated her trade surplus position in the region as a whole.

From 1968 to 1972, a further shift in the trade balance became apparent. During these years the magnitude of Japan's trade surplus averaged nearly $1 billion annually. This again represented more than three times the peak of the previous period. By any measure, Japan realized very large trade surpluses. Needless to say, all of these shifts also point to Pacific Asia's trade running in substantial deficit in terms of Japan. Deficits are more difficult to finance than surpluses. Therefore, an important question to be raised in a later section of this chapter concerns the factors that enabled the Pacific Asian countries to run such large deficits with the Japanese. The discussion here, however, concentrates upon the impact and explanation of this trade on the Japanese trade network.

How important were these trade surpluses to Japan? The answer, of course, depends upon the years for which the question is asked.[1] The data presented in Table 7-2 compare Japan's world trade balance with her corresponding Pacific Asian regional trade balance. The most striking finding is that Japan's overall trade was in deficit every year from 1958 until 1964. There was another large deficit in 1967. For most of the years before 1965, therefore, the Pacific Asian trade was important, though hardly of prime significance. In 1965 and 1966, Japan's world surplus was provided almost completely by the region. In some recent years—especially 1968 and 1970—the regional surplus was clearly much larger than that from the world. By 1972, however, Japan's world trade surplus

Table 7-2
Japan's Regional and World Net Balance of Trade, 1958-1972 (Millions of U.S. Dollars)

	1958	1962	1966	1968	1970	1972
Japan's World Trade Balance	−156	−717	256	−19	436	5,173
Pacific Asian Trade Balance	32	38	236	841	970	825
Pacific Asia As Percent Of World	−	−	92.1	−	222.1	15.9
Less-Developed, Non-Communist Pacific Asian Trade Balance[a]	210	350	662	1,297.5	1,616	2,264
Less-Developed As Percent Of World	−	−	258.1	−	370.8	43.8

[a]Pacific Asia excluding Australia, New Zealand and China.
Source: International Monetary Fund, Direction of Trade, Annual, 1958-1962, 1962-1966, 1964-1968, 1968-1972 (Washington). All data taken and computed from Japanese sources.

easily surpassed the Pacific Asian totals. In sum, it is clear that Japanese balance-of-trade surpluses with Pacific Asia have enabled her to finance significant trade deficits with the rest of the world, especially since 1965.

Few things point up the significance of Japan's highly successful trade expansion more clearly than a comparison of the trade surplus totals from the Pacific Asian region with the balance of foreign trade available from the "rest of the world" sources. This can be done by using the data presented in lines 1, 2, and 4 of Table 7-2. Seen from Japan's perspective, virtually *any* volume of raw materials could be imported from Pacific Asia because of Japan's net surplus position. By the beginning of the 1970s, furthermore, Japan was able to attain levels of trade surpluses that dwarfed even the aggregate levels of trade she had worked during the 1950s to obtain.

This is not the whole story. If the examination is confined to less-developed countries (excluding Australia and New Zealand), and if China is also excluded (on grounds that those trade flows were abnormally affected by political considerations), an entirely different picture emerges. For the nine remaining less-developed countries, Japan succeeded in recording surpluses every year beginning in 1958 at high and rising levels. As lines 2, 4, and 5 of Table 7-2 show, Japan's trade surpluses with just these developing Pacific Asian countries go far to offset her deficits with the rest of the world. To be sure, Japan's deficits in her Australian trade were a major exception. In sum, however, it is clear that the less-developed countries of Pacific Asia provided Japan with a key source of foreign exchange through all three phases of her net world trade balances.

This chapter has up to now concentrated largely upon the overall Japanese trade balance with the Pacific Asian region. The next question is to ask which countries were chiefly responsible for the Japanese surplus and which accounted for significant deficits? Were the trade patterns for each country in the region fairly consistent over time, or were there a large number of switches in the net trade positions?

The principal finding is that the Japanese balance of trade with each of the Pacific Asian countries moved in a remarkably stable, consistent pattern over the 1958-1972 period. Japan was consistently in deficit with only four countries— Australia, New Zealand, Malaysia, and the Philippines. Six countries, on the other hand, including Burma, Hong Kong, Korea, Singapore, Taiwan and Thailand, provided Japan with large sources of foreign exchange surpluses virtually every year. For China and Indonesia, Japan's surplus and deficit positions were, respectively, reversed. Table 7-1 presents all the relevant data. To be sure, the magnitudes of this two-way trade changed enormously, and almost exclusively in an upward direction. However, the clear thrust of this data is to emphasize the remarkable consistency in these trade returns throughout this period.

In terms of respective surplus and deficit magnitudes, it is clear that Korea,

Hong Kong and, in more recent years, Taiwan and Singapore, provided Japan with her largest trade surpluses. In the early 1970s, Japanese exports to each country averaged about $600 million more than her imports. Australia was clearly the largest trade deficit country. In 1972 alone, Japan's trade deficit stood at nearly $1.5 billion—almost triple what it had been just four years before. Indonesia had become the other principal deficit country. Taken together, this data also supports the inference that it is meaningful to discuss and analyze Japanese trade with the region as a whole, since most countries' balance-of-trade patterns were broadly and consistently similar.

The more important comparison for the future, however, is between these recent trade surplus and deficit levels and the levels that will be required if the trade projections discussed in Chapters 5 and 6 between Japan and Pacific Asia are realized. While the Pacific Asian surpluses may no longer be as important to Japan as they had been earlier, reversing the question gives a very different answer for Pacific Asia. The size of these deficits already approach critical levels for several Pacific Asian countries, and future projections point to ever-larger deficits. A key implication of these findings for the future is that the annual deficits have grown so large that they raise fundamental questions about the ability of some countries to finance them at *current* levels, let alone if the trade is permitted to continue to grow.

Earlier chapters showed that exports to the rest of the world from Pacific Asia were creeping upward at rates that fell far short of the trends in their Japanese trade expansion. What factors can be used to explain the financing of these large deficits in Pacific Asia? In the future, how will these countries offset their anticipated trade deficits with Japan?

What these findings point to is that barring any substantial reduction in the expansion of these trade flows, there are only a limited number of opportunities available by which these deficits can be offset. During the last decade, moreover, a principal source of "surplus" foreign exchange to several of these countries was the United States' presence in Vietnam and, subsequently, in Indochina generally.[2] The direct and indirect benefits accruing to the region that stemmed from the United States military involvement began to rise sharply in 1965, and these benefits continued to be realized at very high levels for the next five years. Such activities took the form of direct payments for military assistance, war-related purchases of many industrial products, increased tourism, sales of food products to support and supplement the domestic Vietnamese economy, and the like. These demands diminished sharply as the United States' active involvement in Asia declined.

The economic benefits were not evenly distributed. Most, however, were concentrated upon Korea, Taiwan, Thailand, and Hong Kong—the very countries whose trade deficits with Japan had been the largest in recent years. The foreign exchange earnings for these Pacific Asian countries has been sharply, and adversely, affected by the winding down of the war.[3]

What other alternatives are open to the Pacific Asian countries? How else might they earn or acquire the foreign exchange so that further growth in the Pacific Asian trade would not be endangered, or at least not too severely constrained?

The answers to these questions turn, of course, on Japan providing capital transfers or credits to the region. From official government sources, reparations, accommodating public capital flows, and foreign economic assistance are all potential sources of foreign exchange. In addition, a major argument of the next section will be that Japan has also in recent years acquired both the desire and the capacity to finance major private direct foreign investment to these countries. Thus the answers to these questions largely turn on the movements of capital, rather than goods. Accordingly, the next section of this chapter assesses the possibilities for these sources in turn.

Redressing the Imbalance: Japanese
Financial Flows to Pacific Asia

The central purpose of the remainder of Chapter 7 is to examine the various financial contributions Japan has made to the Pacific Asian countries. More specifically, if the previous section showed that Japan has had a large and growing balance of *trade* surpluses with the region as a whole, this section proposes to examine some of the financial offsets to the net deficit position of the region.

This flow of external resources to the region (from Japan or elsewhere) have taken several different forms. In terms of public aid, these countries have received official grants, reparations and indemnification payments, lending (often financing deferred import payments), and multilateral loans and grants. Direct foreign investment and portfolio investment have also come from private sources, both profit and non-profit.

How great an impact has Japanese public and private development assistance made upon the Pacific Asian region? Seen from Pacific Asia's perspective, of course, an enlarged flow of external resources (whether from Japan or elsewhere) would increase the region's ability to import capital goods and, more generally, improve its economic infrastructure. The large trade deficits most of these countries have experienced in recent years (especially since 1968) have also meant that a continued expansion of their outward-looking development strategies has been seriously threatened. Put somewhat negatively, in the *absence* of a variety of external resources, the region's ability to finance imports would be limited, and that would consequently act as a brake on the countries' efforts to achieve sustained economic growth.[4]

Why has Pacific Asia looked to Japan for financial flows? In part, Japan is geographically and culturally proximate, it has developed an enormous aid-giving capacity in recent years, and the region's balance-of-trade deficits with Japan comprise significant shares of its net deficit position vis-à-vis the world. In part, too, Pacific Asia has looked to Japan because Japan has been willing to extend major contributions to Asian development.[5]

If Japan has been a logical source of aid to Pacific Asia, this ostensible appeal has been reinforced by a strong, long-standing Japanese interest in assisting economic development in Pacific Asia.[6] Partly this interest is directly related to Japan's own economic needs. As long ago as 1961, Prime Minister Ikeda, during a state visit to several countries in the region, asserted that "Asian prosperity is the key to Japan's future prosperity."[7] To this end, he pledged that "Japan will strive to develop Southeast Asia."[8] Japan's underlying motives were not wholly altruistic.[9] From Japan's perspective, aid to Pacific Asia would strengthen ties to many of the economies of a region that is geographically proximate and that has traditionally provided a major market for Japan's exports. The continued growth and development of the region would also facilitate and expand the supply of imported industrial raw materials so vital for Japanese industry.

Finally, part of the explanation underlying Japan's aid motives probably rests upon political and social grounds as Japan attempts to define the role she will assume in Asia.[10] This is because the greatly enlarged foreign exchange resources Japan has had available during the last half-dozen years has enabled her to broaden substantially her financial involvement with the region, in ways that fundamentally have not been possible for three decades or more. In few places is this role more clearly illustrated, if not yet precisely defined, than in the variety and magnitude of the web of Japan's financial relationships with several Pacific Asian countries.

Where during the 1960s Japan concentrated chiefly upon trade and aid, by the late 1960s and early 1970s she had also begun to direct sizeable amounts of private investment to many of these countries.[11]

In sum, Japan's economic cooperation efforts in Pacific Asia have taken a variety of forms. The principal objective of the next several sections of this chapter is to explore the several financial flows from Japan to Pacific Asia. These include both public and private flows, including economic aid, direct private assistance, and export credits. The most interesting questions here are to determine how large these flows were in the past and to speculate on the likely size of the future magnitudes of these capital flows.

Official Japanese Bilateral
Financial Assistance to Pacific Asia

With that brief introduction serving as background, both the Pacific Asian region's inflows of aid, and the Japanese contribution to those totals can now be examined. In previous chapters, twelve Pacific Asian countries were identified and analyzed. In this section, however, only nine developing countries are treated. Australia and New Zealand have been excluded on the grounds that they are already "developed" and therefore not candidates for financial assistance from abroad. Mainland China has also been excluded, though largely on the more narrow grounds that various political considerations kept her from receiving any significant amount of aid from abroad.[a] Those political questions will not, however, concern us in this chapter. The nature of Japan's economic aid to the Pacific Asian region can be seen from an analysis of the aid flows in recent years. These flows are comprised primarily of grants, long-term loans, and short-term credits tied to the purchase of exports from Japan. When foreign assistance as far back as the 1960s is examined, moreover, it should be remembered that Japan's ability and willingness to provide economic assistance was, generally speaking, markedly affected by the successive movements in her own balance-of-payments position. Unlike other developed countries, Japan's ability to make major aid commitments is of very recent origin. On the other hand, the size of Japan's foreign exchange reserves, together with the steady growth in her domestic economy, means that her capacity to increase the flow of financial resources for the developing countries is perhaps without parallel.

The existence of foreign assistance, or the lack of it, has many implications for the successful pursuit of an outward-looking development policy. A key question, therefore, is to estimate how much financial assistance the nine Pacific Asian countries received. Detailed data on official bilateral flows is available from Organization for Economic Cooperation and Development (OEDC) sources for 1960 through 1972, and the findings are shown in Table 7-3. These are summary findings, which include categorical aid covering grant-like flows (sales made in the recipient country's currency), net official grants, reparations, and indemnification payments, official lending, and amortization on official lending.[1 2] The resulting total is thus considered "net," and it covers the official (public) financial flows.

From the aggregate data in Table 7-3, the most striking finding that emerges is that most of these nine countries received very little aid from the world. Korea was the most conspicuous exception, as it received well over $200 million annually. In addition, the financial assistance that did flow into the region was not evenly distributed. In most years, the official bilateral aid flows to Korea were almost as much as the total flows to the other eight countries. While Indonesia and Taiwan were also beneficiaries of fairly sizeable aid flows from the world during these years, Burma, Hong Kong, Malaysia, and Singapore never

[a]Mainland China, of course, dispensed financial and technical economic assistance to many foreign countries, including some in the region. For an analysis and estimation of these Chinese aid flows, see, for example, The United States, Department of State, annual reports on aid flows from the communist bloc to non-communist (or non-aligned) nations. For one such report covering this period, see U.S. Bureau of Intelligence and Research, "Communist States and Developing Countries: Aid and Trade in 1970," RECS-15, unclassified (Washington, September 22, 1971).

Table 7-3
Official Bilateral Aid Flows to Selected Pacific Asian Countries from the World, 1960-1972 (Millions of U.S. Dollars)

Country	1960	1963	1966	1969	1971	1972
Burma	33.89	41.12	15.27	26.07	38.18	40.08
Hong Kong	5.83	5.19	1.74	1.17	3.51	2.78
Indonesia	81.06	104.33	83.60	315.74	547.09	448.10
Korea	–	–	–	328.30	305.25	351.27
Malaysia	13.27	11.33	27.20	28.20	38.04	43.72
Philippines	50.93	21.61	55.40	76.03	63.66	156.39
Singapore	–.33	.43	1.65	14.18	28.09	26.82
Taiwan	110.08	77.96	43.13	15.21	2.91	0.21
Thailand	43.47	34.87	49.13	64.06	57.64	47.66

Source: Data for 1960-1966 taken from Organization for Economic Cooperation and Development (OECD), *Geographical Distribution of Financial Flows to Less-Developed Countries, 1960-1964 and 1966-1967* (Paris, selected years), with the data taken from Asia, South, and Asia, Far East chapters. Data for 1969-1972 taken from OECD, *Development Cooperation, 1973 Review*, pp. 202-3.

participated in very considerable foreign assistance, either on an aggregate or per capita basis. The total aid directed to the region as a whole, however, remained roughly in the same proportion throughout much of this period.

If the Pacific Asian region as a whole did not receive sizeable amounts of foreign assistance from the world, how much did Japan contribute to these countries? Data in Table 7-4 shows Japan's official bilateral financial assistance flows to the nine Pacific Asian countries. Throughout these years, it can be seen that Japan directed very sizeable amounts of economic assistance to the region. The principal recipients were Indonesia, Korea, the Philippines, and Burma. Japan provided little meaningful economic assistance to the remaining countries during those years. In terms of overall magnitudes, Japanese aid rose by more than fivefold from 1960 to 1971. (By way of contrast, Japanese aid to both Indonesia and Korea in 1971 was, by itself, larger than her total aid to the world in 1960.) Geographically, Table 7-4 also shows that Japan steadily distributed between about half and three-quarters of her total aid to these Pacific Asian countries (which means that Japanese foreign economic assistance was much more geographically concentrated than her foreign trade had been).

What has Japan's impact been when examined from the perspective of the Pacific Asian countries? Comparing the findings on Tables 7-3 and 7-4, it is clear that of the nine countries' aid flows, Japan provided a significant fraction of economic assistance to only Burma and, to a lesser extent, the Philippines throughout the 1960-1967 period. From 1970 on, however, the impact of Japan's aid-giving is very different. These tables show clearly that Japanese aid had risen to account for a very sizeable fraction of the aid for virtually all of

Table 7-4

Official Bilateral Aid Flows from Japan to Selected Pacific Asian Countries, 1960-1971 (Millions of U.S. Dollars)

Country	1960	1963	1966	1970	1971
Burma	21.45	27.15	10.34	–	26.7
Hong Kong	–	.01	.03	–	NA
Indonesia	14.28	17.93	50.58	125.8	111.9
Korea	–	5.48	31.18	86.8	124.2
Malaysia	.04	.18	.38	–	12.3
Philippines	27.85	10.75	30.50	19.3	29.6
Singapore	.01	.09	.14	–	6.8
Taiwan	.03	.14	8.84	–	NA
Thailand	.32	3.23	3.66	–	15.5
Japan's Total to World	77.66	128.12	234.78	371.5	432.0

Source: OECD, *Geographical Distribution of Financial Flows to Less Developed Countries, 1960-1964, 1965, and 1966-1967*, data taken from Asia, South, and Asia, Far East chapters. Data for 1970 taken from Japan External Trade Organization, *Economic Cooperation of Japan 1972*, (Tokyo, 1973) p. 22. Data for 1971 taken from OECD, *Flow of Resources to Developing Countries* (Paris, 1973) p. 192.

these countries. Korea and Indonesia were receiving the largest absolute amounts of aid, although Japan's *relative* contribution to the aid of receipts of Burma and Thailand was considerably greater. It is interesting to note that Japan's aid to just two countries, Korea and Indonesia, accounted in both 1970 and 1971 for well more than half of her total aid flows to the world.

Japan's interest in assisting Asian development is put in better perspective when one examines the regional distribution of Japan's official bilateral aid flows over the last decade. Table 7-5 shows Japan's average aid flows to several regions for two recent periods, 1960-1966 and 1968-1970. These data show clearly that the great majority of Japan's economic aid was directed to Asia (though the breakdown here does mix in small amounts to Middle East and South Asian countries as well as the Pacific Asian nations). What is also striking is that Japanese aid rose by more than fivefold between the two periods.

Thus, the magnitude and impact of Japanese aid in recent years has been much more pronounced than in any former period. The data in Table 7-5 confirms that, by 1968-1970 Japan had begun to make significant amounts of financial assistance available to other regions of the world. What these findings point to, especially when taken in conjunction with the easing in Japanese balance-of-trade constraints at about the same time, is that Japan's voluntary, bilateral aid did not really become significant until after 1968. In 1972, by way of comparison, only the United States provided more resources to the less-developed countries and multilateral agencies.[13] These data also support the view

Table 7-5
The Regional Distribution of Japan's Official Bilateral Aid Flows, 1960-1970
(Millions of U.S. Dollars)

Region	1960-1966 Average	1968-1970 Average
Asia	131.41	573.48
Africa	.35	20.38
America	3.82	37.62
Europe	.05	60.76
Oceania	–	.22
Unallocated	.24	34.07
Total	135.87	726.54

Source: Taken from Table 17, OECD, *Development Assistance, 1971 Review* (Paris, 1971), pp. 188-89.

that Japan's aid-giving patterns reflect some of the geographical diversification patterns that trade was undergoing during the period.

Yet the crude magnitudes of the aid flows obscures much that is interesting. Most of Japan's bilateral aid during the early 1960s consisted of reparations payments. These were directed to just four Asian countries, including Burma, Indonesia, the Philippines, and South Vietnam. In addition to those reparations "stricto sensu," Japan also concluded economic cooperation agreements, on a grant basis, with five Asian countries, with Korea being the major beneficiary.[14] Most of these "official" and "unofficial" reparations consisted of products and services awarded by the Japanese government to the recipient countries. They mainly were composed of capital goods, with the two countries involved jointly consulting on the timing and composition of these aid flows.[15]

Only since 1966 has Japan begun to extent significant non-reparations economic assistance to Asia. This has frequently taken the form of providing fairly substantial export credits to less-developed countries through Japanese exporters. Two principal Japanese agencies have been created to deal with these matters. One, the Export-Import Bank of Japan owned by the government, finances exports and imports, makes direct development loans, and extends refinancing credits. The other, the Overseas Economic Cooperation Fund (OECF) under the aegis of Japan's Economic Planning Agency, makes "soft" loans and helps finance the development activities of Japanese firms abroad. Export credits from the OECF have typically been used to finance major purchases of machinery, transport equipment, and agricultural machinery. These flows rose nearly fivefold, to just under $500 million between 1962 and 1970.[16]

In addition to the *financial* flow of resources to the less-developed countries, Japan also instigated a technical assistance program. Under the aegis of the Overseas Technical Cooperation Agency (OTCA), these programs have emphasized technical and professional education, especially in agricultural extension work.[17] Examples include providing advisors and experts, staffing technical cooperation centers in developing countries, sending volunteer workers abroad, initiating pre-investment studies and surveys, and financing travel to Japan for students and trainees. Though these programs may be expanded in years to come, in recent years the technical assistance programs have accounted for a tiny fraction of Japan's total official flows.[18]

The relevance of the Japanese aid-giving patterns to this chapter is straightforward. Since Japan's reparations commitments will very soon be satisfied, what essentially remains are grants, loans, and export credits—and the latter, depending upon the terms of repayment, are not really "aid" anyway. (To the extent that export credits do offer an opportunity to defer the financing and repayment of trade deficits, however, they can provide important assistance to Pacific Asian countries struggling to maintain trade and foreign exchange liquidity, at least in the short run.)

The trends in Japan's aid-giving must be matched against the anticipated requirements of the Pacific Asian countries during the current decade. The principal observation here is that many countries have already developed to the point where they will no longer require significant amounts of general economic assistance. There are exceptions.[b] Burma requires foreign economic aid, although there is a real question as to whether she would currently be able to use it effectively. But countries like Thailand, the Philippines, South Korea, and others are already approaching self-sufficiency, except perhaps for a few key infrastructural projects. China is unlikely to be offered aid. She may also be unlikely to accept it. In the entire Pacific Asian region, in fact, Indonesia emerges as the chief country that both needs and can currently use large-scale economic assistance from Japan.[19]

In the future it is likely that Japan's role in supplying foreign assistance, subject to the exceptions noted above, will largely parallel her current efforts. The future financial resources available to most of these countries will continue to reflect whatever trade imbalances exist by making massive export credits available to them. In addition, it is plausible to speculate that both the terms of these loans and the Japanese preference to support development projects closely tied to her domestic needs may be relaxed somewhat in the years to come.

Other Aid Flows

While most of Pacific Asia's financial assistance has been allocated on a bilateral basis, a number of multilateral agencies have also dispensed net long-term economic aid to these countries. Foremost among them have been such

[b]The Indo-Chinese countries, of course, will continue to need major economic assistance to rebuild their war-damaged countries.

specialized agencies as the International Bank for Reconstruction and Development (World Bank), the Asian Development Bank, and the United Nations Development Program. Most of these agencies have extended a wide variety of commitments, including "hard" loans, "soft" loans, and grants.

How important has multilateral aid been for these countries? Table 7-6 shows, for the nine Pacific Asian countries under scrutiny here, multilateral aid totals from all sources for the years 1960 through 1971. These data come from two sources and may not be fully comparable. Nonetheless what clearly emerges is that while in general official multilateral assistance has not in the past proven an important source of financial assistance for these countries, there are clear signs that it is becoming increasingly important. To be sure, individual countries during some earlier years benefited significantly from these sources. In more recent years, for example, Malaysia, the Philippines, and Taiwan did receive sufficient aid to be somewhat of an exception to these findings. The rising 1969-1971 averages, however, were much larger than comparable totals in the 1960s, and they point to the growing overall importance of the multilateral flows. Further, several of these agencies, including the World Bank and the Asian Development Bank, have begun to provide important coordinating, consulting, and technical services whose value may significantly further economic development in the region.[20] Their long-run impact may consequently be much greater than simply the dollar value of their assistance.

In the future, furthermore, there may be many indications that multilateral aid may steadily grow at the expense of bilateral flows. Freed of possible direct political implications, the specialized multilateral agencies discussed above may have better overall knowledge of where to direct economic assistance than an individual country, especially when the donor country makes grants that are tied to purchases within that country. Several study groups have recognized these advantages and recommended that multilateral aid-giving be strengthened.[21]

Such a multilateral pattern may also prove to be very attractive to Japan in the years to come. The Japanese presence has engendered considerable resentment and even elicited some degree of animosity throughout much of Pacific Asia. Some of this may be due to lingering wartime memories. Partly, too, it may owe something to competitive strains. In some ways, too, Japan's current economic inroads in Pacific Asia have been viewed as another "economic offensive," with parallels to earlier attempts at domination.[22]

From Japan's perspective, therefore, contributions to multilateral aid-giving agencies, which had previously occupied a minor role in her overall aid program, have the potential to become an attractive vehicle by which aid could be awarded without great visibility. Since much of the Japanese activity here would be directed to Pacific Asia, the Asian Development Bank is the logical organization through which she would work. (Japan is currently the largest contributor to the Bank, subscribing in excess of $500 million.) A number of special funds would allow a variety of specific industrial projects to be financed.

Table 7-6
Net Multilateral Capital Flows to the Pacific Asian Countries, 1960-1971

Country	1960	1961	1962	1963	1964	1965	1966	1967	1969-1971 Average
Burma	3.97	2.27	3.19	4.18	2.75	-1.18	.89	-.16	2.6
Hong Kong	–	.20	.09	.26	.28	.03	.03	.03	.1
Indonesia	2.02	5.07	4.79	3.82	3.66	1.64	-2.15	04.35	24.8
Korea	.25	-.37	.48	13.19	2.96	2.39	-.96	-1.96	33.1
Malaysia	1.71	1.20	9.31	1.90	1.95	13.77	19.99	18.79	25.0
Philippines	1.80	.04	4.57	9.75	10.64	18.33	12.21	14.87	30.0
Singapore	.10	.19	.29	.39	*	2.34	10.13	1.99	18.6
Taiwan	-4.60	05.44	-3.50	-1.83	-.30	13.62	17.70	4.49	45.4
Thailand	7.51	10.12	16.58	7.26	3.61	.72	4.51	-.32	39.7

Source: For 1960-1967 OECD, *Geographical Distribution of Financial Flows to Less-Developed Countries, 1960-1964, 1965, 1966-1967*; for 1969-1971 average, OECD, *Development Assistance, 1973 Review*, p. 216-7.

This is not the place to treat this highly complex matter. What can be argued here, however, is simply that to the extent this ill-feeling persists, there is a need to place increasing dependence on consortiums and/or multinational organizations to channel economic assistance.[23] A central theme of this study is that Japan will play an ever-growing role in the region. If this is so, current tensions could be further exacerbated by the growing Japanese presence.

These forces have consequently influenced the pace of multinational agency activity. Thus it is plausible to speculate that Japan's long-term political, as well as the region's economic, interests may best be served by indirect, low-profile patterns of economic assistance to the region through these multilateral organizations.

Private Capital Flows

Japan's net private capital flows have also grown rapidly in recent years. While the official public bilateral and multilateral contributions accounted for the major share of Japanese aggregate external economic assistance, the private flows rose to account for more than a third of the total flows by the beginning of the 1970s. These private capital flows fell within several categories. For Japan, the two principal components were direct private investment and private export credits, both long-term and short-term. Portfolio investment, including development bonds and other long-term lending, comprised a relatively insignificant share of Japan's totals during the 1960s.[24]

The existence of large foreign exchange reserves, growing at a rate of several billion dollars annually, has many implications for Japanese investment policies. What has become clear only within the last four or five years is that Japan now has the financial capability to undertake foreign investments on a very large scale. The purpose of this section, accordingly, is to examine and assess the relative importance of Japanese investment in the Pacific Asian region and to offer a few speculations as to its likely growth in the coming years.

The thesis that Japan's investment can materially affect the region's economics is based on two broad propositions. First, there are the advantages accruing to any country from inflows of foreign capital as a supplement to domestic capital formation. This argument is widely known and requires little discussion here. Second, transfer of capital from Japan to the region can shore up balance-of-payments deficits, particularly in the short run. Taken together, this means that Japan can substantially modify the region's liquidity problem and measurably increase Pacific Asian development prospects by large infusions of direct investment. Whether she does so, of course, depends on a shared perception of the mutual advantages from increased capital flows.[25]

Part of the difficulty turns on adopting a common framework for analysis. This is admittedly a sensitive area. In few places has the rhetoric of the debate so widely outgrown the prevailing economic realities. Data on foreign investments are not widely reported. Even when data are available, there are basic questions of comparability. Should, for example, investment flows be valued at original cost, or at current value? Are retained and reinvested earnings properly a part of this total? Put somewhat differently, is one seeking the sum of past investment flow or, alternatively, is one interested in the present value of the aggregate stock of direct investment? Depending on the question to be asked, quite different answers can emerge.

There is a related difficulty in that there are pressures on both Japan and the recipient country to underreport the magnitudes of these capital flows. Investing companies, for example, may prefer to report lower capital inflows for tax or competitive reasons. Japan, too, may feel that reporting large investment totals contributes to Pacific Asian anxieties about Japanese "aggressiveness" and heightens fears of excessive domination and dependence. For many of these same reasons, joint venture companies in the recipient countries may not wish to report the full extent of their Japanese ties.[c]

A key theme running through many of the discussions of Japanese investment centers upon perceptions of a Japanese economic "invasion" of Southeast Asia. Some commentators even warn against Japan's moving to dominate the region's economies.[26] Yet a careful examination of the data turns up little in support of such assertions. Furthermore, a major contention of this study is that even if projections of the most recent trends made such themes more plausible in the foreseeable future, there would be significant advantages as well as disadvantages for the economies receiving Japanese private capital.

Where have Japan's private investment flows gone in the past? Data on the aggregate magnitudes and region shares of Japan's foreign investment over the period 1951-1969 are presented in Table 7-7. These totals include purchases of security shares and loans for overseas development projects that are controlled by Japanese interests and often closely tied to Japanese import needs; disinvestments are excluded. These data are, of course, subject to the caveats noted above, but the broad picture of the direction of Japanese foreign investment portrayed is at least roughly accurate.

The principal finding from the data is that Japanese investment in Asia represented less than a quarter of Japan's aggregate foreign investment during the period shown. Asia, even broadly defined here as encompassing more than simply the East and Southeast Asian countries, is not even the largest single region towards which Japanese investment has been directed. Japan's investment in North America, by way of comparison, surpassed $700 million. Latin American investment stood larger than $500 million, and it, too, approached the Asian totals. To be sure, Japan did represent a significant source of Pacific Asian investment. What this data does show, however, is that Japanese world investment patterns did not differ perceptibly from her long-standing world trade patterns.

[c]Ian Stewart has noted that in Manila, the Japanese embassy estimated their direct investment at $15 million. *Business Day*, a Philippine publication, estimated Japanese investment to be $23 million. Stewart quotes other business sources as saying that the figure was probably much in excess of $50 million, which he explained in part by the reluctance of local companies with Japanese links to disclose them. See Ian Stewart, "Japanese Stir Asian Resentment," *The New York Times*, January 10, 1972, p. 1.

Table 7-7

Japan's Foreign Investments by Area, 1951-1969 (Totals in Millions of U.S. Dollars)

Region	Magnitude	Percent Share
Asia	604	22.5
Oceania	158.1	5.9
North America	720.4	26.9
Latin America	512.5	19.1
Europe	302.9	11.3
Middle East	306.3	11.4
Africa	78.6	2.9
	$2,682.8	100.

Note: Totals may not add due to rounding.

Source: Taken from Charles Sebestyen, *The Outward Urge: Japanese Investment Worldwide* (London: Economist Intelligence Unit, 1972), p. 20.

There is considerable evidence to suggest that Japanese investment in Asia (and throughout the world, as well) has been growing rapidly during the last four or five years. An examination of some preliminary data covering a five-year period through March 31, 1973, shows clearly that the pace of her private investment flows accelerated sharply. These data are presented in Table 7-8. Among the developing countries in Pacific Asia, Indonesia and Korea have been the principal beneficiaries of this activity, though every country in the region has shared in these flows to some extent. Even if these flows are not precisely comparable with Table 7-7, moreover, the trends in the rough magnitudes emerge unmistakably.

The number of projects built by Japan in the region and their breakdown by sector are presented in Table 7-9. These totals cover basically the same data presented in Table 7-8, and it is reasonable to suppose that the same problems of comparability and full disclosure exist. What is chiefly interesting about these data is that Japanese investment was heavily concentrated in mining and textiles. Manufacturing, not surprisingly, accounted for little more than half of her total investment activity. (Parenthetically, it would be highly instructive to compare the size, technology, and profitability of these Japanese companies with their domestic counterparts throughout the Pacific Asian region.)

Another interesting question is to ask how Japan's investment flows to Pacific Asia compared with the region's total private capital inflows from all sources. It is difficult to construct a precise answer to that question. By taking the findings above together with data on the distribution of the total investment of all developed countries among the less-developed regions for the last six to eight years, however, it is plausible to infer that Japan accounted for roughly 10 to 15 percent of the world's direct investment in Asia.[27] These broad findings sharply

Table 7-8
Japan's Private Investment in Pacific Asia Classified by Country and Year, 1968-1972 (Unit: $1,000)

Country	1968		1969		1970		1971		1972	
	No. of Cases	Value	No. of Cases	Value	No. of Cases	Value	No. of Cases	Value	No. of Cases	Value
Hong Kong	14	987	47	4,808	50	9,259	72	41,192	123	29,459
Indonesia	15	41,665	16	42,827	34	48,635	47	112,409	61	119,319
Korea	4	590	25	10,348	80	17,449	96	28,180	196	146,049
Malaysia	11	2,675	13	5,281	33	14,009	17	12,147	45	13,436
Philippines	9	5,049	8	3,728	11	28,999	17	4,519	23	9,746
Singapore	6	968	11	3,617	26	8,927	47	15,107	72	42,184
Taiwan	97	13,618	91	20,603	61	24,756	22	12,380	37	10,394
Thailand	18	10,233	42	18,701	21	12,656	34	8,646	62	29,582
ASIA	183	77,679	265	196,940	329	167,106	362	236,925	624	401,547

Note: Totals may not add because non-Pacific Asian country data is included in the "Asian" totals.
Source: Approved basis, the Bank of Japan, based on unpublished data obtained from Japan's Ministry for International Trade and Industry (MITI).

Table 7-9
Japan's Direct Investment in Developing Pacific Asian Countries: Industrial Sectoral Totals, 1968-1972 (Unit: $1,000)

Industrial Sector	No. of Cases	Value
Manufacturing		
Foodstuffs	656	28,191
Textiles	233	258,599
Timber & Pulp	56	28,965
Chemical	154	39,686
Iron and Nonferrous Metal	122	63,130
Machinery	118	26,320
Electric Machinery	250	95,767
Transport Equipment	27	29,407
Others	355	76,684
Sub Total	1,380	646,753
Others		
Agriculture & Forestry	69	44,666
Fisheries & Marine Products	32	15,441
Mining	51	254,951
Construction	33	6,246
Commerce	296	35,424
Finance & Insurance	46	79,019
Others	209	64,576
Sub Total	736	500,323
Overseas Branches	206	21,497
Totals	2,322	1,168,572

Source: Balanced basis, the Bank of Japan, based on unpublished data obtained from Japan's Ministry for International Trade and Industry.

call into question allegations concerning a Japanese "invasion." The magnitude of Japanese investment is dwarfed by the long-standing United States and United Kingdom capital flows to the region.

Given the relative investment magnitudes, however, recent trends in the annual rate of increase of Japan's foreign investment do place this data in a somewhat different context. From 1965 to 1970, the average annual growth rate of Japan's direct investment was 29.8 percent.[d] Continuation of approximately

[d]By way of comparison, the U.S. rate of increase was 10.7 percent; the U.K. rate, 14.6 percent; and the West German increase was 20.4 percent. See "Japan's Overseas Investments," *Oriental Economist* 40, no. 740, (1972), p. 20.

this same level of foreign investment increases for a decade or more would clearly change Japan's *relative* position in terms of ownership of foreign investment among other developed countries. Even then, however, projected Japanese totals in 1980 would fall considerably short of *1970* United States and United Kingdom totals—and both the United States and the United Kingdom may be expected to increase the size of their net investments substantially during the current decade.

The relevance of Japan's *past* foreign investment flows to this chapter clearly turns on whether the broad outlines of the past trends can be expected to be maintained. In fact there are many signs of profound changes in prospect as the forces that influence the pace and composition of Japan's foreign investment accelerate. On the one hand, some are arguing, trade can no longer be a fully dependable source of Japan's industrial raw material needs. Thus, an increasingly common view is as follows:

It will no longer be permissible to depend upon foreign interests for supplies of our industrial raw materials—to the extent that now prevails. The more dependent we become, the more we shall be at the mercy of foreign suppliers. . . . In order to secure stable and low-cost supplies of overseas raw materials, it will be essential to invest heavily abroad.[28]

A new dimension of Japan's overseas investment for resources is the so-called "development import" program in which Japanese trading companies supply capital, equipment, and technology to countries that intend to develop natural resources for eventual export to Japan. This approach insures a more secure source of supply for the natural resources Japan will continue to need.[29]

Secondly, due to growing labor shortages and sharply increasing wage levels in Japan, Japanese companies may invest abroad to utilize abundant and comparatively cheap foreign labor at a much faster pace in the future.[30] Pacific Asia may be expected to be a primary beneficiary of such investments. Within the region Korea, Taiwan, Hong Kong, and Thailand would be potentially major recipients of these funds.

Third, it is plausible to suggest that both environmental pressures within Japan and supply rigidities faced by Japanese manufacturers will stimulate additional foreign investment growing out of prospective far-reaching changes in Japan's industrial structure. As JETRO argues:

. . . Japanese industrial structure is also responsible for aggravating the resource procurement and environment problems. Thus a shift in the industrial structure to less resource-using industries will be increasingly needed. For export industries which are heavily resource dependent, consideration should be given to location overseas rather than in Japan.[31]

This move, in addition to meeting some of the most vocal objections from developing countries that Japan set up more processing and fabricating of raw materials abroad, would have the added salutory effect of shifting some highly pollution-causing industrial activities from Japan to considerably cleaner environments.[32]

It is likely that the Japanese yen revaluations supply another major impetus to foreign investment. Little direct evidence of increased investment due to these revaluations is as yet available, but it is possible to speculate on some of the effects. What has happened, of course, is that the Japanese yen has appreciated upwards by a total of some 35-40 percent since 1971 in terms of most of the currencies in the region. For Japanese employers, the initial effect of the yen appreciation is tantamount to roughly a one-third reduction in the wages they must pay foreign workers. The subject of currency revaluations is complex, and the above comments are superficial and meant largely for illustrative purposes. What is contended here is that whatever the economic forces propelling Japanese investment abroad, the currency revaluations will sharply underscore them.[33]

Given these factors and in view of the continuous need for accommodating capital flows to compensate for continuing trade deficits, how large are these capital flows likely to be? Depending upon the forecast, Japanese investment abroad in the coming decade may be as much as ten to fifteen times its present levels.[34] With Japanese domestic growth and balance-of-payments surpluses continuing along current patterns, there are not likely to be any significant economic obstacles in the way of such growth. Far from it, in view of the growing foreign exchange liquidity problems in Pacific Asia discussed above.

Many countries in Pacific Asia remain suspicious concerning Japanese business practices and intentions.[35] Their sensitivities, mixed perhaps with a sense of economic nationalism, remain a key barrier to expanded capital flows. It is beyond the scope of this study to deal with an assessment of country-by-country attitudes toward Japanese investment, even leaving aside the question of whether a meaningful answer to such a complex question can be formulated. The purpose of these comments is simply to point out that a major determinant of future Japanese investment will be the degree of acceptance by the Pacific Asian countries. The region's internal accommodation to these capital flows will be more decisive in influencing the size of future flows than either Japan's interest or her financial capability.[36]

In sum, discussion concerning Japanese investment in the Pacific economies has grown out of all proportion to its current size. Projections of future trends will, however, quite probably result in many Japanese firms becoming more deeply committed and involved economically in the region. Seen from Japan's perspective, many of the factors that make foreign investment attractive in Asia (rich deposits of industrial raw materials, cheap relatively unskilled labor, assured sources of supply, and the like) are at least potentially available in other areas of the world—Latin America, parts of Africa, and even in some developed countries. Japan has a wider range of alternatives. This underscores a basic contention of the study, which is that Japanese investment is probably far more important to the region than, individually or collectively, Pacific Asian investment opportunities are to Japan. If, however, Japan's policies remain in accord with Pacific Asia, it is reasonable to expect that Japan will increasingly replace the United States and Britain as the region's principal source of private foreign capital.

Export Credits and Pacific Asian Indebtedness

Finally, a brief word on private export credits is in order. For Japan, as for most developed countries, the distinction between official and private export credits is usually based upon obscure institutional differences. In many ways, therefore, it is somewhat artificial to attempt to separate the two export credit flows.[37] Nonetheless most published data do separate the official and private flows, and so this study will follow the conventional style. A key feature of export credits, whether private or official, is that they are typically guaranteed by the governments of the exporting countries.

Inadequate data makes it difficult to analyze these flows in any detail. That Japan has been a major supplier of export credits is widely known. There are indications, further, that the majority of Japan's credits have been directed to the Asian region, with about 90 percent of these flows concentrated upon Indonesia, Thailand, and the Philippines.[38] Seen from the Pacific Asian perspective, Japan has also been the largest source of external credits to the region, supplying in recent years about a third of their total. As was true for the official export credits, most of the products financed under these arrangements have consisted of capital goods for development.

It is often argued that the prime stimulus in granting these export credits has been to promote exports from the donor country, rather than to spur development in the recipient country. In this view, export credits represent a form of long-term lending, tied to purchases within a given country, which must ultimately be repaid. Maintenance, service, and replacement parts add to the total in subsequent years. Recent moves by donor countries to extend the maturity dates and lower the interst charges on these credits do not, of course, alter their basic character.[39]

The question of the overall contribution to development assistance contained in extending export credits cannot be answered easily or with great precision. The impact of these resources does differ from the other capital flows discussed above. Without this financing, quite clearly, some imports of capital goods would simply not take place. Yet the repayment burdens are cumulative and can lead to the continual need for the developing country to refinance. Credit provisions themselves can influence the trade. Some distortion in trade probably occurs, in that capital goods are imported at the expense of both domestic and third country sources unable to offer attractive credit financing arrangements.[40] Over the long term, acceptance of export credits can adversely affect the *future* balance-of-payments positions of the developing countries.

In sum, Japanese export credits have in recent years contributed important amounts of financial resources to Pacific Asia. In their absence, Japanese exports would probably not have grown as quickly to the region as they did, particularly during the last several years. Seen from Pacific Asia's perspective, moreover, accepting these credits emphasizes the Pacific Asian commitment to long-term growth. These credits remain a poor substitute for other forms of financial assistance, and some of the Pacific Asian countries may encounter repayment difficulties in the future.

Conclusion

Pacific Asia has traditionally been a trade surplus area for Japan. In particular, the less-developed countries within the region provided major amounts of net foreign exchange that Japan could and did use elsewhere in the world, easing considerably the constraints balance-of-payments deficits would have imposed. Beginning in 1958, several distinct periods could be identified, though the overall trends were both upward and unmistakable. Within the region, of course, the picture was much more uneven among the individual countries. Several countries, notably Korea, Hong Kong, Taiwan, and China, became major surplus countries for Japan, while Australia and Indonesia were the major deficit nations.

Rising Japanese balance-of-trade surpluses cannot really be separated from the parallel growth in the volume of Japanese-Pacific Asian two-way trade analyzed in the previous two chapters. The data in the first section of this chapter indicates the consequence of those trade flows. By the same token, the future prospects for trade surpluses closely follows the prospects for trade itself.

All of this is in terms of Japan. The trade surplus situation for some of the Pacific Asian countries is quite different. With the qualifications noted earlier in the chapter, what are trade surpluses for Japan are quickly transformed into trade deficits for the partner country. A key problem facing most Pacific Asian countries has been how to finance their almost inevitable deficits, particularly when they are so large as to impinge upon the current volume of trade. In addition, United States military presence in Vietnam, and Asia generally, was tapering off. Eliminating or reducing this source of funds, which had provided a major external foreign exchange stimulus since 1965, would be expected to further strain the foreign exchange capacities of some of these countries.

With other sources of earnings less promising in the 1970s, Japanese flows of financial resources, both official and private, became all the more important. The creation and subsequent sharp expansion of a major program in economic assistance by Japan provided much needed grants and export credits and, in so doing, eased in a fundamental way some of the liquidity constraints that followed from the region's net trade imbalance. Several sources of funds were examined, including bilateral and multilateral grants and aid, reparations, export credits, and direct foreign investment and other capital flows. These flows were found to be substantial, and they were growing very rapidly.[e] While the country-by-country data was limited in terms of scope and reliability, it was possible to estimate several different types of these financial flows for the last decade. Some of these financial flows—reparations is a case in point—could be accomplished essentially outside the balance-of-payments framework, since they were closely tied to purchases from Japanese firms. In effect, they represented purchases financed by the Japanese government. This was also true about some other bilateral and multilateral flows. But the rapid rise in direct foreign private investment would not have been possible without Japanese balance-of-trade surpluses. Furthermore, there is some evidence to suggest that a part of these flows would not be as acceptable to the partner countries had they not helped to offset large and growing trade deficits with Japan in these countries.

The Japanese motives were mixed: partly shrewd business, partly a real commitment to help the region's economies develop and prosper, and partly a desire to protect and enlarge her role within these markets and countries. There is little reason to believe that the flow of Japanese capital to Pacific Asia will slow down, let alone disappear, in the immediate future. Both Japan's interest and her financial ability seem unimpaired. The many Japanese forecasts of rapidly rising direct private foreign investment, in particular, provide some assurance that the growth in these flows will be continued.

What effect this will have on the Pacific Asian economies is harder to assess. That these flows can stimulate domestic development, introduce new technology, and help offset the cost of key imports to these countries' domestic and import-competing sectors is not fundamentally in question. What is in question is the response of the Pacific Asian countries to the accelerating Japanese activity. Because of a variety of political and social factors, barriers to an ever-expanding Japanese role have developed, and there is little chance of them disappearing. How often—if at all—will these barriers constrain increases in the various sources of Japanese capital discussed above?

Perhaps the major underlying theme of this chapter is to sharply call into question the customary set of concerns about Japan's economic impact on the developing countries of Asia. It has been conventional to argue that Japan is becoming too large a presence in Pacific Asia. The danger that Japan might come to excessively dominate the economies of these countries is frequently raised. If

[e]In recent years, by combining all sources of financial assistance, Japan's capital assistance has been equal to nearly 1 percent of GNP (.03 in 1970), very close to the Pearson Commission and U.N. targets of 1 percent. See *Oriental Economist* 39, no. 727 (May 1971), p. 3.

anything, the findings here reverse those contentions. It may be that the *real* problem for the developing countries of Pacific Asia would come if, and when, Japan began to *reduce* her economic interests there.

8 Conclusion

The previous chapters have developed and amplified the central theme of this study—to discuss why Japan's import and export trade with Pacific Asian countries grew at such rapid rates from 1958 to the beginning of the 1970s. These greatly expanded trade flows were achieved within commodity trade patterns that remained fairly stable during those years. How were the two regions (Japan and Pacific Asia) able to sustain these rapid gains in trade? How much did this rising trade reflect parallel, and fundamental, changes in their larger economies? Alternatively, was this trade expansion an isolated phenomenon against a background of relative economic stability or even stagnation?

The Japanese-Pacific Asian Economic Framework

If trade with Japan was growing very rapidly for the Pacific Asian countries, their world trade levels were also rising rapidly. It was argued that these countries had, with the exception of China and possibly Burma, adopted very outward-looking, trade-conscious development strategies. A key problem for Pacific Asia generally was that its growth in trade was lagging somewhat behind world trade levels during these years. Also, because most exports remained highly concentrated among the established categories of industrial raw materials and food products, the region was developing few major exports outside of its traditional framework. While this pattern was common to many developing regions, Pacific Asian trade, when measured against only that of the other less-developed countries, more than held its own. Equally important, foreign sales grew somewhat faster than domestic output. Since marginal domestic income and price elasticities of demand for the great majority of their exports were not large, these results tended to confirm the success of the outward-looking strategies.

Yet it was fundamental to Chapter 3 that little of this would have been true had it not been for Japan. It came as no surprise to find that trade with Japan grew at rates that easily exceeded the region's comparable world totals. The central finding here was the steadily increased share of Japan in every country's trade. During these years, exports to Japan rose by a factor of six, to well over $4 billion, while imports rose to nearly $7 billion. Some of this could be explained by the fact that the developed countries generally assumed greater importance in the Pacific Asian region's trade network. As Chapter 2 showed, for all the increasing shares attributed to the developed countries, Japan's share of even this market was rising steadily. In terms of Pacific Asian imports, both structural and, in particular, competitive gains shifted rapidly in Japan's favor. What was at least ostensibly surprising in these results was that Japan accounted for much greater shares of Pacific Asian exports even though the commodity composition of this trade was unchanged. Pacific Asia, as a region, continued to export its traditional products; what was different was that these countries were just much more successful. Several explanations were subsequently offered in Chapter 6.

Japan's trade patterns did not appear to have changed much during these years. The trade volume, of course, rose enormously. Between 1958 and 1972, Japan's share of the world's trade more than doubled. It would commonly be expected that such rapid rates of growth would result from a very trade-oriented economic policy. Japan was naturally conscious of the potential gains from trade. If anything, however, Japanese trade dependence actually declined slightly during the last ten to fifteen years. Japanese gains abroad were more than balanced by very sharp rises in domestic output generally.

How important was the Pacific Asian region to Japan? The evidence presented in Chapter 3 showed that these ten or twelve countries collectively accounted for about a quarter of Japan's trade during the last two decades, slightly more for exports and slightly less for imports. Since Japanese exports were increasingly directed towards industrial countries, these findings meant that exports to Pacific Asia, when measured only against other non-industrial regions, grew considerably in importance. Import shares from Pacific Asia and from industrial versus non-industrial countries generally moved within a narrow range and ended virtually unchanged. What was principally surprising here was that Japanese demand for the Pacific Asian industrial raw materials was maintained at such a high level. Chapters 5 and 6 were devoted to attempts to explore some of the factors that helped explain these trade patterns.

A final question was whether Japan's composition of exports and imports was substantially modified during the period under consideration. Did Japan's trade with Pacific Asia constitute a different commodity pattern than her trade with the rest of the world? In general, the answer was no. Exports to Pacific Asia reflected the same high concentration among machinery, transport equipment, and manufactures that characterized Japan's exports to the rest of the world. Broadly speaking, the import patterns consisted chiefly of industrial raw materials and food products. Although rapidly rising aggregate totals disguised it somewhat, Japanese imports from the region were not in recent years as diversified as her imports from the rest of the world. While the evidence was sketchy, there were signs that a principal explanation of Japanese import trends was that earlier raw material-saving industrial patterns had been halted or even reversed. Part of this was due to the continued spread of heavy resource-using

Japanese industry. The very stable import price trends, set against a background of steadily rising Japanese domestic prices, did nothing to discourage these trends. In sum, this summary evidence suggested that a pattern of unchanging demand and gradually shifting supply marked Japan's trade with the Pacific Asian region.

In a general way, the broad outlines of Japanese-Pacific Asian trade did not change greatly during this period. Central to this discussion were the enormous increases of these trade flows. Against this background of success there was little need—or at least little pressure—for the Pacific Asian countries to develop new products or greatly expand trading contacts with third countries.

Yet many observers were beginning to feel that a continuation of these trade patterns constituted a major barrier against Pacific Asian domestic structural change. This feeling was buttressed by the stirrings of economic nationalism that were being articulated in many parts of Pacific Asia. The growing trade dependence upon Japan made most of the developing Pacific Asian countries highly vulnerable to changes in Japanese needs. For many, consequently, trade diversification was a prudent strategy because it served both as a hedge against any interruption in Japan's import demand patterns and as a stimulus to domestic manufacturing expansion.

Growth and Demand for
Foreign Trade

The core chapters of this study attempted to explain how this enormous increase in the two-way trade was made possible. Chapter 4 was devoted to presenting the quantitative theoretical model by which these trade flows were to be analyzed. The next two chapters presented the detailed empirical findings. For the period that began in 1958, Japan's impact on Pacific Asia was examined. Trend projections for most countries were clearly sizeable. The structural demand coefficients accounted for only about a tenth of Japan's gains, as demand for Japan's key export products was generally growing in the Pacific Asian countries. If textiles, which had in earlier decades featured prominently in Japanese sales abroad, were excluded, however, the structural gains were even more pronounced. The major factor accounting for Japan's very rapid gains in exports, however, was her competitive gains, and those chapters also attempted to put forward reasons why that was so.

Was the Japanese export performance in Pacific Asia an isolated phenomenon? Could much of this success be explained on grounds that Japan was particularly "interested" in this region to the comparative exclusion of other parts of the world? Must one look to, for example, the political or even strategic considerations that underlay the grand designs for "Pacific Asia" that were briefly discussed? On balance, the answers to these questions are no. When

Japanese exports to Pacific Asia were contrasted with their exports to the rest of the world, Japanese trade gains with Pacific Asia were only slightly larger, proportionately, than her rising trade with the rest of the world. For Japan, the Pacific Asian trade was not "something special." Instead, within the context of the enormous world growth in Japanese exports, Pacific Asia barely held its own.

There was one potentially major disturbing portent in these findings. Japan had become so successful—so competitive—that by 1970 she often accounted for more than two-thirds or three-quarters of these countries' total imports in the commodities that constituted her key commodity exports. Maintaining these market shares, let alone further expanding them, would be difficult throughout the years ahead. Future Japanese export prospects in Pacific Asia will consequently be more closely tied to the growth in Pacific Asia's import capacity for many of these commodities. Japanese import commodity concentration, on the other hand, was not excessive, and it did not generally constitute a problem. It even declined slightly in several countries over the decade.

Pacific Asian exports to Japan, on the other hand, were in many ways channeled within the relatively narrow mold they had traditionally been confined to. These exports grew rapidly enough to roughly maintain their postwar shares of Japanese imports. The key to these increases was the structural demand coefficients. Contrary to widely held expectations, Japanese demand for industrial raw material imports continued to be fairly strong. The competitive effect coefficients were large and positive for many countries in the region, which showed that Pacific Asia succeeded in maintaining a competitive position in her established raw material and food exports.

There was little evidence that the pattern of the region's exports to Japan had shifted to emphasize more of the labor-intensive, light manufacturing products that these countries had started to export. Much of this was explained by Japanese protectionist policies rather than Pacific Asian supply rigidities. Pacific Asian export prospects in the 1970s thus depended chiefly upon two factors: (1) Japanese industrial growth and its accompanying demand for raw material imports, and (2) Japanese import liberalization for both light manufactures and food products.

In emphasis of a central theme of this study, by the early 1970s Japan was becoming the dominant trading partner for most Pacific Asian countries. Because Japanese exports were to most countries much greater than Japanese imports, the steady growth of trade resulted in rising trade surpluses for Japan, and large deficits for more than half the countries in the region. By 1970, it was becoming clear that there was no easy way by which the developing countries could finance their rising deficits. This meant, of course, that future two-way trade would be closely tied to Pacific Asia's ability to sell to, as well as buy from, Japanese markets.

How could this constraint be removed? A principal alternative was for Japan to send accommodating *capital* inflows to the developing countries in the region to at least partially offset their trade deficit outflows. After presenting the country-by-country trends in the balance of trade, Chapter 7's chief purpose was to explore the various official and unofficial capital flows moving from Japan to Pacific Asia. Reparations, of course, had constituted most of Japan's capital flows until 1965. The principal findings of these sections were that (1) Japanese financial flows were growing enormously after 1965, with many of these resources being directed to Asia, (2) there was a rising propensity in favor of multilateral rather than bilateral forms of official assistance, and (3) Japan was extending very large amounts of export credits to help finance the balance of trade deficits. Perhaps the most striking finding, however, was that direct private foreign investment was not only growing very rapidly, but that a concensus of published forecasts called for approximately a tenfold increase during the decade of the 1970s. In practice, this would mean that Japan's equity position in many foreign countries would be as dominant as Japanese commerical relationships are at present. These capital flows, of course, are closely related to Japan's newly expressed determination to be less closely dependent upon foreign countries for economic needs. Yet there is mounting evidence that this foreign investment will not be limited to producing natural resources, but that it will be extended to many manufacturing and service sectors as well.

Appendix

Appendix

Throughout this study a wide variety of trade and other economic data has been presented. Much of it was taken from statistics furnished by the originating country, either directly or through international agencies such as the United Nations or the International Monetary Fund. Some portions of the study, particularly Chapters 5 and 6 make very precise, detailed use of the data on trade flows. Thus, it is useful to have some idea of the basic accuracy of this data in order to ask if the empirical results discussed here are suspect because the underlying data is either not accurate or not reliable.

It is virtually impossible to assert that the detailed trade returns, and to a lesser extent the other data, are in some absolute sense "accurate." Much of the other (non-trade) data was impressionistic, and it was used to illustrate and shape the broad economic aggregates for the countries discussed in this book. What was principally wanted was an understanding of the trends and of the quantitative changes in these respective economies over time. For those purposes, these data were largely sufficient.

Thus the real question turns upon the detailed trade data. How accurate, within some limit, is this data? Equally important, how accurate must it be before any importance can be attached to the findings of the study?

In answering that question, one criterion is that the trade data for country i's exports to j should be comparable to j's imports from i. This is not to imply, however, that the totals would be the same. Indeed, several discrepancies are normally present that together virtually insure that the totals would not be identical, though they may still be comparable. One major factor is, of course, the fact that exports are customarily reported f.o.b. while import totals are reported c.i.f.[1] It has been customary to estimate a 10 percent correction for transportation charges, though such a rule-of-thumb may frequently obscure deviations of considerable magnitude.[2]

Secondly, there are systematic differences in the timing and the methods of reporting imports and exports, varying by country. In terms of designation of shipment, for example, one country may elect to record trade on the basis of the destination on the ticket of the shipment, while another country might use a customs clearance basis. Luey has shown that there are at least nine methods currently used to designate trading partners, and there may well be more.[3] Many of these differences ultimately turn upon the question of re-exports. As and if entrepot trade is a major factor—as it has been in some of this Pacific Asian trade—differences in designation by consignment can account for a significant degree of discrepancy in comparing trade returns. No real purpose is served by discussing these alternative ways of classifying trade flows in greater detail. Rather, what must be emphasized is that potentially large discrepancies can exist in the export of i, import of j comparisons even if all countries report their data accurately.

There is a third source of difference between the reported trade totals whose influence is not so easily eliminated. Under this category are grouped all the sources of bias that occur when errors, lags in reporting time, foreign exchange conversion factors, non-comparable classification criteria and the like are used.[4] Common to all of these potential pitfalls is that they throw into question the comparability of the trade data for any pair of countries during a given year.

Finally, faulty estimating techniques, insufficient inspectors and unreported trade (smuggling) and corruption can also be present.[5] Such factors typically lead to one or both of the partner countries underreporting their trade receipts.[a] The motivation is widely held to be a desire to avoid customs taxes or duties or to minimize receipts, the escape from none of which would be promoted by over-reporting. That such factors are endemic and persistent does not ease the inherent difficulties of data problems that are widely held to be of major proportions.

There is no simple, unambiguous *a priori* way to test for accuracy. If only Japanese data were used, one would have greater confidence in the consistency and accuracy of the trade returns. Some recent empirical studies have held that, within Southeast Asia, the intraregional trade suffers from far more discrepancies than the data for trade with developed countries.[6] For the non-Japanese data, accordingly, it is plausible to speculate that the trade returns are likely to contain a somewhat greater bias.

The purpose of these comments, however, is not to put forth claims in support of the reliability of this trade data—nor, for that matter, to assert that the data is *not* reliable. Rather, since the empirical results were intuitively reasonable, perhaps the most that can be said is that the findings provide the interlying detailed trade data with a degree of credibility.

---

[a]Over-reporting would be equally serious for these purposes, but it has remained largely a hypothetical problem, being confined typically to cases where it is desired to transfer capital from one country to another where such flows are constrained or forbidden. Overstating imports (or understating exports) becomes a vehicle for facilitating capital movements.

Notes

Notes

Chapter 1
Introduction

1. For a representative forecast that the export sectors of these countries would grow too slowly to meet their development needs, see United Nations, *Economic Survey of Asia and the Far East, 1959* (New York and Bangkok: Economic Commission for Asia and the Far East, 1967), p. 101.

2. Reed Irvine, "Some Lessons of the Development Decade," *Asian Survey* 10, no. 7 (1970), pp. 552-62.

3. Ministry of International Trade and Industry (MITI), *Tsusho-Soron (Foreign Trade White Paper: General Survey)*, Tokyo, 1963, pp. 333-5, quoted in Robert Ozaki, "Japan's Role in Asian Economic Development," *Asian Survey* 7, no. 4 (1967), pp. 237-44.

4. Kogoro Uemura, President of the Japan Federation of Economic Organizations (Keidanren), "Challenge for Responsible Partnership," speech delivered in Washington, D.C., June 15, 1971 and reprinted by the United States-Japan Trade Council. He asserted that Japan's relative trade dependency ranks her only 62nd among 76 IMF nations in the world.

5. Robert Guillain, *The Japanese Challenge: The Race to the Year 2000*, trans. by Patrick O'Brian (New York: J.B. Lippincott, 1970), especially pp. 138-60. Also see Uemura, "Challenge for Responsible Partnership," and Louis Kraar, "How the Japanese Mount That Export Blitz," *Fortune* 82, no. 3 (1970), pp. 128ff.

6. See, for example, D.G. Keesing, "Outward-Looking Policies and Economic Development," *Economic Journal* 77, no. 306 (1967), pp. 303-20; Hla Myint, "The 'Classical Theory' of International Trade and the Underdeveloped Countries," *Economic Journal* 68, no. 270 (1958), pp. 317-37; and "The Inward and Outward-Looking Countries of Southeast Asia," *The Malayan Economic Review* 12, no. 1 (1967), pp. 1-13.

7. Dick Wilson, "PAFTA and NAFTA," *FEER* 55, no. 2 (1967), pp. 54-58, discusses the proposed Pacific Area Free Trade Association and the North Atlantic Free Trade Association. *ASPAC* (Asian and Pacific Council, with nine members including Thailand, Japan, Taiwan, South Korea, Philippines, South Vietnam, Malaysia, Australia, and New Zealand) and its formation of the Asian Development Bank are cases in point. For a slightly different version, see Kiyoshi Kojima, "A Pacific Economic Community and Asian Developing Countries," *Hitotsubashi Journal of Economics* 7, no. 1 (1966), pp. 13-37.

8. See also Robert Guillain, *The Japanese Challenge*, especially chapters 1-12, pp. 218-78; Herman Kahn, *The Emerging Japanese Superstate: Challenge and Response* (Englewood Cliffs, N.J.: Prentice-Hall, 1970); and Eisaku Sato, "Pacific Asia," *Pacific Community* 1, no. 1 (1969).

9. Guillain, *The Japanese Challenge*, pp. 235-9.

10. Kayser Sung, "Interview with Takeo Miki," *FEER* 55, no. 2 (1967), pp. 52-54. See also Guillain, *The Japanese Challenge*, pp. 235-78 for a full discussion of the strategy and its mutual benefits.

11. In this regard, see especially Kiyoshi Kojima, "Asian Developing Countries and PAFTA: Development, Aid, and Trade Preferences," *Hitotsubashi Journal of Economics* 10, no. 1, (1969), pp. 1-17.

12. For a discussion of these matters, see Laurence Olson, *Japan in Postwar Asia* (New York: Praeger Publishers, 1970). Some political considerations are discussed in Akira Iriye, *Across the Pacific* (New York: Harcourt, Brace & World, 1967).

Chapter 2
Trade and the Japanese Economy: The Contribution of Pacific Asia

1. See, for example, an early view of Ichiro Nakayama, "Boekishugi to Kokunai Kaihatsushugi" ("Foreign Trade Method and Domestic Development Method") and *Nihon Keizai no Kao (Aspects of Japanese Economy)* (Tokyo: Nihonhyosonsha, 1953) arguing strongly for trade, both taken from Hisao Kanamori, "Economic Growth and Exports," in L. Klein and K. Ohkawa, *Economic Growth: The Japanese Experience Since the Meiji Era* (Homewood, Ill.: Richard D. Irwin, 1968), p. 303. The latter article offers a good historical view of both sides of the trade controversy. See also Miyohei Shinohara, *Growth and Cycles in the Japanese Economy* (Tokyo: International Publications Service, 1962), especially p. 70.

2. See also "Japan, A Special Strength," a supplement in *The Economist* (March 31, 1973), p. 54, and Robert Guillain, *The Japanese Challenge: The Race to the Year 2000*, trans. by Patrick O'Brian (New York: J.B. Lippincott, 1970).

3. See Kanamori, "Economic Growth and Exports," p. 303.

4. A basic reference here is Kazushi Ohkawa and Henry Rosovsky, *Japanese Economic Growth: Trend Acceleration in the Twentieth Century* (Stanford, Calif.: Stanford University Press, 1973).

5. Kiyoshi, Kojima, for example, estimated that import dependence would rise to an "expected average" of 16 percent during the early 1960s; further trade dependence was expected to be high as a concomitant to industrialization, although the latter finding was qualified as textiles (with a high import coefficient) declined and chemicals and heavy industry (with low import coefficients) increased, respectively, in importance as the structural composition of exports changed. See Kojima, "Economic Development and Import Dependence in Japan," *Hitotsubashi Journal of Economics* 1, no. 1 (1960), pp. 29-51.

6. Japan ranks no higher than 62nd among 76 nations of the IMF; her dependence is less than any industrial country in Europe. Kogoro Uemura, "Challenge for Responsible Partnership," in a speech in Washington, D.C. in his capacity as president of Japan's Keidanren (June 15, 1971).

7. Robert Guillain, *The Japanese Challenge*, especially p. 218. Guillain argues that ". . . it is a mistake to suppose, as so many people do, that Japan derives its wealth and strength from foreign trade. In fact, Japanese manufacturers do not make their money abroad but on the home market" (p. 218).

8. Hollerman asserts that Japan's "actual" trade dependence is, and continues to be great, even though the nominal M/GNP and X/GNP ratios are low and generally falling. Leon Hollerman, *Japan's Dependence on the World Economy* (Princeton, N.J.: Princeton University Press, 1967), p. 18.

9. H.S. Houthakker and S. Magee, "Income and Price Elasticities in World Trade," *Review of Economics and Statistics* 51, no. 2 (1969), pp. 111-25.

10. A major proponent of this view is Ragnar Nurkse, *Equilibrium and Growth in the World Economy* (Cambridge, Mass.: Harvard University Press, 1961), especially chapter 11, "Patterns of Trade and Growth." See also Gunnar Myrdal, *Rich Lands and Poor* (New York: Pantheon Books, 1957), especially chapter 5, "International Inequalities," pp. 50-66. Trade prospects for less-developed countries grow only sluggishly, he argues, due to ". . . inelastic demands in their export market, often also a demand trend which is not rising very rapidly, and excessive price fluctuations." Nurkse, *Equilibrium and Growth in the World*, p. 52.

11. However, the matter is not unambiguously straightforward. See Alexander Cairncross, "International Trade and Economics Development," *Kyklos* 13, no. 4 (1960), pp. 545-58; and Gerald Meier, "International Trade and International Inequality," *Oxford Economic Papers* 10, no. 3 (1958), pp. 277-85, for reservations on the usefulness or the applicability of the trade model sketched above.

12. Hisao Kanamori, "Economic Growth and the Balance of Payments," in R. Komiya (ed.), *Postwar Economic Growth in Japan*, trans. by R. Ozaki (Berkeley: University of California Press, 1966), pp. 69-94; and Kiyoshi Kojima, "Trade Arrangements Among Industrial Countries: Effects Upon Japan," in Bela Belassa (ed.), *Studies in Trade Liberalization* (Baltimore, Md.: Johns Hopkins Press, 1967), pp. 177-216.

13. See Hisao Kanamori, "Economic Growth and Exports," p. 307.

14. Korea and Formosa accounted for 27 percent of Japanese imports from 1934-1936; China, for 10 percent; Oceania, 7 percent, and all of Southeast Asia, for 17 percent. Kanamori, "Economic Growth and Exports," p. 307. The limitations cited earlier for comparative exports data hold equally for these important figures.

15. The key reference here is the Japan Economic Research Center, *Japan's Economy in 1980 in the Global Context: The Nation's Role in a Polycentric World* (Tokyo, 1972, abridged translation).

16. Japan Economic Research Center, *Japan's Economy in 1980*, especially p. 62, presents an excellent discussion of Japan's non-tariff trade barriers. For related commentary, see also "Japanese Agriculture: Groping for a Path to Modernization," *Oriental Economist* 35, no. 694 (1967), especially p. 625; Warren Hunsberger, *Japan and the United States in World Trade in Asia: Developments since 1926–Prospects for 1970* (New York: Praeger Publishers, 1966), especially chapter 6, "Trade Barriers in the ECAFE Region," pp. 134-52. It should be also noted that if quotas, licenses, and the like are in fact more import than tariffs or price differentials, the stimulatory effect of Japan's revaluations since August 1971 will be proportionately limited.

17. A recent Foreign Trade White Paper noted that Japan now has only forty items on its residual import restriction list. The White Paper pledged that Japan would continue to liberalize trade, both in response to Kennedy Round tariff-reduction programs and unilaterally, particularly for developing countries. See "Foreign Trade," *Oriental Economist* 39, no. 739 (1971), pp. 36-37 for a summary of these trends. See also Kiyoshi Kojima, "A Pacific Asian Community and Asian Developing Countries," *Hitotsubashi Journal of Economics* 7, no. 1 (1966), for a projection of future trade patterns, and Hisao Kanamori, "The Impact of Japanese Economic and Trade Growth on Asian Trade and Trade Policies," in Kiyoshi Kojima, *Economics Cooperation in the Western Pacific* (Tokyo: Japan Economics Research Center, Paper No. 20, June 1973) pp. 57-68.

18. See Hisao Kanamori, "Economic Growth and the Balance of Payments," especially p. 91.

19. See Warren Hunsberger, *Japan and the United States in World Trade*, especially chapter 7, "The Geography of Japan's Foreign Trade," pp. 179-240; and Kyung-Mo Huh, *Japan's Trade in Asia*.

20. See, for example, Japan Economic Planning Agency, *New Long-Range Economic Plan of Japan (1961-1970): Doubling National Income Plan* p. 76. The same general conclusions were put forward by the United Nations, *Economic Survey of Asia and the Far East, 1969* (New York and Bangkok: Economic Commission for Asia and the Far East, 1960), pp. 89 ff.

21. Kanamori, "Economic Growth and the Balance of Payments," pp. 91-92, offers a careful discussion. See also, Kiyoshi Kojima, "Trade Arrangements Among Industrial Countries: Effects upon Japan," p. 186.

Chapter 3
Pacific Asian Trade Flows: The Influence of Japan

1. Gunnar Myrdal, *Asian Drama* (New York: Pantheon Books, 1968), vol. 1, chapter 13, pp. 581-672. It should be noted that the data supporting Myrdal's

arguments, which are summarized on pp. 581-3, includes countries like India and Pakistan that are not examined in this study.

2. Prebisch is a principal exponent of this view, see Raul Prebisch, "Commercial Policy in the Underdeveloped Countries," *America Economic Review*, 49, no. 2 (1959). See also Hans Singer, *International Development: Growth and Change* (New York: Dobbs, Ferry, 1964).

3. In a footnote on p. 582, Myrdal notes three possible exceptions: rubber for Malaya, and rubber and oil for Indonesia. Myrdal, *Asian Drama*, p. 582.

4. Ibid., pp. 582-3.

5. Ibid., p. 583.

6. Hla Myint, *Southeast Asia's Economy: Development Policies in the 1970's* (New York: Praeger Publishers, 1971) especially pp. 73-88, and *Economic Theory and the Underdeveloped Countries* (New York: Oxford University Press, 1971), especially Parts II and IV. See also D.B. Keesing, "Outward-Looking Policies and Economic Development," *Economic Journal* 77, no. 306 (1967), pp. 303-20. For a discussion of the dynamic benefits to capital formation and development growing out of exporting products for which domestic demand is close to zero, see Oscar Braun, "The External Economic Strategy: Outward- or Inward-Looking?" in Dudley Seers and Leonard Jay, *Development in a Divided World* (London: Penguin, 1970), pp. 151-73.

7. Hla Myint, *The Economics of the Developing Countries* and *Southeast Asia's Economy: Development Policies in the 1970's*, pp. 73-88.

8. For a good discussion elaborating on this and other arguments, see Hla Myint, "The Inward and Outward-Looking Countries of Southeast Asia," *The Malayan Economic Review* 12, no. 1 (1967), pp. 1-13.

9. This point was originally recognized and developed by Paul Rosenstein-Rodan, "Problems of Industrialization of Eastern and South-Eastern Europe," *The Economic Journal* 53, no. 211 (1943). See also Myint, *The Economics of the Developing Countries*, (New York: Praeger Publishers, 1964), especially chapters 2 and 3.

10. A full quantitative discussion of trade patterns among countries of different size and levels of economic achievement is contained in Simon Kuznets, *Modern Economic Growth* (New Haven, Conn.: Yale University Press, 1966), chapter VI, especially pp. 300-59 and Kuznets, "Quantitative Aspects of the Economic Growth of Nations: IX Level and Structure of Foreign Trade: Comparisons for Recent Years," *Economic Development and Cultural Change*, Part II, vol. 13, no. 1 (1964). See also Karl Deutsch and Alexander Eckstein, "National Industrialization and the Declining Share of the International Economic Sector," *World Politics* 13, no. 2 (1961).

11. The classic statement in Hla Myint, "The Gains from International Trade and the Backward Countries," *The Review of Economic Studies* 22, no. 58 (1954-1955), pp. 129-42. See also Myint, "The 'Classical Theory' of International Trade and the Underdeveloped Countries."

12. Hla Myint, *Southeast Asia's Economy: Development Policies in the 1970's*, chapter 4, pp. 73-88. This is part of a summary of a major Asian Development Bank study of the economic prospects for the Southeast Asian region in the decade ahead. See also Joseph W. Dodd, "The Colonial Economy 1967: The Case of Malaysia," *Asian Survey* 9, no. 6 (1969), pp. 438-46.

13. Not all would agree upon an external strategy for the future. Irvine, for example, argues that in view of the region's poor export prospects, import substitution should be the key strategy. Reed Irvine, "Some Lessons from the Development Decade," *Asian Survey* 10, no. 7 (1970), pp. 552-62.

14. See Kiyoshi Kojima, Saburo Okita, and Peter Drysdale, "Foreign Economic Relations," published as chapter IV in Asian Development Bank, *Southeast Asia's Economy in the 1970's*, (New York: Frederick A. Praeger, 1971) p. 254.

15. Alexander Eckstein, *Communist China's Economic Growth, and Foreign Trade* (New York: McGraw-Hill, 1966), and Feng-hwa Mah, "Foreign Trade," in A. Eckstein, *Economic Trends in Communist China* (Chicago: Aldine-Atherton, 1968) offer extended discussions of antarky as a strategy in China's foreign trade.

16. See John Badgley, *Asian Development: Problems and Prognosis* (New York: Free Press, 1971), especially introduction and chapter 1. A good general reference is John Kendrick, *Economic Accounts and Their Uses* (New York: McGraw-Hill, 1972).

Chapter 4
A Method for Analyzing Trade Flows

1. For a good standard treatment of the theory of the international trade that covers these and other theoretical developments, see Charles P. Kindleberger, *International Economics* (Homewood, Ill.: Richard D. Irwin, 1973). A more mathematical treatment may be found in I.F. Pearce, *International Trade* (New York: W.W. Norton, 1970).

2. Gottfried Haberler, "Some Problems in the Pure Theory of International Trade," *Economic Journal* 60, no. 238 (1950), pp. 223-40.

3. See Hollis Chenery and L.J. Taylor, "Development Patterns: Among Countries and Over Time," *Review of Economics and Statistics* 50, no. 4 (1968), pp. 391-416; and Simon Kuznets, *Modern Economic Growth*, (New Haven, Conn.: Yale University Press, 1966) especially chapter 6.

4. Paige and Bombach, for example, prepared estimates of industrial cost comparisons between the United States and United Kingdom for 1950. They defined cost as value added net of depreciation, however, which would seem to include profits in costs—undesirable in that relative profits are among the things such a study would hope to identify and isolate, rather than burying profits as a

part of overall costs. Furthermore, by measuring "cost" in terms of value added, the costs of raw or lightly fabricated materials that entered at an earlier stage of the productive process would seem to be ignored. See D. Paige and G. Bombach, *A Comparison of National Output and Productivity of the United Kingdom and the U.S.* (Paris: Organization for European Economic Cooperation, 1958).

5. An example of the survey approach is a study by Theodore Gates and Fabian Linden, *Costs and Competition: American Experience Abroad* (New York: N.I.C.B., 1961). Prepared for the National Industrial Conference Board, it relied on responses supplied by 147 manufacturing firms with plants in both the United States and foreign countries.

6. For a useful review of some of the relevant literature here, see Richard E. Caves, *Trade and Economic Structure: Models and Methods* (Cambridge, Mass.: Harvard University Press, 1967), esp. pp. 268-82.

7. See, for example, W.W. Leontief, "Domestic Production and Foreign Trade: The American Capital Position Re-examined," *Economia Internationale* 7, (1954), pp. 9-38; and Leontief "Factor Proportions and the Structure of American Trade: Further Theoretical and Empirical Analysis," *Review of Economics and Statistics* 38, no. 4 (1956), pp. 386-407.

8. For an early example of these attempts, with reference to Japan (covering 1955) see Seiji Naya, "Natural Resources, Factor Mix, and Factor Reversal in International Trade," *American Economic Review* 57, no. 2 (1967) pp. 561-70. See also K. Arrow, N. Chenery, B. Minkas, and R. Solow, "Capital-Labor Substitution and Economic Efficiency," *Review of Economics and Statistics* 43, no. 87 (1961), pp. 225-50. It should be noted that these authors assert that their study indicates that relative international factor intensities are not independent of factor prices. In any case their answers are consequently not unambiguous in signaling international specialization.

9. Bela Belassa, "An Empirical Demonstration of Classical Comparative Cost Theory," *Review of Economics and Statistics* 45, no. 3 (1963), pp. 231-38.

10. G. MacDougall, "British and American Exports: A Study Suggested by the Theory of Comparative Costs," Part I, *Economic Journal* 61, no. 244 (1951), pp. 694-8. It is interesting to note parenthetically that this attempt, like many of the others, relies on the relatively rich data resources of Atlantic industrial countries.

11. Belassa, "An Empirical Demonstration of Classical Comparative Cost Theory," p. 233.

12. Ibid., pp. 236, 237. Belassa subsequently found that no relationship between wage rations and export shares could satisfactorily be established, and that adding as explanatory variables both wage levels and unit costs to productivity levels did not significantly alter the earlier results in any conclusive fashion.

13. Since relative wage comparisons were limited to the United States and the United Kingdom, the generality of the findings appears to be limited. As

representative of the considerable literature here, see Karl Forchheimer, "The Role of Relative Wage Differences in International Trade," *Quarterly Journal of Economics* 62, no. 1 (1947), pp. 1-30; and I. Kravis, "Availability and Other Influences on the Commodity Composition of Trade," *Journal of Political Economy* 64, no. 2 (1959), p. 146.

14. Donald Keesing, "The Impact of Research and Development on United States Trade," *Journal of Political Economy* 75, no. 3 (1967), pp. 303-20.

15. Ibid. See also W. Gruber, D. Mehta, and R. Vernon, "The R & D Factor in International Trade and International Investment of U.S. Industries," *Journal of Political Economy* 75, no. 1 (1967), pp. 20-37.

16. Irving B. Kravis and Robert E. Lipsey, *Price Competitiveness in World Trade* (New York: Distributed by Columbia University Press, 1971), and "International Price Comparisons by Regression Methods," *International Economic Review* 10, no. 2, (1969), pp. 233-246.

17. Kravis and Lipsey, *Price Competitiveness in World Trade*, especially chapter 5.

18. See, for example, several discussions of non-price variables in Kravis and Lipsey, *Price Competitiveness in World Trade*. See also United Nations, *Non-Tariff Distortions of Trade* (New York: Committee for Economic Development, 1969).

19. An excellent discussion with good generality is Charles P. Kindleberger, *American Business Abroad*, Lecture I (New Haven, Conn.: Yale University Press, 1970), especially pp. 1-36.

20. For a good discussion on the impact that, for example, Australia's natural resources have had vis-à-vis their trade with Japan, see M.P. Narayana Pillar, "The Kalgoorlie Trail," *Far Eastern Economic Review* 63, no. 12, (1969), pp. 532-4.

21. Bela Belassa, "Trade Liberalization and 'Revealed' Comparative Advantage," *Manchester School of Economic and Social Studies* 36, no. 2 (1965), p. 103.

22. H. Tysznski, "World Trade in Manufactured Commodities, 1899-1950," *Manchester School of Economic and Social Studies* 19 (1951), pp. 272-304.

23. For a brief discussion of two other straightforward applications of this basic method, see S. Spiegelglass, "World Exports of Manufactures," *Manchester School of Economics and Social Studies* 27, no. 2 (1959) pp. 111-39; and United Nations, *United Nations Economic Survey of Asia and the Far East, 1967*, Part I, "Policies and Planning for Exports" (New York and Bangkok: Economic Commission for Asia and the Far East, 1968), pp. 15-38.

24. Bela Belassa, "Trade Liberalization and 'Revealed' Comparative Advantage," pp. 90-123. This method was later used by a number of economists to measure the impact of proposed trade liberalization measures on several industrial countries. See Bela Belassa, ed., *Studies in Trade Liberalization* (Baltimore, Md.: Johns Hopkins Press, 1967).

25. J.M. Fleming and S.C. Tsiang, "Changes in Competitive Strength and Export Shares of Major Industrial Countries," *International Monetary Fund Staff Papers*, vol. 5, no. 3 (1956-1957), pp. 218-48.

26. Ibid., p. 218.

27. In conversations with the author. The major reference is I.R. Savage and Karl Deutsch, "A Statistical Model of the Gross Analysis of Transaction Flows," *Econometrica* 28, no. 3 (1960), pp. 551-72, especially 552. See also Leo A. Goodman, "Statistical Methods for the Preliminary Analysis of Transaction Flows," *Econometrica* 31, no. 1-2 (1963), pp. 197-208.

28. Belassa, "Trade Liberalization and 'Revealed' Comparative Analysis," p. 103. See also Belassa, *Studies in Trade Liberalization*.

29. For a thorough treatment of many of the factors underlying "competitiveness," as it is used here, see J.M. Fleming and S.C. Tsiang, "Changes in Competitive Strength and Export Shares in Major Industrial Countries," p. 218.

30. See William Baumol, *Economic Theory and Operations Analysis* (Englewood Cliffs, N.J.: Prentice-Hall, 1965) pp. 202-5; or R.E. Baldwin, "Commodity Composition of Trade: Selected Industrial Countries," *Review of Economics and Statistics* 40, no. 1 (1958), special supplement, pp. 5-50.

31. Fleming and Tsiang, "Changes in Competitive Strength and Export Shares in Major Industrial Countries," especially pp. 218-22.

Chapter 5
Japanese Exports to Pacific Asia:
Empirical Results and Future Prospects

1. There is an enormous literature on these points. See, for example, Michael Michaely, "Concentration in Imports and Exports: An International Comparison," *Economic Journal* 68, 272 (1958), pp. 722-36, for a representative approach. Michaely argues that a large number of classifications ought to be utilized.

2. Hollis Chenery and L.S. Taylor, "Development Patterns Among Countries and Over Time," *Review of Economics and Statistics*, 50, no. 4 (1968), pp. 391-416, offers good treatment of these matters for a large number of countries.

3. Morihisa Emori. "Japanese Trading Companies: Their Functions and Roles," in Pierre Uri (ed.), *Trade and Investment Policies for the Seventies: New Challenge for the Atlantic Area and Japan* (New York: Praeger Publishers, 1971), pp. 111-24.

4. Morihisa Emori, "Japanese Trading Companies: Their Functions and Roles," offers an extended discussion of their general role. See also Louis Kraar, "How the Japanese Mount That Export Blitz," *Fortune* 82, no. 3 (1970), p. 105.

5. "Japan Trade Center," a statement put out by the *Japan Trade Center Information Service*, No. 4609 (Tokyo and New York, 1971), pp. 1-4.

6. Saburo Okita, "Economic Development in the 1970's—Japan and Asia," (Tokyo: Japan Economic Research Center, Center Paper No. 18, 1972).

7. Herman Kahn, *The Emerging Japanese Superstate: Challenge and Response* (Englewood Cliffs, N.J.: Prentice-Hall, 1970) repeatedly makes this point, especially in his long appendix. See also Robert Guillain, *The Japanese Challenge: The Race to the Year 2000*, trans. by Patrick O'Brian (New York: J.B. Lippincott, 1970), especially pp. 138-60; and Louis Kraar, "How the Japanese Mount That Export Blitz," p. 105.

8. This section relies upon Japan Economic Research Center, *Japan's Economy in 1980 in the Global Context: The Nation's Role in a Polycentric World* (Tokyo, 1972).

9. The Japan Economic Research Center's projection calls for the developing countries of Southeast Asia (not strictly analogous to the region analyzed here) to increase at an annual rate of 8.7 percent and China at 11.2 percent. See Japan Economic Research Center, *Japan's Economy in 1980*, p. 2. Leon Hollerman notes that the annual ECAFE's meeting declared that attainment of an average growth rate of 6 or 7 percent was considered feasible for the decade ending in 1980. Leon Hollerman, "Liberalization and Japanese Trade in the 1970's," *Asian Survey* 10, no. 5 (1970), p. 432n. See also, Herman Kahn, *The Emerging Japanese Superstate*, p. 133 for a "surprise-free projection" of 7 to 8 percent.

10. Hollerman, "Liberalization and Japanese Trade in the 1970's," p. 432.

11. Japan Economic Research Center, *Japan's Economy in 1980*, p. 9.

12. Kahn, *The Emerging Japanese Superstate*, p. 141. These prospects are detailed on pp. 133-43, and in the appendix, pp. 218-34.

13. Kraar, "How the Japanese Mount That Export Blitz."

14. Masaya Miyoshi, "Japan's International Trade and Investment Policies for the 1970's," in Pierre Uri (ed.), *Trade and Investment Policies for the Seventies: New Challenges for the Atlantic Area and Japan* (New York: Praeger Publishers, 1971), pp. 125-65.

15. For example, see Barry Pearton, "Koreans Face Hard Facts," *FEER* 74, no. 45 (November 6, 1971), p. 37; and Richard Halloran, "Koreans Bitter about U.S. Trade Policies," *The New York Times* (December 11, 1971), p. 43.

16. Ahn Kwang Ho, President of KOTRA (the Korean Trade Promotion Corporation), argued that he could envisage future adjustments permitting Mainland China to play a role in this regional trade configuration, a striking economic and political departure for South Korea. Pearton, "Koreans Face Hard Facts," p. 37.

Chapter 6
Pacific Asian Exports to Japan:
New Gains for Traditional Commodities

1. See, for example, United Nations, *United Nations Economic Survey of Asia and the Far East 1959* (New York and Bangkok: Economic Commission for

Asia and the Far East, 1960); and Japan Economic Planning Agency, *New Long-Range Economic Plan of Japan, (1961-1970)* (Tokyo: Office of the Prime Minister, 1961), p. 70.

2. This would be revised upward if Japan would liberalize her imports to permit Pacific Asia to export non-primary products. United Nations, *United Nations Economic Survey of Asia and the Far East 1959*, p. 91. See also Warren Hunsberger, *Japan and the United States in World Trade* (New York: Harper & Row, 1964), pp. 226-8.

3. Kiyoshi Kojima, *Japan and a Pacific Free Trade Area* (Berkeley, Calif.: University of California Press, 1971).

4. See also Kiyoshi Kojima, "Non-Tariff Barriers to Japan's Trade," *Hitosubashi Journal of Economics* 13, no. 1 (1972).

5. See Hisao Kanamori, "The Impact of Japanese Economic and Trade Growth on Asian Trade and Trade Policies," in K. Kojima (ed.), *Economic Cooperation in the Western Pacific* (Tokyo: The Japan Economic Research Center, 1973).

6. For a view of intensive export concentration as a basic outgrowth of the Asian colonial experience, see Joseph W. Dodd, "The Colonial Economy, 1967: The Case of Malaysia," *Asian Survey* 9, no. 6 (1969), pp. 438-46.

7. See Koyishi Kojima, "Asian Developing Countries and PAFTA: Development, Aid, and Trade Preferences," *Hitotsoubashi Journal of Economics* 10, no. 1 (1969), pp. 1-17. See also Kojima, ed., *Pacific Trade and Development* (Tokyo: The Japan Economic Research Center, 1968) and *Pacific Trade and Development II* (Tokyo: The Japan Economic Research Center, 1969).

8. See JETRO, *Foreign Trade of Japan, 1971* (Tokyo, 1971), a condensation of the 23rd White Paper on the Foreign Trade of Japan, prepared by the Ministry of International Trade and Industry and published by the Japan External Trade Organization. See also Osamu Shimomura, "Balance of Payments Constraints on Economic Growth," *Oriental Economist* 36, no. 690 (1968), p. 24.

9. As Hunsberger argued, "To get imports is the main object of Japanese foreign trade . . . exports . . . are not basically ends in themselves but the means by which the Japanese nation provides itself with imports." Warren Hunsberger, *Japan and the United States in World Trade*, p. 105.

10. Tatsunosuke Takasaki, Minister of Japan's MITI, had articulated this view much earlier. *Far Eastern Economic Review* (1958), p. 1.

11. See K. Kojima et al., "Foreign Economic Relations," in Asian Development Bank, *Southeast Asia's Economy in the 1970's*, (New York: Frederick A. Praeger, 1971), pp. 267-70 on this point.

12. For one view emphasizing the limits on trade expansion caused by supply rigidities in many Pacific Asian countries, see Hiroshi Kitamura, "Economic Development and Regional Cooperation in Southeast Asia," in United Nations, *Economic Bulletin for Asia and the Far East* 20, no. 2 (1969), p. 4.

13. Herman Kahn, *The Emerging Japanese Superstate: Challenge and Re-*

sponse (Englewood Cliffs, N.J.: Prentice-Hall, 1970), p. 116. Kahn generally argues that what he calls the Non-Communist Pacific Asian region, which considerably overlaps the countries examined here, will participate in much greater shares of Japanese trade in the 1970s with major foreign investment the key vehicle.

14. See, for example, Japan Economic Research Center, *Japan's Economy in 1980 in the Global Context: The Nation's Role in a Polycentric World* (Tokyo, 1972), especially pp. 51-55.

15. This is discussed more fully in Robert Guillain, *The Japanese Challenge: The Race to the Year 2000*, trans. by Patrick O'Brian (New York: J.B. Lippincott, 1970), p. 223.

16. Ibid. The Japan's MITI's 23rd White Paper on Trade, taken from JETRO, *Foreign Trade of Japan, 1971*, p. 31, also stresses this point.

17. Hiroshi Kitamura, "Economic Development and Regional Cooperation in Southeast Asia," pp. 1-8.

18. Ibid., p. 4.

19. Japan's MITI's 23rd White Paper on Trade, in JETRO, *Foreign Trade of Japan, 1971*, p. 25.

20. Japan Economic Research Center, *Japan's Economy in 1980*, p. 4.

21. Ibid., Table 4, p. 9.

22. Derek Davies, "The New Empire," *FEER*, 71, no. 13 (1971), pp. 29-30.

23. Nihon Keizai Shimbun, "Natural Resources of Japan," *Japan Economic Journal* 9, no. 467 (1971), p. 20.

24. Japan Bureau of Statistics, *Statistical Handbook of Japan, 1970* (Tokyo: Office of the Prime Minister, 1970), p. 103, plus calculations by author.

25. Ibid., p. 64.

26. See, for example, "Japanese Agriculture: Groping for Path to Modernization," *Oriental Economist*, 35, no. 684 (1967), pp. 621-5.

27. Takashi Saski, Governor of the Bank of Japan, emphasized both the pressures from abroad and the benefits in terms of reducing domestic inflation, reported in *The New York Times*, May 29, 1971, p. 28. See also, Joseph Reday, "Far East Business," *Oriental Economist* 39, no. 727 (1971), pp. 40-43.

28. D.B. Keesing, "Outward-Looking Policies and Economic Development," *Economic Journal* 77, no. 306 (1967), pp. 303-20, discusses the case for emphasizing exports of manufactures relatively early in development; he sees the major advantages as upgrading training and labor skills ("human" capital) and easing the introduction of new technology.

29. Kakuei Tanaka, MITI Minister, said that a major new timetable on import liberalization would be presented to the current Diet Sessions, although he emphasized that liberalization should be carried out in accordance with Japan's long-range industrial and agricultural policies, and not because of pressure from other countries. "Schedule Prepared for Import Liberalization," *Japan Trade Bulletin* (JETRO), no. 694 (February 11, 1972), p. 1. In September 1971, the

Japanese government announced a detailed eight-point trade liberalization program. See "Government Implements Eight-Point Program on International Economic Policy," in the *Japan Trade Center's Information Service*, No. 4611 (September 1971), pp. 1-5. See also Joseph Reday, "Far East Business," *Oriental Economist* 39, no. 727 (1971), p. 31; and Leon Hollerman, "Liberalization and Japanese Trade in the 1970's," *Asian Survey* 10, no. 5 (May 1970), pp. 427-37, especially p. 435.

Chapter 7
The Balance of Trade and
Financial Flows

1. Masaya Miyoshi, "Japan's International Trade and Investment Policies for the 1970's," in Pierre Uri (ed.), *Trade and Investment Policies for the Seventies: New Challenges for the Atlantic Area and Japan*, (New York: Praeger Publishers, 1971), especially p. 125-47. For a good discussion of this question emphasizing the earlier postwar period, also see Miyohei Shinohara, *Growth and Cycles in the Japanese Economy*, published under the auspices of the Institute of Economic Research, Hitotsubashi University (Tokyo: International Publications Service, 1962), especially pp. 110-50.

2. See Emile Benoit, "Impacts of the End of Vietnam Hostilities and the Reduction of British Military Presence in Malaysia and Singapore," in Asian Development Bank, *Southeast Asia's Economy in the 1970's*, (New York: Frederick A. Praeger, 1971), pp. 582-671. George Viksnins, "United States Military Spending and the Economy of Thailand," *Asian Survey* 13, no. 5 (1973), pp. 441-57, examines the case of Thailand.

3. Shim Jae-Hoon, "The High Cost of Peace," *Far Eastern Economic Review* 71, no. 6 (1971), p. 37; and see Se Jin Kim, "South Korea's Investment in Vietnam and Its Economic and Political Impact," *Asian Survey* 10, no. 6 (1970), pp. 519-32. See again Benoit, "Impacts of the End of Vietnam Hostilities and the Reduction of British Military Presence in Malaysia and Singapore," especially pp. 631 and 651.

4. Henry Scott Stokes, "The Economic Invasion Myth," *FEER* 71, no. 13 (1971), pp. 49-50, stresses the view that expanded trade from the region can no longer be financed internally. For an examination of Thailand's foreign exchange problems, see "Trade-Gap—Ever Wider," *FEER* 74, no. 46 (1971), pp. 39-40.

5. Japanese technology and capital will continue to move abroad as long as they are welcomed. Takaski Ikara, "Japan's Economic Position in the World," *Pacific Quarterly* 1, no. 4, (1970), p. 629.

6. See JETRO, *Economic Cooperation of Japan* (Tokyo, 1973), for a good discussion of Japanese economic cooperation in Pacific Asia.

7. Taken from Kazuo Takita, "An Asian Common Market," *Far Eastern Economic Review* 34, no. 11 (1961), p. 535. Ikeda here stressed the mutual benefits from the two-way trade, as well as pledging aid.

8. Ibid., p. 535.

9. For a good discussion of the underlying rationale of Japanese aid, see Kiyoshi Kojima, "Japan's Foreign Aid Policy," *Hitotsubashi Journal of Economics* 6, no. 2 (1966); or J. Alexander Caldwell, "The Evolution of Japanese Economic Cooperation, 1950-1970," in Harald Malmgren (ed), *Pacific Basin Development: The American Interests* (Lexington, Mass.: D.C. Heath, 1972).

10. As Kojima says, ". . . political unrest and disillusionment among developing countries, particularly in neighboring regions, create anxieties in Japan." Kiyoshi Kojima, "Japan's Foreign Aid Policy," p. 45. See also Zbigniew Brzezinski, *The Fragile Blossom: Crisis and Change in Japan* (New York: Harper & Row, 1972), especially pp. 61-93.

11. See JETRO, *Japan Into the Multinationalization Era* (Tokyo, 1973), especially Chapter IV, "Japanese Enterprises in Southeast Asia," pp. 27ff. See also JETRO, *Economic Cooperation of Japan.*

12. For a detailed discussion of the precise coverage in these categories, see OECD, *Geographical Distribution of Financial Flows to Less-Developed Countries, 1966-1967* (Paris, 1968), pp. VII-VIII. This series presents considerably disaggregated findings in each of these categories.

13. Taken from data in Table 1, OECD, *Development Assistance, 1973 Review* (Paris, 1973), pp. 180-1. Japan accounted for about 14 percent of the developed countries' total bilateral economic assistance in 1968-1970.

14. OECD, *Resources for the Developing World: The Flow of Financial Resources to Less-Developed Countries, 1962-1968* (Paris, 1969), pp. 118-20.

15. Ibid., p. 120. For a full and thoughtful discussion of the Japanese reparations question, see Laurence Olson, *Japan in Postwar Asia* (New York: Praeger Publishers, 1970), pp. 13-62. Olson provides accounts of the reparations agreements and an analysis of the background to the settlements.

16. For a good discussion of both the Japanese agencies involved and the dollar magnitudes, see OECD, *Resources for the Developing World*, pp. 117-22. For 1969 and 1970 data, see OECD, *Development Assistance, 1971 Review*, pp. 168-71.

17. OECD, *Resources for the Developing World*, p. 120.

18. Ibid.

19. These comments rely heavily upon an unpublished paper by Dwight Perkins.

20. *Partners in Development: Report of the Commission on International Development*, The Pearson Report (New York: Praeger Publishers, 1969), especially pp. 208-30; and United Nations, *Development Assistance to Southeast Asia* (New York: Committee on Economic Development, 1970), pp. 54-55, are two widely known examples.

21. Ibid., pp. 29-32 and appendices.

22. Ian Stewart, "Japanese Stir Asian Resentment," *The New York Times*, January 10, 1972, p. 13.

23. Ibid. See also, Robert Ozaki, "Japan's Role in Asian Economic Develop-

ment," *Asian Survey* 7, no. 4 (1967), pp. 237-44.

24. OECD, *Development Assistance*, chapter VI, "Private Capital Flows," pp. 87-102, plus appendix tables.

25. For a fuller discussion of these matters, see *Partners in Development*, especially chapter 5, "Private Foreign Investment," pp. 99-123.

26. See, for example, James Sterba, "Japan Tightens Her Economic Grip of Nations of East and South Asia," *The New York Times*, August 28, 1972, p. 1.

27. See OECD, *Development Assistance, 1971 Review* pp. 88-89.

28. Kamekichi Takahashi, "The Japanese Economy: Tasks of a New Dimension," *Oriental Economist* 39, no. 730 (August 1971), p. 17.

29. Sueyuki Wakasugi, "Japanese Traders Face Tough Global Problems," *Pacific Community* 4, no. 2 (1973), pp. 226-35.

30. "Are Japanese Foreign Ventures Profiting?" *Oriental Economist* 39, no. 728 (1971), pp. 14-17.

31. JETRO, *White Paper on International Trade: Japan, 1973* (Tokyo, 1973), p. 37.

32. Harald Malmgren, "Japan, the U.S. and the Pacific Economy," *Pacific Community* 4, no. 3 (1973), pp. 307-25.

33. Ibid., Malmgren argues that the enlarged Japanese presence will strengthen her interdependence with the region.

34. The Industrial Bank of Japan estimates that between 1972 and 1977, new overseas Japanese investments will total $6 billion, of which $2.7 will be directed towards acquiring and developing natural resources. By 1980, Japanese corporate investments abroad are expected to top $25.7 billion. Koji Nakamura, "Spend More, Earn More," *Far Eastern Economic Review* 73, no. 35 (1971), p. 29. In Asia alone, a report by the Japanese Industrial Structure Deliberative Council, an advisory body, predicted that Japanese investment in Asia would rise tenfold by 1980 from its current $700 million total, although others were quoted as saying that estimate was too low. Ian Stewart, "Japanese Stir Asian Resentment," p. 13. Of them all, Herman Kahn has forecast the highest future levels. Kahn has estimated a Japanese investment of $5 to $10 billion in non-Communist Pacific Asia by the later 1970s and early 1980s, assuming nothing disturbs the stability of the area. Herman Kahn, *The Emerging Japanese Superstate* (Englewood Cliffs, N.J.: Prentice-Hall, 1970), p. 141.

35. Yoshida Makoto, "How We Look to Southeast Asia," *Japan Quarterly* 18, no. 1 (1971), pp. 32-33.

36. Ibid.

37. OECD, *Development Assistance*, p. 96.

38. United Nations, *Development Assistance to Southeast Asia*, pp. 35-36; and OECD, *Resources for the Developing World: The Flow of Financial Resources to Less Developed Countries, 1962-1968*, p. 124.

39. See the brief discussion in the United Nations, *Development Assistance to Southeast Asia*, pp. 32-36, especially p. 35.

40. OECD, *Development Assistance*, pp. 96-99.

Appendix
Pacific Asian Trade Data

1. Though in the comparisons that follows, Australia and New Zealand data for imports were also reported f.o.b. and not c.i.f., thus understating the size but not the relative shares of imports, assuming that shipping, insurance and handling charges were uniform among all exporters to Oceania. With respect to Japan, if not to the remaining Pacific regions, it may be inferred that in view of the two countries relatively close proximity and the fact the composition of Australian and New Zealand imports is not heavily biased in favor of the kind of product that is not heavily biased in favor of the kind of product that is large and bulky with respect to total value, so that transportation costs may be expected to be considerable, the "normal" 10 percent estimates for c.i.f. may slightly overstate the true costs, thus imparting a slight upward bias to Japan's trade share. For a more detailed discussion of transportation costs in trade, see Carmellah Moneta, "The Estimation of Transportation Costs in International Trade," *Journal of Political Economy* 67, no. 1 (1959), pp. 41-58.

2. See Carmellah Moneta, "The Estimation of Transportation Costs in International Trade," *Journal of Political Economy* 67, no. 1 (1959), pp. 44ff. This study, it should be noted, was heavily concentrated around Western European trade returns. A brief discussion of one suggested treatment of mainland Chinese trade data argues that a correction of 5 percent is the right order of magnitude. See Robert L. Price, "International Trade of Communist China, 1950-1965," taken from *An Economic Profile of Mainland China*, studies prepared for the U.S. Congress Joint Economic Committee (1967), pp. 583-609, especially the Methodological Supplement, pp. 607ff.

3. Paul Luey, "On Discrepancies in Trade Statistics of Trading Partners," *The Malayan Economic Review* 16, no. 1 (1971), pp. 13-23, especially p. 20.

4. Paul Luey, "On Discrepancies in Trade Statistics of Trading Partners," *The Malayan Economic Review* 16, no. 1 (1971), p. 15ff.

5. For a detailed discussion of these difficulties with respect to the Southeast Asian countries, see Seiji Naya and Theodore Morgan, "The Accuracy of International Trade Data: The Case of the Southeast Asian Countries," *Journal of the American Statistical Association* 64, no. 326 (1969), pp. 452-67.

6. Naya and Morgan report that the bias is not so much regional as between developed and developing countries; further actual data often falls within accepted ranges for most developed countries. See Seiji Naya and Theodore Morgan, "The Accuracy of International Trade Data: The Case of the Southeast Asian Countries," *Journal of the American Statistical Association* 64, no. 326 (1969), pp. 456-58.

Bibliography

Bibliography

Arrow, K., N. Chenery, B. Minkas, and R. Solow. 1961. "Capital-Labor Substitution and Economic Efficiency." *Review of Economics and Statistics* 43, no. 87.

Ashbrook, Arthur G., Jr. 1972. "China: Economic Policy and Economic Results, 1949-1971." In U.S. Congress, Joint Economic Committee, *People's Republic of China: An Economic Assessment.* Washington, D.C.

Badgley, John. 1971. *Asian Development: Problems and Prognosis.* New York: Free Press.

Baldwin, R.E. 1958. "Commodity Composition of Trade: Selected Industrial Countries." *Review of Economics and Statistics* 40, no. 1. Cambridge, Mass.

Baumol, William. 1965. *Economic Theory and Operations Analysis.* Englewood Cliffs, N.J.: Prentice-Hall.

Belassa, Bela. 1963. "An Empirical Demonstration of Classical Comparative Cost Theory." *Review of Economics and Statistics* 45, no. 3. Cambridge, Mass.

_____. 1965. "Trade Liberalization and 'Revealed' Comparative Advantage." *Manchester School of Economic and Social Studies* 36, no. 2. London.

_____. 1967. *Studies in Trade Liberalization.* Baltimore, Md.: Johns Hopkins Press.

Benoit, Emile. 1971. "Impacts of the End of Vietnam Hostilities and the Reduction of British Military Presence in Malaysia and Singapore." In Asian Development Bank, *Southeast Asia's Economy in the 1970's.* New York: Frederick A. Praeger.

Braun, Oscar. 1970. "The External Economic Strategy: Outward- or Inward-Looking?" In Dudley Seers and Leonard Jay, *Development in a Divided World.* London: Penguin.

Broadbridge, Seymour. 1964. *Industrial Dualism in Japan: A Problem of Economic Growth and Structural Change.* Chicago: Aldine-Atherton.

Brzezinski, Zbigniew. 1972. *The Fragile Blossom: Crisis and Change in Japan.* New York: Harper & Row.

Caldwell, J. Alexander. 1972. "The Evolution of Japanese Economic Cooperation, 1950-1970." In Harald Malmgren (ed.), *Pacific Basin Development: The American Interests.* Lexington, Mass.: D.C. Heath.

Cairnscross, Alexander. 1960. "International Trade and Economics Development." *Kyklos* 13, no. 4. Basel, Switzerland.

Caves, Richard E. 1967. *Trade and Economic Structure: Models and Methods.* Cambridge, Mass.: Harvard University Press.

Chenery, Hollis and L.J. Taylor. 1968. "Development Patterns: Among Countries and Over Time." *Review of Economics and Statistics* 50, no. 4. Cambridge, Mass.

Davies, Derek. 1971. "The New Empire." *Far Eastern Economic Review* 71, no. 13. Hong Kong.

188

Deutsch, Karl and Alexander Eckstein. 1961. "National Industrialization and the Declining Share of the International Economic Sector." *World Politics* 13, no. 2. Princeton, N.J.

Dodd, Joseph W. 1969. "The Colonial Economy, 1967: The Case of Malaysia." *Asian Survey* 9, no. 6. Berkeley, Calif.

Eckstein, Alexander. 1966. *Communist China's Economic Growth, and Foreign Trade.* New York: McGraw-Hill.

Economist, The. 1973. "Japan, A Special Strength." London.

Emori, Morihisa. 1971. "Japanese Trading Companies: Their Functions and Roles." In Pierre Uri (ed.), *Trade and Investment Policies for the Seventies: New Challenge for the Atlantic Area and Japan.* New York: Praeger Publishers.

Far Eastern Economic Review. 1971. "Trade-Gap—Ever Wider." In vol. 74, no. 6. Hong Kong.

_____. 1973. *1973 Far Eastern Economic Review Asia Yearbook.* Hong Kong.

Fleming, J.M. and S.C. Tsiang. 1956. "Changes in Competitive Strength and Export Shares of Major Industrial Countries." *International Monetary Fund Staff Papers* vol. 5, no. 3. Washington, D.C.

Forchheimer, Karl. 1947. "The Role of Relative Wage Differences in International Trade." *Quarterly Journal of Economics* 62, no. 1. Cambridge, Mass.

Gates, Theodore and Linden Fabian. 1961. *Cost and Competition: American Experience Abroad.* New York: National Industrial Conference Board.

Goodman, Leo A. 1963. "Statistical Methods for the Preliminary Analysis of Transaction Flows." *Econometrica* 31, no. 1-2. Amsterdam.

Gruber, W., D. Mehta, and R. Vernon. 1967. "The R & D Factor in International Trade and International Investment of U.S. Industries." *Journal of Political Economy* 75, no. 1. Chicago.

Guillain, Robert. 1970. *The Japanese Challenge: The Race to the Year 2000.* Translated by Patrick O'Brian. New York: J.B. Lippincott.

Haberler, Gottfried. 1950. "Some Problems in the Pure Theory of International Trade." *Economic Journal* 60, no. 238. New York.

Halloran, Richard. 1971. "Koreans Bitter about U.S. Trade Policies." *The New York Times*, December 11.

Hasluck, Paul. 1967. "Australia and Asia." *Oriental Economist* 35, no. 680. Tokyo.

Hollerman, Leon. 1967. *Japan's Dependence on the World Economy.* Princeton, N.J.: Princeton University Press.

_____. 1970. "Liberalization and Japanese Trade in the 1970's." *Asian Survey* 10, no. 5, Berkeley, Calif.

Houthakker, H.S. and S. Magee. 1969. "Income and Price Elasticities in World Trade." *Review of Economics and Statistics* 51, no. 2. Cambridge, Mass.

Huh, Kyung-Mo. 1966. *Japan's Trade in Asia: Developments Since 1926—Prospects for 1970.* New York: Praeger Publishers.

Hunsberger, Warren. 1964. *Japan and the United States in World Trade.* New York: Harper & Row.

Ikara, Takaski. 1970. "Japan's Economic Position in the World." *Pacific Quarterly* 1, no. 4. Seattle, Wash.

International Economic Review. 1969. "International Price Comparisons by Regression Methods."

International Monetary Fund. Selected Years. *Direction of Trade: A Supplement to International Financial Statistics.* Washington, D.C.

_____. *Direction of Trade, Annual, 1958-1962, 1962-1966, 1964-1968, and 1968-1972.* Washington, D.C.

_____. 1971. *International Financial News Survey* vol. 23, no. 48. Washington, D.C.

Iriye, Akira. 1967. *Across the Pacific.* New York: Harcourt, Brace & World.

Irvine, Reed. 1970. "Some Lessons of the Development Decade." *Asian Survey* 10, no. 7. Berkeley, Calif.

Jae-Hoon, Shim. 1971. "The High Cost of Peace." *Far Eastern Economic Review* 71, no. 6. Hong Kong.

Japan Bureau of Statistics. 1971. *Statistical Handbook of Japan 1970.* Office of the Prime Minister. Tokyo.

Japan Economic Planning Agency. 1961. *New Long-Range Economic Plan of Japan, 1961-1970.* Office of the Prime Minister. Tokyo.

Japan's Economy in 1980 in the Global Context: The Nation's Role in a Polycentric World. Tokyo. Japan Economic Research Center.

Japan External Trade Organization (JETRO). 1971. *Foreign Trade of Japan.* Tokyo.

_____. 1973a. *Economic Cooperation of Japan.* Tokyo.

_____. 1973b. *Japan Into the Multinationalization Era.* Tokyo.

_____. 1973c. *White Paper on International Trade: Japan, 1973.* Tokyo.

Japan Industrial World. 1972. "Outlook on Natural Resources Problems." In vol. 4, no. 1.

Japan Trade Center Information Service. 1971. Nos. 4609 and 4611. Tokyo and New York.

Japan Trade Bulletin. 1972. no. 694. Tokyo: JETRO.

Kahn, Herman. 1970. *The Emerging Japanese Superstate: Challenge and Response.* Englewood Cliffs, N.J.: Prentice-Hall.

Kanamori, Hisao. 1968. "Economic Growth and Exports." In L. Klein and K. Ohkawa, *Economics Growth: The Japanese Experience Since the Meiji Era.* Homewood, Ill.: Richard D. Irwin.

_____. 1966b. "Economic Growth and the Balance of Payments." In R. Komiya, *Postwar Economic Growth in Japan.* Translated by R. Ozaki. Berkeley: University of California Press.

_____. 1973. "The Impact of Japanese Economic and Trade Growth on Asian Trade and Trade Policies," in Kiyoshi Kojima, (eds.), *Economic Cooperation in the Western Pacific.* Tokyo: The Japan Economic Research Center.

Keesing, D.B. 1967a. "Outward-Looking Policies and Economic Development." *Economic Journal* 77, no. 306. New York.

_____. 1967b. "The Impact of Research and Development on United States Trade." *Journal of Political Economy* 75, no. 3. Chicago.

Kendrick, John. 1972. *Economic Accounts and Their Uses.* New York: McGraw-Hill.

Kim, Se Jin. 1970. "South Korea's Investment in Vietnam and Its Economic and Political Impact." *Asian Survey* 10, no. 6. Berkeley, Calif.

Kindleberger, Charles P. 1970. *American Business Abroad.* New Haven, Conn.: Yale University Press.

_____. 1973. *International Economics.* Homewood, Ill.: Richard D. Irwin.

Kitamura, Hiroshi. 1969. "Economic Development and Regional Cooperation in Southeast Asia," in United Nations, *Economic Bulletin for Asia and the Far East* 20, no. 2. Economic Commission for Asia and the Far East. Bangkok.

Kojima, Kioshi. 1960. "Economic Development and Import Dependence in Japan." *Hitotsubashi Journal of Economics* 1, no. 1. Tokyo.

_____. 1966a. "Japan's Foreign Aid Policy." *Hitotsubashi Journal of Economics* 6, no. 2. Tokyo.

_____. 1966b. "A Pacific Economic Community and Asian Developing Countries." *Hitotsubashi Journal of Economics* 7, no. 1. Tokyo.

_____. 1967. "Trade Arrangements Among Industrial Countries: Effects Upon Japan," in Bela Belassa (ed.), *Studies in Trade Liberalization.* Baltimore, Md.: Johns Hopkins Press.

_____. 1968. *Pacific Trade and Development.* Tokyo: The Japan Economic Research Center.

_____. 1969a. "Asian Developing Countries and PAFTA: Development, Aid, and Trade Preferences." *Hitotsubashi Journal of Economics* 10, no. 1. Tokyo.

_____. 1969b. *Pacific Trade and Development II.* Tokyo: The Japan Economic Research Center.

_____. 1971. *Japan and a Pacific Free Trade Area.* Berkeley, Calif.: University of California Press.

_____. 1972. "Non-Tariff Barriers to Japan's Trade." *Hitotsubashi Journal of Economics* 13, no. 1. Tokyo.

_____, Saburo Okita, and Peter Drysdale. 1971. "Foreign Economic Relations." In Asian Development Bank, *Southeast Asia's Economy in the 1970's.* New York: Frederick A. Praeger.

Kraar, Louis. 1970. "How the Japanese Mount that Export Blitz." *Fortune* 82, no. 3. Chicago.

Kravis, I. 1959. "Availability and Other Influences on the Commodity Composition of Trade." *Journal of Political Economy* 64, no. 2. Chicago.

Kravis, I. and Robert E. Lipsey. 1969. "International Price Comparisons by Regression Methods," *International Economic Review* 10, no. 2.

_____. 1971. *Price Competitiveness in World Trade.* Distributed by Columbia University Press, New York.

Kuznets, Simon. 1964. "Quantitative Aspects of the Economic Growth of Nations: IX Level and Structure of Foreign Trade: Comparisons for Recent Years." *Economic Development and Cultural Change*, Part II, vol. 13, no. 1. Chicago: University of Chicago Press.

_____. 1966. *Modern Economic Growth*. New Haven, Conn.: Yale University Press.

Leontief, W.W. 1954. "Domestic Production and Foreign Trade: The American Capital Position Re-examined." *Economia Internationale* 7. Barcelona, Spain.

_____. "Factor Proportions and the Structure of American Trade: Further Theoretical and Empirical Analysis." *Review of Economics and Statistics* 38, no. 4. Cambridge, Mass.

Luey, Paul. 1971. "On Discrepancies in Trade Statistics of Trading Partners." *The Malayan Economic Review* 16, no. 1. Singapore.

MacDougall, G. 1951. "British and American Exports: A Study Suggested by the Theory of Comparative Costs." Part I. *Economic Journal* 61, no. 244. New York.

Madison, Argus. 1969. *Economic Growth in Japan and the U.S.S.R.* New York: W.W. Norton.

Mah, Feng-hwa. 1968. "Foreign Trade." In A. Eckstein, *Economic Trends in Communist China*. Chicago: Aldine-Atherton.

Makoto, Yoshida. 1971. "How We Look to Southeast Asia." *Japan Quarterly* 18, no. 1. Tokyo.

Malmgren, Harald. 1973. "Japan, The U.S., and the Pacific Economy." *Pacific Community* 4, no. 3. Victoria, Australia.

Meier, Gerald. 1958. "International Trade and International Inequality." *Oxford Economic Papers* 10, no. 3. London.

Michaely, Michael. 1958. "Concentration in Imports and Exports: An International Comparison." *Economic Journal* 68, no. 272. New York.

Miyoshi, Masaya. 1971. "Japan's International Trade and Investment Policies for the 1970's," in Pierre Uri (ed.), *Trade and Investment Policies for the Seventies: New Challenges for the Atlantic Area and Japan*. New York: Praeger Publishers.

Moneta, Carmellah. 1959. "The Estimation of Transportation Costs in International Trade." *Journal of Political Economy* 67, no. 1. Chicago.

Myint, Hla. 1954-1955. "The Gains from International Trade and the Backward Countries." *The Review of Economic Studies* 22, no. 58. Edinburgh, England.

_____. 1958. "The 'Classical Theory' of International Trade and the Underdeveloped Countries." *Economic Journal* 68, no. 270. New York.

_____. 1964. *The Economics of the Developing Countries*. New York: Praeger Publishers.

_____. 1967. "The Inward and Outward-Looking Countries of Southeast Asia." *The Malayan Economic Review* 12, no. 1. Singapore.

_____. 1971a. *Economic Theory and the Underdeveloped Countries*. New York: Oxford University Press.

Myint, Hla. 1971b. *Southeast Asia's Economy: Development Policies in the 1970's.* New York: Pracgcr Publishers.

Myrdal, Gunnar. 1957. *Rich Lands and Poor.* New York: Pantheon Books.

———. 1968. *Asian Drama.* New York: Pantheon Books.

Nakamura, Koji. 1971. "Spend More, Earn More." *Far Eastern Economic Review* 73, no. 35. Hong Kong.

Naya, Seiji. 1967. "Natural Resources, Factor Mix, and Factor Reversal in International Trade." *American Economic Review* 57, no. 2. Evanston, Illinois.

——— and Theodore Morgan. 1969. "The Accuracy of International Trade Data: The Case of the Southeast Asian Countries." *Journal of the American Statistical Association* 64, no. 326.

Nurkse, Ragnar. 1961. *Equilibrium and Growth in the World Economy.* Cambridge, Mass.: Harvard University Press.

———. 1971. *Development Assistance, 1971 Review.* Paris.

Organization for Economic Cooperation and Development. 1969. *Resources for the Developing World: The Flow of Financial Resources to Less-Developed Countries, 1962-1968.* Paris.

———. 1973a. *Development Cooperation, 1973 Review.* Paris.

———. 1973b. *Flow of Resources to Developing Countries.* Paris.

———. *Geographical Distribution of Financial Flows to Less-Developed Countries, 1960-1964, 1965, 1966-1967.* Paris.

———. Selected Years. *Economic Surveys: Japan.* Paris.

Ohkawa, Kazushi and Henry Rosovsky. 1973. *Japanese Economic Growth: Trend Acceleration in the Twentieth Century.* Stanford, Calif.: Stanford University Press.

Okita, Saburo. 1972. "Economic Development in the 1970's—Japan and Asia." Center Paper No. 18. Tokyo: Japan Economic Research Center.

Olson, Laurence. 1970. *Japan in Postwar Asia.* New York: Praeger Publishers.

Oriental Economist. 1967. "Japanese Agriculture: Groping for a Path to Modernization." In vol. 35, no. 684. Nikonbashi, Tokyo.

———. 1971a. "Are Japanese Foreign Ventures Profiting?" In vol. 39, no. 728. Nikonbashi, Tokyo.

———. 1971b. "Foreign Trade." In vol. 39, no. 739. Nikonbashi, Tokyo.

———. 1972a. "Japan's Overseas Investment." Nikonbashi, Tokyo.

———. 1972b. *Japan Yearbook, 1971.* Tokyo.

Ozaki, Robert. 1967. "Japan's Role in Asian Economic Development." *Asian Survey* 7, no. 4. Berkeley, Calif.

Paige, D. and G. Bombach. 1958. *A Comparison of National Output and Productivity of the United Kingdom and the U.S.* Paris: Organization for European Economic Cooperation.

Partners in Development: Report of the Commission on International Development. The Pearson Report. New York: Praeger Publishers.

Pearce, I.F. 1970. *International Trade.* New York: W.W. Norton.

Pearton, Barry. 1971. "Koreans Face Hard Facts." *Far Eastern Economic Review* 74, no. 45. Hong Kong.

Pillar, M.P. Narayana. 1969. "The Kalgoorlie Trail." *Far Eastern Economic Review* 63, no. 12. Hong Kong.

PRC, International Trade Handbook. 1973. Washington, D.C.

Prebisch, Raul. "Commercial Policy in the Underdeveloped Countries." *American Economic Review* 49, no. 2. Evanston, Illinois.

Price, Robert L. 1967. "International Trade of Communist China, 1950-1965," in U.S. Congress, Joint Economic Committee, *An Economic Profile of Mainland China*, Vol. II. Washington, D.C.

Reday, Joseph. 1971. "Far East Business." *Oriental Economist* 39, no. 727. Nikonbashi, Tokyo.

Rosenstein-Rodan, Paul. 1943. "Problems of Industrialization of Eastern and South-Eastern Europe." *The Economic Journal* 53, no. 211. New York.

Sato, Eisaku. 1969. "Pacific Asia." *Pacific Community* 1, no. 1. Tokyo.

Savage, I.R. and Karl Deutsch. 1960. "A Statistical Model of the Gross Analysis of Transaction Flows." *Econometrica* 28, no. 3. Baltimore, Md.

Sebestyen, Charles. 1972. *The Outward Urge: Japanese Investment Worldwide.* London: Economist Intelligence Unit.

Shimbun, Nihon Keizai. 1971. "Natural Resources of Japan." *Japan Economic Journal* 9, no. 467. Tokyo.

Shimomura, Osamu. 1968. "Balance of Payments Constraints on Economic Growth." *Oriental Economist* 36, no. 690. Nikonbashi, Tokyo.

Shinohara, Miyohei. 1962. *Growth and Cycles in the Japanese Economy.* Tokyo: International Publications Service.

Singer, Hans. 1964. *International Development: Growth and Change.* New York: Oceana Publications, Dobbs Ferry.

Spiegelglas, S. 1959. "World Exports of Manufactures." *Manchester School of Economics and Social Studies* 27, no. 2. London.

Sterba, James. 1972. "Japan Tightens Her Economic Grip of Nations of East and South Asia." *The New York Times*, August 28.

Stewart, Ian. 1972. "Japanese Stir Asian Resentment." *The New York Times*, January 10.

Stokes, Henry Scott. 1971. "The Economic Invasion Myth." *Far Eastern Economic Review* 71, no. 13. Hong Kong.

Sung, Kayser. 1967. "Interview with Takeo Miki." *Far Eastern Economic Review* 55, no. 2. Hong Kong.

Takahashi, Kamekichi. 1971. "The Japanese Economy: Tasks of A New Dimension." *Oriental Economist* 39, no. 730. Nikonbashi, Tokyo.

Takasaki, Tatsunosuke. 1958. *Far Eastern Economic Review.* Hong Kong.

Takita, Kazuo. 1961. "An Asian Common Market." *Far Eastern Economic Review* 34, no. 11. Hong Kong.

Tysznski, H. 1951. "World Trade in Manufactured Commodities, 1899-1950." *Manchester School of Economic and Social Studies* 19. London.

Uemura, Kogio, President of the Japan Federation of Economic Organizations (Keidanren), "Challenge for Responsible Partnership," a speech delivered in Washington, D.C., June 15, 1971 and reprinted by the United States-Japan Trade Council.

United Nations. 1959. *United Nations Economic Survey of Asia and the Far East, 1959*, selected numbers. Economic Commission for Asia and the Far East. Bangkok and New York.

_____. 1967. *United Nations Economic Survey of Asia and the Far East, 1967*, selected numbers. Economic Commission for Asia and the Far East. Bangkok and New York.

_____. 1960. *Non-Tariff Distortions of Trade*. Committee for Economic Development. New York.

_____. 1970. *Development Assistance to Southeast Asia*. Committee for Economic Development. New York.

_____. 1972. *Handbook of International Trade and Development Statistics, 1972*. Conference in Trade and Development. New York.

_____. Selected Years. *Commodity Trade Statistics, Series D*, vols. VII-XX, assorted numbers. Statistical Office. New York.

_____. Selected Years. *Yearbook of International Trade*. New York.

Usack, A.H. and R.E. Batsavage. 1972. "The International Trade of the People's Republic of China," in U.S. Congress, Joint Economic Committee, *People's Republic of China: An Economic Assessment*. Washington, D.C.

U.S. Bureau of Intelligence and Research. 1971. "Communist States and Developing Countries: Aid and Trade In 1970." Unclassified, RECS-15. Washington, D.C.

U.S. Department of State. Various Years. *Battle Act Report*. Mutual Defense Assistance Control Act of 1951. Washington, D.C.

Viksnins, George. 1973. "United States Military Spending and the Economy of Thailand," *Asian Survey* 13, no. 5. Berkeley, Calif.

Wakasugi, Sueyuki. 1973. "Japanese Traders Face Tough Global Problems." *Pacific Community* 4, no. 2. Tokyo.

Wilson, Dick. 1967. "PAFTA and NAFTA." *Far Eastern Economic Review* 55, no. 2. Hong Kong.

Index

Gross national product (GNP), growth
  rates for, 49-50
  and exports, 15
  imports and, 48
  increase in, 99
  Japan's, 11, 12
  for Pacific Asia, 50t
  per capita, 13
  postwar trade shares of, 18
  raw materials in, 34n
Growth, industrial, 33-37
  of Pacific Asian trade, 42-52

Haberler, Gottfried, 62
Hegemony, economic, 4
Hollerman, Leon, 99
Hong Kong, aid flows to, 140t, 141t
  C.E. factor for, 87, 88t
  exports of, 43t, 53t, 55t, 57t, 105,
    106t, 108t, 110t
  foreign exchange earnings for, 136
  GNP of, 50t
  import coefficients from, Japan, 86t
  imports of, 44t, 54t, 56t, 85t, 93t
  Japanese exports to, 20
  Japanese import coefficients from,
    112t
  Japanese imports from, 21t, 120t,
    122t
  Japanese private investment in, 149t
  and Japanese trade, 22t, 133t
  multilateral capital flows to, 145t
  textile industry in, 88
  and trade surpluses, 136
Houthakker, H.S., 18

Ikeda, Prime Min., 138
Import dependency ratios, 18
Import flows, 125
  and export trends, 24
Import mix, for Pacific Asia, 85
Imports, categorization of, 66
  commodity composition of, 31t,
    119-124
  commodity demand patterns for, 73
  concentration of, 92
  future trends in, 127
  growth of, 72, 123
  Japanese, 3, 8, 10t, 23, 29, 31, 33
    non-industrial countries share of,
      25
  Pacific Asian shares of, 22t

market shares of, 92
non-industrial, 29
from Pacific Asia, 20t, 103
Pacific Asian, 42, 43-44, 84-88
patterns of, 79
prewar, Japanese, 23
reporting of, 165
restrictions on, 33
source of, 28
and terms of trade, 17t
world, 10t, 43-44, 52, 91
Income, determination of, 62
  export, 18
Increase, of Japanese trade, 8
Indebtedness, Pacific Asian, 153-154
Index numbers, Laspreyre, 76
  Paasche, 76
India, and trade flows, 27n
Indices, consumption, 33
Indonesia, aid flows to, 140t, 141t
  deficit of, 154
  economic assistance for, 143
  export dependency ratios for, 47t
  export prices of, 51t
  exports of, 43t, 51, 57t
  exports to Japan of, 53t, 55t, 105,
    106t, 108t, 110t
  foreign assistance for, 139
  GNP of, 50t
  import dependency ratios for, 48t
  imports of, 44t, 54t, 56t
  Japanese exports to, 20t
  Japanese import coefficients from,
    112t
  Japanese imports from, 21t, 121t,
    124
  Japanese private investment in, 149t
  and Japanese trade, 22t, 23, 133t
  multilateral capital flows to, 145t
  petroleum export of, 117
  reparation payments to, 142
  terms of trade of, 51
Industrial countries, 24
  Japanese trade with, 25t, 26. See
    also Developed countries
Industrial goods, 63
Industrialization, Japanese, 3
Industry, capital-goods, 49
  expansion of, 16
  Japanese, 33, 97
  labor-intensive, 129
  textile, 83

200

About the Author

Thomas R. Kershner is associate professor of economics and chairman of the Economics Department at Union College. He received the Ph.D. degree from Harvard University. Dr. Kershner has taught at Harvard University and Union College and has served as a consultant to government and industry. He is a frequent contributor to a number of professional journals.

DATE DUE

DEC 11 '80			
NOV 5 '81			
GAYLORD			PRINTED IN U.S.A.